The Radical Soap Opera

David Zane Mairowitz

The Radical
Soap Opera

An Impression of the American Left
from 1917 to the Present

Wildwood House London

First published 1974
Copyright © David Zane Mairowitz, 1974

Wildwood House Ltd
1 Wardour Street, London W1V 3HE
ISBN 0 7045 0102 3

Printed in Great Britain by
Biddles Ltd, Guildford, Surrey

Gary: Do you like Americans?

Perowne: Five years ago you would still impress them by showing them a reproduction of Van Gogh. Two years ago you had to show them the real thing. Now you have to give them his ear.

HEATHCOTE WILLIAMS, *AC/DC*

Scenario and
Cast of Characters

Programme Notes

This book is the product of a private continental drift. Living in England for over eight years, I have tried to look at my American past, its cultural myths and my own political involvement, through an adopted 'European eye'. Distance now affords me the luxury of irony.

This is not a history of the American Left movement, but rather an impressionistic 'staging' of some of its more emphatic moments. From this side of the Atlantic the basic theatricality of the movement seems all the more apparent; I have merely imposed a structure on it.

I believe that pinning down and defining the American Left is an impossible task. Therefore I have accepted as inevitable the very American confusion between groups and effects that are 'leftist' and those which are 'left-ish'.

The intention is not objectivity. I have consciously avoided the autobiographical road taken by many other accounts of the same subject. But the choice and arrangement of events, the peculiar and diversified cast of characters and the imposition of artificial rhythms and climaxes on history indicate very personal attitudes towards the material. The information contained here belongs to historical fact and analysis; the obsessions are my own.

I would like to thank the following people for their help:
The Reading-Room Staff of the British Museum, John Chioles, John and Eileen Allman, Lawrence Pitkethly, John Lahr, Deborah Rogers, John Thomas, Peter Stansill, Claus Clausen, Jenni Pozzi, Annabel Whittet, Dieter Pevsner, Mrs G. Mairowitz, Elliott

and Norma Sullivan, Richard Neville, Eric and Eileen Kaufman and Fred Zentner of The Cinema Bookshop, Great Russell Street, London.

The special kind of 'push' I received from Betty Anne Clarke, Judith Burnley and Harvey Matusow revived, at critical moments, the flagging spirits of my work.

My most lasting thanks go to Oliver Caldecott, the 'Godfather' of this book, without whose trust it probably wouldn't exist.

DZM

London, 1973

Acknowledgements

I would like to thank the following people who either read the manuscript at various stages, advised in one way or another, provided crucial personal accounts of their own participation in the American movement or were simply there when I needed them:

The Reading-Room Staff of the British Museum, John Chioles, John and Eileen Allman, Lawrence Pitkethly, John Lahr, Deborah Rogers, John Thomas, Peter Stansill, Claus Clausen, Annabel Whittet, Dieter Pevsner, Mrs G. Mairowitz, Elliott and Norma Sullivan, Richard Neville, Eric and Eileen Kaufman and Fred Zentner of The Cinema Bookshop, Great Russell Street, London.

The special kind of help I received from Betty Anne Clarke, Jenni Pozzi, Judith Burnley and Harvey Matusow revived, at critical moments, the flagging spirits of my work.

My most lasting thanks go to Oliver Caldecott, the 'Godfather' of this book, without whose trust it probably wouldn't exist.

Curtain Raiser

When young American leftists – Yippies, Zippies, Zoupies and Straights – came to the Miami Beach presidential conventions in 1972 they were searching for their 'lost' political initiative. They hoped to gain a foothold inside a system whose shins they had kicked for a decade, to win a new home in the Democratic Party and to warm up to a comforting father in George McGovern. McGovern had begun his move for the Top Banana limelight four years earlier when he engineered a new procedure for choosing convention delegates from minority groups – who would naturally be more sympathetic to him than to established candidates. Yet he managed to give the new shock troops the impression that their enthusiasm alone had swept him – and, by implication, themselves – to the brink of power. Many were led to believe, once again, that they could break fresh ground in the re-building of America; others, more seasoned and bitter, sniffed just another pipe-dream, but came along for the razzle-dazzle. Whatever anyone might find here, however, it could never measure up to the intensity of political experience just passed. Win or lose, there was nothing new under the Florida sun, nothing to lend a bit of fresh dimension to the action. Unless, perhaps, you counted the Grandma syndrome.

It was a surprising alliance. The over-65s who make up the bulk of the Miami Beach population and the under-30 invaders had, at the very least, a common bugaboo: the parents in-between. The old folks, now burdensome to their middle-aged sons and daughters, were farmed out to this final resting-place. They would stagnate here until the end, getting an occasional visit from their offspring, a postcard, a request to sign the insurance policy. The demonstrators discovered they could relate to the old people (whom they'd ignored pretty much before), because they were not trying to 'make it' in the capitalist world any longer, just 'hanging out' like they were, living off the State, plenty of time to kill. Once the elders got over their initial fear (instilled in them by a middle-aged media) they warmed to the grandchildren, moving into their camp where the music and carnival atmosphere brought them more fun and attention than they'd had since being written off. They shared watermelon and dope, danced, sang, observed with wonder the freaks and nudes and drag queens and farcical angries who were now part of the permanent road-company of the Left. Some found long-lost relatives over whose long hair they could wax paralytic. Others got 'politicized', not merely to oppose the Government, but to partake of the Great Liberation they'd heard about with trepidation and now watched with delight. For – why not? – weren't the very old entitled to more than just a premature burial out here in the lost horizon of pink-stucco America? Geriatric's Liberation made fantastic sense in this new culture which seemed to embrace all interest groups and disenchanted waifs and strays. The rights of the aged had long since been ignored, and 'Grey Panther' organizations were already forming in some states following the trails blazed by women, homosexuals, Puerto Ricans and vampires. It wasn't just a need for higher pensions or wider coffins, but the recognition that they were still very much alive, that they wanted more than bed-pans and insulin, that they were ready for a little hotcha-cha, would smoke a joint and shake that thing and – perhaps, perhaps – renew that long-forgotten spring in the loins.

The young were turned on by the fact that many of the senior citizens could think back to a time when the Republic was not so dreary a place, when the culture flourished, when the 'voice of the people' had, to some small degree, a contactable ear in Government. It was precisely what the demonstrators came there to achieve, having had no taste of it in their lifetimes or seen evidence of it in their parents'– a more responsive, pro-human, people-serving State. Together the new allies could get high on the sentiment.

But in 1972 the two groups had something more crucial in

common – retirement from active life. The young were there, of course, to enter another 'new era' in the history of their movement; but even the potential of 'influence' in the Democratic Party could not obscure the fact that the best years of their State-smashing lives were behind them. The Democratic Convention – despite its new look – was oh so conventional. For revolutionaries it was cinemascope reduced to the TV screen, a constricting and sudden narrowing of vision. The whole affair had the air of old-timers out for a final fling before admitting the inevitable.

Many had gone as far as they could in the realm of powerful experience, altering consciousness and breaking into hidden crypts of personality. A good handful had already written their revolutionary memoirs. Others of their movement were out to pasture, back to the land, tilling the soil and scratching their sage-whiskers far from the famous street-battles which marked their active days. All that was consigned to memory now, even memories were growing memories. If the last-ditch effort at political comeback should prove a failure, the troops could easily slip into reclining beach chairs, letting the sweat of revolt drift off them and disperse out over the Florida Keys. They could stop right where they were and pass out where all the years of struggle led up at last to that much-promised place in the sun.

Many left turns lead to those beach chairs. In a sense, the leftist movement stops here for breath, jettisons its debris and pauses in its commitment before moving on. Having to decide where it will go or why is not entirely awkward or frivolous. Its history, spreading back to the 1920s when it became a significant force, is not so much a tale of achievement as an unending pattern of re-definition and change of mind. European leftists seem to hold on to a basic set of (chiefly Marxist) doctrines, despite changes in emphasis and tone over the years. These are too business-like and tradition-bound to go through the perpetual revolutions within the revolution and labyrinthine soul-searchings that mark their American brothers-in-struggle. Nor are they so easily sidetracked from political work by excitements of the cultural climate.

But the American Left begins with such Europeans, devoted

Socialists seduced and disarmed by the New World. They and their sons after them strove to build the international Socialist revolution *while* trying to learn to be Americans. The two drives were bound to cross-fertilize, even though they often appeared to be in direct opposition. These immigrants were as susceptible as anyone else to the lure of indigenous cultural fictions. They could not escape the very capitalist myths or soap-powder jingles they hoped to eradicate. The American mirror was too attractive to shatter, and they never got far beyond its glitter. American leftists, whether old, new, Marxist-Leninists, Trotskyites, Maoists or freaks, are Americans first and foremost. And, despite its internationalist claims and lip-service to an occasional theoretical approach, the US Left, in all its incarnations, owes as much homage to the B-movie as to Karl Marx. This is not to disparage it, but to pinpoint the root of its desires and motives.

The American movement has always been wide open to external impressions like a moonscape catching meteorites. These can be powerful ideas out of popular psychology, glitterings from the Star System of Hollywood or Washington or sensations drummed up by exploitative media. Often the Left has been able to politicize these effects and turn them into useful tools of propaganda. But, more often, the movement itself is deflected, its political course altered and its internal workings confused. Popular mythology has changed the very nature of protest over five decades and, with increasing intensity, the political acts of the Left beg to be judged for performance value and its treatises as best-selling literature. This phenomenon is not true of the movement as a whole, for there are (and always will be) hard-core workers who never stray from the 'correct' path. Civil Rights and other black movements, as well as early union and working-class struggles, demonstrate a basic conservatism of purpose which does not allow for much political kinkery. But a significant element of white middle-class leisured rebels has always paraded and pranced, capturing the publicity and notoriety of protest. Those who make spectacle out of rebellion are not always in the vanguard so much as front-stage centre, rehearsing the various soft-shoe routines they have picked up from the ongoing American repertoire:

Autobiography. The heart's-core of the deal – as expressed in both the best and worst American cinema, theatre, fiction, comic books – is that you can *win* esteem in the critical eye of the world. Yes, even you, Joe Blow, can rise to the top of the Somebody Sweepstakes or play the romantic lead in the film version of your own life. This used to be called American dreaming, but it can't always be measured in the amassing of greenbacks, nor has it retained the nobility expressed by Jefferson and the founding fathers. It runs down now to a preoccupation with exposing your self. This achievement of personality status and pride is in natural opposition to classic Marxist doctrine. The movement becomes, as a result, a series of dialogues between the impulse to determine your own salvation and hand-me-down ideologies rooted in collectivization, selflessness and obedience to the Party line.

Poets, writers, psychologists, actors, madmen and shamans are always drawn to the fringes of the American Left, and the movement has never been so rigid it couldn't accommodate them as 'left-ish' people, fellow-travellers or groupies. But their general impact has been to twist the Left away from Marxism, inch by inch. They add fuel to the fire of the personal quest, urging that each comrade find his *own* voice with which to shout his anguish, rage, frustration, slogans and – oh yes – political programme. Once found, this voice identifies you with the common struggle, but in your own terms: I am the movement. There follows an acting out of autobiography, the public *movement* of your political life. It's a life played for keeps, with contours, a beginning, middle and end. One guy's lonely ride down the highway to the New Order. You might 'find yourself' in the class struggle and 'be somebody' by shining out in the revolution. It's your coming-out party, your anti-social debut.

When he is finished or simply too exhausted, the gentleman of protest can still stake his claim to a piece of the Fame Pie by writing down his autobiography. This has always been a standard American way of rubbing dirty laundry in the face of others, but in the service of rebellion it takes over the function of the political manifesto. You simply manifest your private version of events and collect the royalties. Even in the gut of the revolutionary surge of the sixties, the market was filled with memoirs of personal psychodramas that had occurred only months before in the guise of social cataclysm. Almost exclusively these were fables of our guy as he emerges from darkness to light, from liberal naïvety to revolutionary wisdom, the motion of the movement turning in a still unsettled eyeball.

Therapy. If American dreaming appears to follow through, from time to time, on its promise that everyone can better himself, it still doesn't provide a true means by which a guy can be distinguished. You can bust out of your trap only to find every other Palooka busting out of his. Rising above your public disgrace requires a strategy. Before you can get to be 'somebody' you have to find out 'who you are'. To find out who you are means broadening your awareness. Gaining awareness means gathering experience. To get experience, you need the correct *method*. But stop right there; rest assured there will be swarms of medicine-men waiting at the gates of the Republic to sell you just such a remedy.

There are a thousand-and-one therapies, miracle-cures and short cuts to the Truth which Americans seem to devour like no other race on earth. Inside their labyrinth lies the promise of getting down to the *real you* by carving away all that is sham and pretence. In most popular therapies this means ridding yourself of games and 'masks'; it can be as painful as a snake shedding its skin. Socially it makes virtue equal to honesty, encounter, confrontation, being 'up-front', letting it all hang out, pulling down all the dams and defences and opening up the dark night of your soul to other humans. The morality play called Analysis.

Many American therapies and salvation syndromes are perfectly legitimate, but they tend to be self-perpetuating. The effect of endless scoopings in the soul can be like narcotics – thrilling but debilitating. The problem for a political movement comes in trying to turn all the groping into concrete action, into quality performance. From its early days, however, the Left got enmeshed in Freud, in the kind of pseudo-psychology practised in acting seminars, in the general pressure of the search for the 'real'. A classic pattern saw people go from the analyst's couch to the Communist Party and back to the couch again, or the other way round. The thought behind it was that making better people is a stepping-stone to making that famous Better World. The sentiment made scrambled eggs of hard-core leftist discipline; almost all major struggles from the building of the Communist Party to the dismantling of the Students for a Democratic Society refer back to this issue. The question was whether the capitalist order and the bourgeois consciousness that propped it up were driven by laws of economic determinism or by 'hang-ups' and neuroses begotten and nourished (usually) at Mama's teat.

Melodrama. The big Dream comes to imply, above all else, the *failure to get it.* You can see the very point at which it begins to sour by watching American literature disgrace it. It builds a new breed of losers chasing a tease; the impossibility of truly 'making it' brings only suffering. It's a perfect set up for a big Weep. The earliest forms of American entertainment were influenced by those late eighteenth-century European melodramas where the musical accompaniment actually expressed or heightened the actor's emotions. Carried into the trembly terrain of Hollywood this becomes pure 'emotionalism', an excess of display forced down the spectator's throat simply to mesmerize him. This device doesn't merely exploit escapist fantasies or provide magical cinematic mirrors. It is a powerful instrument of the senses by which we exorcize our demons and through which we may perhaps one day orchestrate the Last Judgement.

The Left was far more attracted to this steamy brew than to social expression that might have served its political ends. The so-called 'social dramas' of the Depression came straight from the heart, reinforcing American values through a gut-spilling yearning for a better deal. On the silver screen the Left capitalized on the sensitive, concerned, speak-my-mind, air-my-grievance mentality that already existed. The tough guys who didn't let nobody push them around were made into paragons of social rebellion. Even then, the desired effect of their revolt on the audience was more often the tear than the raised fist.

If the Republic relies on overstatement and the 'impossible' stratagem, if a truth is meant to be embellished and overplayed, such extravagance can certainly serve the purposes of a struggle against the social order. Revolutionaries are already into over-dramatizing by the very nature of their task. When the struggle must be equal to the barbarity of American power, you've got a gusher: soap opera.

Righteousness. Your investment in the personality stakes requires a return on capital. The therapeutic fiction takes on a further obsession – keeping *everyone else* open, honest, real. This is the natural imperialism of the American spirit. So we witness the rampage of the favourite game: ripping away the mask, exposing the fraud, busting up the illusion, extracting the bitter truth from the bullshit. It swaggers undaunted across the cultural spectrum from Eugene O'Neill to Watergate.

Around this 'moral' core the Left weaves its own *counter-mythology*. Opposed to the delusion that was the Dream comes the chimera called the Revolution. Scratching away the mask of power, to show that the promise of dignity for every man cannot be fulfilled, becomes the fervent crusade of the movement. The very thought of whipping the Power, despite its incredible entrenchment, lends a tingle to the spirit. With right on our side, how can we not but overcome . . . someday.

The best place for the Left to display its morality was in the consciousness-raising business. And why not? If the media traditions could reflect and foster the macho-fascistic fantasies of a gun-toting, woman-whopping right-wing majority, why shouldn't they also service a minority of State-smashers? Asking this question led to the first major fall of the movement. It got too close for comfort to the central-fiction clearing-house of Hollywood. This was a primary fortress of value-reinforcement, and the State had a monopoly here.

After the end of the Second World War the culture was already solidifying its ethic of Middle America/Silent Majority, a populace responsive to the whims of power, obedient and dulled. The insurance policy for it was being drawn up in the closets of the Right. The movement was already damaged by the loss of a working-class base and its difficult marriage with the Soviet Union. Its attempt to define its tenuous purpose collapsed under pressure of the Red Scare. All that remained to build on was sanctimoniousness, keeping the boys stout and sturdy against the odds.

American revolutionaries of the sixties tend to think their movement 'began' somewhere in the early part of that decade, a wholly new attempt at political strategy with little reference to the movement that 'died' some years before as a result of witch-hunting. This 'New Left' blossomed out of non-violent and anti-liberal sentiments. It displaced the old accent on the working-class with any number of alternative focal points shifting ceaselessly. Tactics generally gained a new militancy. But only a pitiful sense of history can declare a prior movement defunct. Just as it has come out of past mistakes and triumphs, it is applied, it succeeds or misfires and passes again into a new batch of political cocoons. These may be dormant for a spell, but they are always evolving and informing the future, always *in movement*. The big splash of the sixties contained in it all the previous history of the American Left: the glories, the defeats, the fantasies, the hunger for sensation. It was a *reactive* explosion to the effects of the Red Scare on the parent generation and against the mass defection from political life. Because the thrill of revolt had run down to middle-class silence and liberal boredom, it had to be revived. When it came it blew the roof off the respectful acceptance of power with all the fury of moralistic rancour. It was the last outpost of the great fictions, a conceit to suit the overkill of the moment: confrontation between the races, the generations, the sexes. Here was the gathering of personality turf on which to parade. The society seemed blasted open, exposing its wounds, anything was possible; the desire to take part, or rather partake, not to mention *take apart*, was overwhelming. It appeared to be the opening breakdown for a great shakedown.

Yet the early seventies show the right-wing at the zenith of its power, despite massive internal corruption and scandal. Persecution of the Left opposition is again an *underhanded* business. Witch-hunting has become electronic, but its goals remain constant – to stifle the protest voice and beef up the Silent Majority. A certain nasty *déja vu* feeling pervades the air and brings the mid-fifties home to roost. Even the kingpin of repression and gatherer of the leftist spoils is the very same public man. This sameness and other recurring patterns of protest history give the lie to some of the fabled originality of times just gone by. For if the Left has arrived at virtually the same dead 'end' again, it may be possible it got there in the same tried and true manner.

The 'New Left' never really shook off the 'old', nor could it if only for the fact that one generation was parent (often literally) to the other. Ghosts haunted the younger revolt at every stage of its activity. These were not merely the slogans of the fathers visited upon the sons, nor even the great pretence to a socialist Utopia which crept in where it made little sense. More than that, a counter-mythology built up in earlier generations passed down its influence. It was a ready-made phalanx of heroes and villains, fervent songs and phantasms of victory into which the young leftists could pour their own fresh obsessions. It was designed to give the *appearance* where there could be no *real* political power. At the centre is an original bobbin of Americana pushing out a thread which links the first awkward attempts at organizing the unions right up to bombs in the toilets of the Pentagon. In the unravelling appears a series of disjointed identity-games covering some fifty years of America-bashing. We also find here the fables that revolutionaries tell themselves and the ritual dramas they play out to occupy the time while waiting for Lefty.

The Romance of Treason

'*Ladies and Gentlemen. It is with novel and bewildering feelings that I find myself in the New World . . .*' 1909; Sigmund Freud's first words in a lecture series at Clark University in Worcester, Massachusetts. Some few Americans, after listening to him, were left with a novel and bewildering 'new world' of emotional possibilities destined to inform their lives in a powerful way. Here was sublimation, free association, the sexual instincts of children, the analysis of dreams – ideas that would shortly take root in the culture and blossom in a thousand variations. These ideas would come to challenge set assumptions and private fears which made for rigidity of self-expression – fears related to sex and other natural impulses. One member of the audience had heard Freud before – in Vienna, 1896 – and came now to witness the development of his theories of sexuality. This was the Russian writer and anarchist, Emma Goldman, the notorious 'Red Emma' who, by pure coincidence, was scheduled to deliver some lectures of her own in Worcester at the same time. Unlike Freud, she was denied a public platform by police and by an outraged press that referred to her as 'Satan'. One important reason for this (although neither the Doctor nor his hushed assembly would have realized it) was that she had already tried to put Freud's theories into practice and interpreted them as tools for changing the unjust orders of the world.

Both of these Europeans had hopes of having an impact in the United States. Psychoanalysis was still subject to suspicion and repression in the clinics of Europe, and Freud saw his invitation to America as a sign of its future acceptance. He was excited by the potential for and openness to a sense of experiment he assumed to be there. After his first dose of the Republic, however, he had his *doubts; he saw the US as a colossal 'mistake'. He was appalled by the easiness of local manners (which, ironically, became easier due to his influence), by the lack of culture, the sexual hypocrisy, the rotten cooking that caused havoc in his intestines and the absence of public toilets in which to empty the spoils of his overworking prostate. Above all, he feared that American 'vulgarity' would abuse the work he had built up for decades. He had already been warned, before his lectures, not to stress too heavily his theory of dreams; Americans were practical, commercial-minded people who would want to know, first and foremost, how to make his discoveries pay off.*

Emma arrived in America (1886) full of expectation of a better life, having escaped from Tsarist tyranny and Cossack atrocities. Instead, she only saw immigrants treated like cattle, she received starvation wages for medieval working conditions and experienced perpetual cop brutality and harassment. Because she spoke her mind on all these things, she later gained an overblown reputation for incitement, and was viciously thwarted as she made her speaking tours through the US. On one of the Worcester nights, while Freud was enjoying indoor comforts, public esteem and an enthusiastic press, Goldman was forced to speak to a small crowd on a private lawn. Years later she was glad that 'anarchism was heard there, not under the Stars and Stripes, but under a more appropriate canopy – the limitless sky and the myriads of glittering stars . . .'

For a brief second their roads had crossed in a small, conservative New England town before diverging again forever. Emma had always been deeply impressed by the Doctor and carried forward his message to justify a broad sweep of freedom from government control, freedom from marriage-chains, the total emancipation of women, a better deal for children, prisoners and immigrants – a political spectrum that would have shocked the conservative Freud. His goal was the health of the body, not the body politic. But there were some, like Emma, who would argue the one was unthinkable without the other. Her anarchism, or even the imported communism soon to make its mark, would never prove sufficient in themselves in the struggle against American injustice. First would have to come a freedom of expression for every man and woman, one that could accommodate the needs of personality. This might be found, with

*some effort, in the lovely box of wonders Uncle Freud had left
behind.*

1

At many stages over half of this century protest against the
American state of things has looked like a pageant of self-promotion. Classical economic motivations have, of course, been
instrumental in giving shape to reactions against governmental
injustice. But American activism has been stymied at every turn
by the sheer impossibility of its task; it has no real hope – nor has
it ever had any – of overturning the capitalist colossus. All of the
left-wing movement's attempts at gaining concrete political power
have been easily crushed; most of its dreams for changing American consciousness are sheer pretence. As the movement is faced,
decade upon decade, with these bleak facts, it turns increasingly to
activities in strictly cultural fields and builds itself elaborate
fantasies of political significance in lieu of the real thing. Appropriately, a single man's reaction to the political stone wall and to
his own helplessness is to turn his radical impulses towards re-
designing himself. This has come to be more and more the case as
America loses the concept of a traditional proletariat, and the
'working-class' turns conservative. Rebellion is then left chiefly
to the middle-classes whose anger-base is generally non-economic.
Most often a man's motives for political involvement can be
traced to American bourgeois desires for 'self-discovery' and
the revelation of this self on a public platform.

Modern American protest almost always has in it an element of
'romanticism' and often nostalgia for a mythological America
that may once have existed in principle. The theoretical reference
to it was laid down by the First Fathers and their famous founding doctrines. Jefferson's distrust of authority in general worked
against the natural reverence for the State found in most European societies. His feeling that governments ought to be forced
from power when they ignore the will of the people delivered up a
spine of rebellion which subsequent generations of State-smashers
have called upon to lend legitimacy to their efforts.

Yet, in the twentieth century, this tradition of perpetual vigilance in the name of the American Revolution has come to be culturally suppressed and instinctively checked; national upheaval seems a fearful, unnatural phenomenon. The great freedoms, the vaunted 'equality', even the curious 'happiness' that Jefferson jammed into the framework of the people's government – all these cannot be more than secondary considerations for a nation with a voracious commercial will. As the deification of Gross National Product came into being, it was only natural that the individual and his 'spiritual' needs would have to knuckle under. Where the new industrial expansionism expanded out of human scale, stealing patches of land and putting factories there, later combining these as monopolies and, ultimately, a spider-web of megacorporations, a whole new definition of freedom was in order. For the cultural goal of such a Business State was an efficient, highly productive, unquestioning middle-class society. This would clearly be in conflict with the old romance of liberty; dark people would still demand equal rights, workers a better deal and every man his pursuit of happiness. But the system developed safetyvalves for these, and could dam up immediate needs with sops; in time, even long-range 'happiness' could be doled out – a measure of equal opportunity, an increase in standard of living, at last even a 'working-class' home with two colour TVs, two latest-model cars and a freezer full of steaks.

What could not be spared, however – now gathered up in relatively few hands – was power. The most promising of all the original promises seemed to be that every man had the right to have an effect on the social and political environment. One way to achieve status, of course, was through the amassing of personal wealth; even where this was not possible, the *power* of manifesting yourself to the public and achieving 'fame' in the community was a truly American alternative. But what was once a Grand Vision for accommodating such social influence now became a Grand Design to foster anonymity, compliance and cowardice in the face of authority. The commercial State had to de-mystify, debase and render powerless *any* potential challenge to its proper functioning. In the early part of the century American Power concentrated on squashing labour demands and demonstrations.

But it could just as easily learn to turn its cannons at the sons of the bourgeoisie rising to claim their traditional place in the sun.

The full recognition of the de-personalization process carried with it an overwhelming sense of disappointment, of having been cheated, the feeling that the bond proffered by original principle was not honoured. In the face of this, a more visionary brand of rebellion sought to re-define cultural values, to get back to some imagined primal state of grace, to re-dream America. It looked back to a time of pioneer spirit and open space and 'pure' democracy – the anti-face to industrialism. In the late nineteenth and early twentieth centuries writers and poets began to demand payment on their American Dream-bonds and tried to create a mythology that would once again herald the sanctity of the *person*. This meant, first of all, discovering a wholly American voice. For the understanding was that a man's claim to social power – despite his class or status – was what made him distinctly *American*.

Chief rabble-rouser in this tradition was the poet Walt Whitman. Whitman believed that an indigenous culture would first of all need to dispel the lingering shadow of Europe. He especially hated the sham, the social masks and pretence which Americans had come to associate with the Old World. It was necessary for the US to 'cease to recognize a theory of character grown of feudal aristocracies, or formed . . . from any ultramarine full-dress formulas of culture, polish, caste, etc., and . . . promulgate her own new standard . . . appropriate to the modern, the democratic, the west . . . Ever the most precious in the common.' It was a nitty-gritty America Whitman conjured up, full of massive-thighed lumberjacks and superwomen who could drop a master race of children without a squeal. Natural stuff. But Nature weren't no English tea party no more, with nightingales and trellises and scones. No, sirree, America was voluminous with volcano-stock, blasting up gushers of rock-lava to build biblical-like cities. In the heart of such cities stood the impressive Individual Man, part of a great human chain of similarly heroic 'comrades'. Together the races of these States would, through brain and brawn and poetry, give example to the world (and annex Canada and Cuba). Stand up for America.

Whitman's words had the spinal ring of Jefferson or Tom Paine but, like them, he could only address *future* generations with his ecstatic optimism. He had witnessed the Civil War and could not reconcile it with his hopes. In 1870 he laid down the components of his gloom-filled vision: 'The underlying principles of the States are not honestly believed in (for all this hectic glow, and these melodramatic screamings) . . . What penetrating eye does not everywhere see through the mask? . . . The men believe not in the women, nor the women in the men . . .' Still, all these faults would disperse once America could fulfil its own nature. This bombast and jingoism served to influence a whole flock of mini-Walts, believing that the Republic still had seed-potential for reviving the promise and even building the new Jerusalem. It was rhapsodic vision that also inspired protest movements and gave background to specific demands for a better deal. In this dream-state the culture would be delivered from money-consciousness, Mammon would be sent packing and the individual would again inherit his rightful place at the pivot of the American social conscience.

Nostalgia for an American 'paradise lost' is for pipe-dreamers. The logic of a continent so full of natural resources and capacity for land expansion is, and always was, pragmatic and materialistic. The desires of a single man or even the spiritual needs of the nation tend to become luxury, often aberration. Moreover, a closer look at the founding doctrines dampens romanticism and shows a concentration on business, land and private property. Jefferson, practically on his deathbed, expressed his life-long fear of the abstract: 'These dreams of the day, like those of the night, vanish in vapour, leaving not a rack behind. The business of life is with matter. That gives us tangible results. Handling that, we arrive at the knowledge of the axe, the plough, the steamboat and everything useful in life . . .' A concept like Manifest Destiny could be disguised romantically as ' . . . the right . . . which Providence has given us for the great experiment of liberty and federated self-government . . .'; but it was, in fact, a super land-grab and genocide of Indians, the rampage of the first breed of real-estate developers and landlords. Even the shirking of European manners was related to economic requirements. If the foundation of the new culture was business, then it had little time for social graces; its priorities (at least in principle) had to be plain-dealing and the dominion of currency.

One poet and re-definer of American values who understood this was Ezra Pound. Pound, like Whitman, sought to locate the truly American voice. In 1912, he saw this coming about through an American *Risorgimento*. But it was not some blissful pioneer panorama where burly buckaroos exercised their demo-crassy. Rather, it recognized the jingle of coin and the thrill of commerce. He believed there were serious casualties in American expansionism and also in the over-concentration on individual motivations. History was not a series of events haphazardly chained together, but the play of economies in conflict. Yet America was fast winding towards its manifestly destined place at the centre of the universe, at the heart of historical time, and had no use for the subtle strategies of Old World materialism.

Pound's own myth-making was designed to get the Republic back onto a more useful track. His particular protest – a more or less right-wing one – was not against the loss of spiritual values under capitalism. Such values could only be revived after the common man stopped being mystified by monetary mechanics. Pound wrote in 1935:

> The state has credit.
> Distribution is effected by little pieces of paper.
> If you don't watch these, you will be slaves. If
> you don't know how they are made; who makes them;
> who controls them; you will be diddled out of your
> livings, as millions of dead men have been diddled,
> as millions of live ones are being.

This was hardly a call to arms, yet it inadvertently put Pound among the growing legions of enemies of the State. He gave a series of wartime speeches on Italian radio beginning in 1941, in which he tried to lay down his peculiar context for a new social order. His warcry was against 'usury' and the gang of high-level Jews – including Roosevelt – who were bleeding America dry. He also claimed that Mussolini was the new Jefferson, and that the financial salvation of America depended on an understanding of President Van Buren's autobiography.

What Pound considered a re-definition of American principle, the US Government called treason. He was made to pay dearly for broadcasting his angry patriotism. After the liberation of Italy in 1944 he tried to get to the American Army to see if he could help out in any way. For that gesture, he was put into a cage at Pisa and ultimately incarcerated in a Washington DC mental asylum.* He remained there until 1958, considered too insane to stand trial; his lawyer claimed Pound could not understand how he had committed treason.

Pound rose up angry only to receive razzberries. Despite his world stature, he gained his place as a clown in the circus of American protest. In his own way he demonstrated the romantic vision; he hoped in the end to re-make America in his own highly distorted image. He saw his social power in a microphone – as would many after him – and wanted only to express a private patriotism. While a prisoner in Pisa, he said: 'I was not sending axis propaganda, but my own . . .' Incapable of rising above his poet's sense of prophecy, his politics reduced to a *cri de coeur*.

The idea of completely re-dreaming America was, naturally, an intellectual luxury. The ordinary man with a grievance needed to be simply relieved of his social dilemma, delivered from his impotence. He did not need to overhaul the system, merely to learn how to take from it his rightful share of the pursuit of happiness stakes. But to get to this edge of rebellion, it was necessary for him to find a clear means of self-expression, a way in, as it were, to the societal ear. Theodore Dreiser's novel, *An American Tragedy* (1925), zeroes in on just such an American outsider – called Clyde

---

*This was not the end of the retribution for Pound. In 1947 he won the Bollingen Prize for his *Pisan Cantos* (written in his cage), and this led New York's Senator Javits to demand an investigation. As late as 1972 the trustees of the University of Maine reversed a decision to award him an honorary degree; Pound was prepared to return from his fourteen-year exile to accept it, but the trustees reminded the world he was a 'traitor and a known anti-Semitic'.

Griffiths – one who *ought* to be blowing his top but has no voice and no channel for his protest.

An American Tragedy is an historically pivotal exposition of hard-luck Americana. It was written at a time when Freud's ideas were just coming into fashion and before Dreiser himself dipped his toes in the waters of American Communism. It was a moment when many 'liberal' Americans began to recognize the de-personalization process, but could neither understand its source nor figure out how to combat it. Dreiser is loath to blame Clyde Griffiths' problems entirely on a hostile social environment, so he commingles personal and social determinations to produce the hero's actions. The societal landscape sets up his hunger to be somebody, only to offer him no food in the long run. He is given a high-speed injection of capitalist prospect to keep him alert, but when he is defeated he has no strength of character to fall back on. He is frozen in his tracks at almost every stage of his 'rise', amazed by the dull, dulled by the truly amazing, a victim not merely of the class structure but of his dread of the very experi-ence he craves. He has become a sub-zombie of the new com-mercialism, and intuits that he will pay the price for trying to shine out in America.

Clyde Griffiths is a classic victim, in this case overwhelmed by social climbing, Puritanism, his own sexual overdrive, limousines and murder. He hails from a poverty-stricken background, re-vivalist ministers for parents; is stunned by the glitter of sharp clothes and silver dollars; thinks he needs money to sleep with girls; works for a rich uncle; falls for a factory girl, puts her in the family way; falls for a richer girl, plots to kill the first girl, can't even arrange that properly and 'accidentally' kills her; gets caught (of course), he hasn't even covered his tracks well; is brought to trial (the necessary humiliation of the striving ego); mouths the prepared remarks of his attorneys while on the witness stand; breaks under the strain of the DA's sadistic prosecution; cannot voice his own defence; is sentenced to death; goes soul-searching in the death house; receives, as a reward for his desire for public renown, a juicing in the Electric Chair.

He has *cause* enough to shriek. His background prevents him from pursuing his happiness, a grim social morality hampers his lascivious inclinations, he is bullied into guilt by a ruthless legal system and, at the last, has no societal aid in expressing his 'innocence' or the appeal against his sentence. His voice is cramped by a social fear specially bred in him. He cannot say 'no' or protest his perpetual punishment except to desire some dramatic satisfaction to lift him clear.

2

For the 'Clyde Griffiths' who needed to vent his social frustrations, the new communism seemed to provide a working channel.

This was not the case in the first part of the century when political activity amounted to a batch of disorganized, uninspired interest groups. Labour unions generally acted independently of (and often at cross purposes with) each other. Native American unionists had little feeling for those political movements which spoke of 'workers of the world'. Early forms of European socialism in America were wholly alien and conflicted with indigenous methods of industrial action. Even Friedrich Engels recognized the US would have to blunder into its own version of a socialist Utopia, not quite the one he and Marx had mapped out. In 1887 he felt that his *Communist Manifesto* was 'far too difficult for America at the present time. The workers over there . . . are still quite crude, tremendously backward theoretically . . . as a result of their . . . special American nature . . .' Most American trade unions fought for concrete demands without the sense of international solidarity, extending membership and power only to keep up with the development of capitalist industry. So, too, a worker would usually measure himself not as a representative of an oppressed class, but as a guy looking for a better deal like everyone else was. The only source of political theory came into the unions via immigrant groups who had a natural grounding in the internationalist position. Most of these were brought over for the purpose of beefing up the American labour force to meet increasing production demands. They had a basis for comparison, and saw that labour's servile situation was strategically the same the world over. But they could not readily explain this to native labourers. They often did not speak English, lived in ghettos, united politically only according to nationality and generally steered clear of American workers. Where the occasional European agitator was able to expound socialist doctrine, he was shunned or ostracized. These foreigners sought refuge inside the Socialist Party, but many were already fighting to establish their American place, and only the most desperate were really willing to rock the boat.

The only significant militant labour force in the first decades of the century was the I W W (International Workers of the World or 'Wobblies'). They believed that broader political issues could not be divorced from the question of immediate union demands, and hoped to organize all American (and, one day, international) workers into one strong union. But most workers were content to look after their own needs and live on the dramatic tension that existed from one strike to another. Few believed – even if they were interested in the prospect – that governmental power could be toppled, and thus they shied away from suggestions of a united American political movement.

Events in Russia, circa 1917, changed all that. Suddenly the news started pouring in that a small political party had seized control of a backward, entrenched country in the name of the proletariat. Soon after, similar leftist revolutions broke out in Hungary and Bavaria and there were rumblings elsewhere. The thrilling success of the Bolsheviks quickly inflamed American hotshots, impelling them like cannonballs towards the creation of their own movement.

In the first years there was a ready-made rallying point for the Left. The US Government had reacted to the Russian Revolution with a blockade and an attempted military intervention. European Communists, who had already begun to solidify around the Russian example, now struggled to protect the Bolshevik victory. This made *internal* opposition to the US Government vital, both in terms of disseminating pro-Soviet propaganda and in making trouble at home to distract the forces of intervention. In 1917 an 'American Red Guard' was formed to go over and fight for the

Bolsheviks. But the Guard made the mistake of asking for permission from the US War Department and, since the American Government was hatching its own plans for the Reds, the request was naturally denied.

Impatience was now the order of the day. Because the native version of the great struggle had been conceived in awe, the proper *means* for arriving at the revolutionary threshold never held as much excitement as the desired *end*. Before the hard work could even begin, the absurd fantasy of a great American Bolshevik Revolution was implanted – if it could happen in Russia, it could certainly happen here.

The American Communist Party, therefore, was born under the influence of the Russian Revolution, and its future was charted by the movements of that ruling planet. Socialist immigrants in the US at last had a vantage from which to insist themselves into leadership of the Left; Bolshevism seemed to prove their life-long theoretical arguments. But the old Socialist Party was far too tame and insular to carry out this overdue international destiny. In June 1919 a group of Europeans attempted to take over a socialist National Left-Wing Conference; when they failed to achieve a majority they stormed out to form their own party (a dramatic pattern that would repeat itself often thereafter). The immigrants considered the group of Americans who defected with them too dim-witted to run a US party; this arrogance caused a split within the split so that the breakaway from the Socialist Party was immediately two-pronged. Both new parties believed in the need for making the international socialist revolution. Both opposed the temporary demands of the unions, and even fought bitterly with the IWW over the value of single-issue strikes. The only difference was a national one: the Europeans made up the Communist Party while the Communist Labor Party was composed of Yanks.

While the new groups lived off Bolshevik glory, they already began to slide into political ineffectiveness. Just four months after their formation, Attorney-General Palmer's broad crackdown on all troublemakers forced the Communists underground. A series of raids and round-ups resulted in convictions, deportations and hundreds of court cases. Here the Europeans had the advantage of a clandestine tradition. The CP destroyed its membership cards, changed all names and cut down the risk factor by dividing into small groups of ten. Those who stayed were considered the stalwart 'cadres', the loyal nucleus around which the Party could always regenerate itself. The Communist Labor Party, on the other hand, was seriously weakened and its wide-eyed American idealism crushed in the onslaught of repression. A political existence that was not above board did not suit their 'American nature'; many cracked and ran.

Just as the CP began to patch its wounds from the raids, it suffered an internal rupture. The last hold-out Americans who had stayed under its protective wing finally rebelled, just as the others had; they wanted, naturally, more 'action' and less socialist theory. This breakaway group called itself, typically, the 'official' Communist Party, put out a newspaper called the *Communist* (as did the 'other' CP) and absconded with the files of the old organization. Soon after, these Americans merged with the remnants of the Communist Labor Party to form the United Communist Party.

It was evident, even in the first months, that all these factions could never unite themselves into a movement. If allowed to go their own way, they would have gained new heads *ad infinitum*. But such anarchic communism in the US was of no use to the international movement and, in January 1920, the first of many messages arrived from the Communist International (Comintern) in Moscow asking the American groups to pull their socks up. This first request was more or less shrugged off; but soon it became a firm order and the American parties, in their adoration of the Soviets, had to agree. In May 1921 a shotgun wedding was ordered in which the CP and the CLP/UCP married to form the new Communist Party of America.

But Moscow's own theoretical development brought another kind of chaos inside the new unity. In the first few years after the Bolshevik Revolution, American workers had left the old reactionary unions, to work instead through the Communist parties. So bitter was the antagonism to these unions that the parties even ignored a very significant wave of militant strikes that took place in 1919. Now the Comintern thought it wise to reverse course and try to work from within the unions. Also the Party was advised to enter into American elections as a vehicle for propaganda. This was a logical, pragmatic development for Soviet Communism; but for American radicals it seemed a total reversal of the tough, heroic revolutionism that had motivated them. They expressed disappointment. It was then that Comrade Lenin put his finger on a central button in the 'American nature': he admonished leftists who were too emotionally involved in the struggle and had not mastered the art of *strategically* cooling off. It was vital to learn this lesson in order to escape the perpetual dream-state of living the revolution before it actually happens.

The new policy came to a head in June 1921, when the Russians urged the still underground Party to legalize. The point was to build a mass organization of workers, and this was impossible from a clandestine position. In December the Workers Party of America was established; the first of many legal 'front' groups the Party would throw up in years to come. The Russians claimed that American workers were not yet ready for socialist Utopias, and their political inexperience would have to be taken into account. This was a major admission, which meant that the impending American revolution would have to be postponed. A disillusioned group broke off in early 1922, claiming the Party was no longer militant and had compromised its dedication to revolutionary violence. It called itself the 'real' Communist Party and even set up its own legal front, the United Toilers of America. The Communist Party itself was not to be outdone and split itself into two more hostile camps over the question of legalizing; many felt you could not be truly revolutionary unless you were illegal.

The factionalism persisted, even down to fist fights and security clampdowns against opposition groups at meetings. But the Party reached a major crisis in 1923 when the Comintern calmly announced that US capitalism was in a state of imminent collapse, and that the workers must be nudged over the edge of their desperation into rebellion. While some Party members were willing to carry out any order the Russians cared to deliver, many simply could not reconcile this one with the reality they saw around them.

The new prosperity of the Coolidge Administration showed a mammoth rise in corporate profits and industrial expansion. Employees owned stock in companies and received adequate pensions and insurance benefits. Wages, too, were increasing at a fast enough pace to keep most workers fairly content. Not only was it impossible, in these conditions, to establish a strong working-class base, but union membership was on the decline, some million and a half less than a peak reached in 1920. The Left could do little more than turn its revolutionary enthusiasm to fighting itself.

But now a major power struggle was building to a climax in the Soviet Union, and its enormous implications would throw the American Left off course yet again. Stalin had been moulding the Comintern to his own ends since 1923, on the theory that the Soviet Union had to begin consolidating its strength instead of emphasizing Communist revolutions elsewhere. The chief opposition was Trotsky, who hoped to maintain the original impetus of revolution on an international scale. Because the Comintern generally issued orders, but kept the American Party ignorant of its internal manipulations, there was immense disorientation in the US Left. Americans did not know the complex issues involved, nor did they know that Comrade Trotsky's star was rapidly falling. Hardly had some realized they were 'Trotskyites' when they found themselves expelled from the Party in 1928. Now the most famous leftist rivalry began to rip through the American Party with astonishing ferocity. After the first expulsion, other CP members were given one week to state, in writing, their attitude towards Trotskyism. Those who hesitated or asked for more information were summarily expelled. It was now forbidden for loyal members to talk to Trotskyites, and all personal friendships with the renegades had to be terminated. The famous syndrome of Stalinist thugs breaking up Trotskyite meetings began almost immediately.

It was clear to anyone who could see the forest for the trees that you kept your place now only by soliciting Stalin's favour. The Party was taking on a new military precision, and there was no room in it for serious factions. It had done everything but function effectively for ten years. Now the difficult birth was over.

The Stalinized Party became the dominant force in the American Left for nearly two decades. Authority and inspiration were now vested solidly in the Comintern. The Party gained a new disciplinary imperative and a penchant for ritual purification. The invited repentances and apologies, the charges and counter-charges, the internal paranoia, the cutting away of dissidents all tended to strengthen the running of the operation. But it meant that the wholly 'foreign' perspective would again play tug-of-war with 'American nature'. The new discipline required a mental and moral stamina that did not come easy for American Communists; because of this, the Party could never fully harness its independents or curb a stubborn streak of libertarianism in the rank and file.

The psychological keynote of the new Party line was impersonality. The suppression of self-concern was designed to build an organization free of factions, based on solidarity. You were not meant to be 'a somebody' here, but rather a blank cheque at the disposal of the cause. As put by William Z. Foster, then head of the American CP: 'I am for the Comintern from start to finish. I want to work with the Comintern and if the Comintern finds itself criss-cross with my opinions, there is only one thing to do and that is change my opinions to fit the policy of the Comintern.' The classic theme of communist rationality was now pitted against natural American spontaneity, expressiveness, moodiness and feelings that were 'irrelevant' to greater goals. The importance of personal relationships was played down because these tended to interfere with Party work and could create a relaxation of revolutionary effort. 'Friendship' was distinguished from 'comradeship', the one referring to private distractions, the other to Party loyalties. You were not encouraged to have social relationships outside the organization, especially with renegades and opponents of the CP. Comrades whose husbands or wives had not joined up were strongly urged to recruit their mates. Promiscuity was frowned upon, and fidelity to one's mate sometimes insisted on. Homosexuality was considered an illness that needed curing before Party work could be carried out. But this was not an arbitrary morality, designed merely for the sake of efficiency. By allowing frustrations to build up under the guise of 'meaningful' self-denial, the Party could assume the role of supreme comforter and also bolster its authority.*

The Party also gained power through 'mystification' of its members. By creating its own 'official reality' it could keep people politically confused and in a state of tension. Yesterday's truth could simply be abandoned when it was no longer convenient or it proved embarrassing. Names of 'renegades' were eliminated from Party histories and political tracts. The constant vigilance against Red-baiters and turncoats always made the ordinary Communist question his own loyalty.

But power-play and distrust were chiefly the domain of those with aspirations to high-level positions in the Party. It was not always clear to the rank and file that there were secret businesses going on in the backrooms. Nor were they – except perhaps at moments of internal crisis – subjected to such a rigorous discipline that they were utterly compromised as individuals. In the 1930s the CP had a raging hunger for membership, and did not want to frighten people off. Indeed, the organization hardly discriminated in the recruiting of members; its strategy was to find people who had an initial interest and then *make* them into Communists. Most people who joined the CP had never read the Marxist classics, and they did not normally receive a theoretical education once inside the group. They were made to feel that the professionals at the top were looking after the economics, while they were supposed to be content to raise funds and sell the *Daily Worker* door to door. It could not be otherwise when the bulk of the membership joined out of some abstract 'concern', feeling the world deserved a better deal than capitalism was giving it. It did not matter all that much that the specific remedy was Marxian socialism.

The Party seems to have preferred things this way, perhaps

* This idea was stated by Freud who believed that sexual morality created weaklings of a 'follower' mentality. His disciple, the onetime Communist, Wilhelm Reich (see V), carried this notion much further, showing the suppression of natural impulses to be the psychological foundation of totalitarian systems – notably Hitler's and Stalin's.

needing loyalists and hard-core workers much more than classical Marxists who would no doubt question the constant shifts of Party line.

If it did not stress socialist doctrine, the CP did set up propaganda programmes for its members. Its National Training Schools had the function of instilling Party psychology as an alternative to pre-existing personal orientations. The tactics employed at these schools were similar in some ways to post-psychoanalytic therapies of later years, primarily in the goal of eliminating personality barriers. One Communist teacher, described by an ex-Party member, 'used to enrage and attack people, then suddenly lighten up with a joke – then suddenly attack again. The object was to break down independence of judgement and character . . . He broke one man completely one day – and then sat up all night speaking softly and "inspirationally" to him.'

Eventually, many would drop out of the Party because of its increasing lack of warmth, and the organization would continue to rigidify around a tighter nucleus. But for the depressed period of the early thirties it appeared to be the best organized and winningest channel for rebellious opposition to the State. The socialists – what was left of them – were limp and respectable, 'Bolsheviks with a shave'. The Trotskyites had inherited the leftist factional tradition, content with baiting their beastie 'Stalinoids' but incapable of seizing political initiative. Despite its new look, the Party seemed like it could even be a champion against authoritarianism, and began to represent the Utopian aspirations of American dreamers – many of whom had joined out of private feelings of pacifism, hatred of injustice or just plain rebellion.

The Party's 'mysticism' also had its positive aspects. The new religion of Stalinism could fulfil the hero-worshipping and faith needs of thousands. It established not merely a new 'reality' of fact and history, but also a heroic mythology where the wisdom of the Comintern or the splendour of the Red Army or the superiority of Soviet culture or the glory of the Five Year Plan played key roles. There was also a complementary demonology which rated capitalists and fascists pretty high, though not so high as socialists or CP renegades. As for Leon Trotsky and his crew, well, Judas Iscariot didn't know the half of it. All this was wrapped in the mystic ring of the words 'The Party', hypnotic and suggestive, rendering instant reactions of loyalty and/or ecstasy.

But the CP did not always have to mesmerize. It asked for Party loyalty even above the family or lover, but often it got such dedication voluntarily. It provided comforts which the family structure could not. The deliberate creation of social clubs as adjuncts to the political centre catered to victims of the loneliness of the urban landscape. In the early thirties most members of the CP were still immigrants or the children of immigrants; their loyalty came out of an obvious alienation from American culture. For them the Party was a community of 'outsiders'; they had anticipated American Dream-myth only to find more ghettos, humiliation and Depression. For Communist bachelors the rumour was out (despite the subsequent Puritanism) that Red girls were free lovers, marriage was a bourgeois frame-up and you might get laid without regret by putting your name down. The Party could often be a *party*, a total 'hootenanny' of experience, a human refuge in the midst of rat-race America.

The Party was also – by its very nature as opposition to the *status quo* and social 'normality' – a catch-all for strange bed-fellows. Weirdos and Bohemians naturally haunted the fringes, expecting that in such a revolutionary band they might find a home for their particular public platform.* In the fifties many Red-baiting psychoanalysts were quick to suggest that reasons for joining the CP were often attributable to neurotic aberrations. For example, it was discovered that where a dominant American mama existed, our boy might run into the arms of the Party seeking a strong, authoritarian father substitute. Power-freaks could hope to gain ascendancy in an organization that encouraged distrust, spying and informing. Others signed up because they

---

* Many of these who could not bear CP discipline thought to find more sympathy among Trotskyites. James Cannon, a top Trotskyite, warned against admitting 'freaks always looking for the most extreme expression of radicalism, misfits, windbags, chronic opportunists . . .' In voicing these fears, Cannon was perhaps prophetic about the future role of the leftist fringe: 'They are going to mark our organization as something freakish, abnormal, exotic . . .'

had pent-up hostility to express or because they were rejected by the outside world. Certainly such atrocity stories can be found wherever there is a revolutionary party. At the same time, it seems clear that the American CP did come to imply, for many, an important form of individual therapy. The most common relation to the organization and its aims was a personal one, and whatever compulsions put a man into its vanguard embrace, they were seldom related to hard-core politics.

The goal of Communist rationality was dependent on reducing emotional displays. Any excess, be it joy or rage or depression, was thought harmful to clear-headed work. If you failed in your task, it was not cause for weeping or doldrums; a little self-critical Stalinist enema would clean out the mistake. If you scored a success for the Party it was not cause for whoops of ecstasy or dancing in the street. What could you do next to better it? Win or lose, it was disastrous to let down the momentum of the political function by any form of excitement.

For the man who needed to publicize his role in making the better world, Communist rationality was disappointing. There was little hope of bringing the Party in line with the American obsession for becoming a Man. The revolutionary bravado that suggested itself after 1917 was slowly dimming to a muffle. 'Clyde Griffiths' had just begun to raise his voice; now some far-away commissar put a finger to his lips.

Still, the authoritarian hand could stifle only so much enthusiasm. The Party had to accept that many rank and file could not and would not respond according to Communist precision. There were, first of all, large numbers of Eastern European Jews and their children to take into account; even the Party could not eradicate traditions of breast-beating and powerfully expressed feelings. It was this very sentimentalism that brought such comrades into the fold. Equally, there was a new American spontaneity and emotional honesty inspired by Freud; to many novice revolutionaries it seemed part and parcel of the same liberating spirit that gave rise to Bolshevism.

Freud did not invent the new open city of personality. He merely gave theoretical shape to an amorphous bustle of excitations, many of which derived from the 'freedoms' made possible by commercial prosperity in the 1920s. Because his ideas were publicized at a time when natives and immigrants alike were looking into their 'American nature', Freud seemed to provide some useful digging tools. The folkloric notion of 'speaking your mind' was coming back into vogue; he literalized it. Psychoanalysis was a method of self-discovery based on 'complete candour', the idea that the self is most clearly revealed when the mind exercises least control over impulses. The patient was meant to let his most suppressed thoughts flow out into words without making a critical selection from his revelations. It was the sort of thing only coloured folks were supposed to do, but which anti-repressive whites were fast learning.

Freud did not intend his work to be taken as a signal for a Brave New World of exposure and political freedom. His interest was in the elimination of neurotic symptoms to cure mental disorders. Indeed, he stressed that the unlimited flow of powerful instincts could be dangerous when transferred from the psychoanalyst's couch to daily life; in the late twenties he went so far as to say these should be checked to avoid conflict with the demands of civilization. But the Freud who gained a foothold in American popular fictions, in the cinema and the theatre, in the private psychodramas of millions of guys and gals, was interpreted as having encouraged going naked psychologically and letting it all hang out. In 1925 he wrote that psychoanalysis 'has suffered a great deal from being watered down . . . many abuses which have no relation to it find a cover under its name, and there are few opportunities for any thorough training in technique or theory'. Freud's intentions and world-view were overlooked once it was discovered how his science could be marketed.

While America was experiencing the new upsurge of immediacy and personal confession, it was impossible for the Left not to be touched in some powerful way. The massive frustrations which built up throughout the gestation period of social agitation, the constrictions of the Puritan ethic and of Communist discipline combined with the pressure to elevate your self and *make your stand* – all this worked in favour of the need to struggle with your own immediate past rather than that abstraction called history.

In this sense, Freudian thinking brought many headaches for the Party. Here you were not a product of the clash of economic forces – as Marx had it – but rather a being with conscious will and choice, whose social distress could be traced to neuroses originating in the first five years after birth. These neuroses hampered the easy fulfilment of normal functions and, in order to *act* properly, you had first to trace the source of your dilemma. Technically, this involved the aid of an analyst in liberating repressed data from the unconscious. Such professional fellows posed a real threat to the comforting, power-holding function of the Party. But even more dangerous was the wholly un-political way in which many members now began to perceive themselves; with a little knowledge of the basic rules, you might even learn to analyse yourself and determine the course of your own character.

Once you eliminated the psychological blocks to your liberation, you could develop, at last, your *character*. 'American nature' had updated the Old World notion of 'self' which implied an integration of personal, distinctive traits seen against a broader spectrum of the world, a living definition of one's place in history. The cut-price version reduced this to something called 'personality' or 'character', having as its final aim making the subject presentable. It was now possible to speak of politicians, movie stars and others as 'personalities', and draw from them a fund of instant associations. Personality had the strictly American virtue of being acquired property; you might say someone 'had' personality – thereby implying he could also be without it. Self, however, as it was interpreted in European fiction and psychology, had no commercial value and could not be hastened through therapy. It existed in varying degrees of eccentricity or obscurity; it could be built up over a lifetime with enormous effort.

Yet, there was no time for life-long projects. The social scene talked of liberation and looked like revolution. *Your* voice and *your* character could give fight to the rotten state of the world. And subsequently the witch-hunters and political sadists who throttled the Left for the next decades did not always distinguish the hardcore leftist from the protestor who did not necessarily want to overthrow the Government, but only find himself. The

latter was becoming a genuine threat because he was an inveter-
ate questioner of the bourgeois psychology that buttressed
capitalist economy. The Power was not amused at the potential
for revolutions in the family structure, the work ethic or sexual
morality. 'Clyde Griffiths' had reached deep into his personal
well and pulled up, with his character, unexpectedly, a kind of
treason.

3

While the Left was struggling to define the nature of its future
operation, the Power was already mapping out its own scenario
for crushing it. Up until 1917 radicals were generally handled by
strike-breakers, vigilantes or the cop on the corner. But the Russian Revolution compelled the Woodrow Wilson Administration
(as well as all successive presidencies) to insure against a similar
performance at home. The fear of Bolshevism could only be
eliminated at conspiratorial level by an alerted *Federal* government.

Since it was faced with an undirected jumble of rebellion, the
Government's first major wave of national repression in 1919 cast
a wide net and swept in unionists, socialists, Communists, as well
as the just plain dissatisfied. Many of these were members of
immigrant anarchist groups, believing in their traditional mutual
aid, freedom from government interference and free-thinking on
most public and private matters. Aside from the occasional bomb
incident, most anarchists presented no real political or civil
threat. Still, they often wrote and disseminated ideas that had
enough intrinsic appeal to cause some worry among public officials. Also, their influence was strong among foreign workers
who could not speak English. These were not subject to the conservative brain-washing of the mass media, but were receptive to
the hundreds of small foreign-language publications put out by
the anarchist press.

Since most anarchists had no concrete 'programme', they usually came into the more abstract – but equally dangerous – field
of re-making social mythology. They spoke to the liberation of
personality and provoked the worst fears of repressed American

Puritanism. When, in 1919, Attorney-General Palmer justified his Red raids to the Senate Judiciary Committee, he emphasized a typically self-righteous manifesto issued by a Spanish anarchist group in New York. The voluptuousness of its poetics offended his sensibilities: 'Oh, governments! Associations of corruption, dens of assassins, adulterers of purity, deformers of angelic innocence . . .' These would be overrun by the sacred 'redeeming ideal, which illuminates the clouds, and sheds its fecundating rays . . . which offers a prosperous and infinite robustness to life, dignified and purified by the balm, the fragrance, the delight of free love, saturated and fortified by its germs of maternity . . .'

There was nothing in the language of an immediately dangerous nature, nor had the anarchists involved committed any acts of violence. Yet they were brought to trial for publishing only poesy posing as politics. Although they were acquitted, Palmer cited this as a test case for his scheme because it suggested a *spirit* that had to be crushed. The US was still drawing itself up from a history of lawlessness, hoping to build a streamlined, panic-free society. Anarchists – especially greasy foreign ones – represented to the popular mind the very essence of social chaos-making.

One of the most feared of naturalized anarchists was Emma Goldman. Her ferocious and uncompromising revolutionary passion embarrassed capitalists and Communists alike, but won her a coterie of intellectual and famous admirers like Theodore Dreiser. The stories of her exploits were shared and exaggerated by both her champions and detractors – her theatrical actions for political effect, her political actions for theatrical effect. Because of her notoriety she became politically useful to Palmer. When the Attorney-General brought his case against radicals to the Senate in 1919, he made Emma the star attraction, knowing her name alone would play upon the worst fantasies of his audience. Yet, because her legal transgressions were only minor ones, Palmer was forced to nail her by intellectual implication – setting a precedent for later witch-hunters. Her ideas being so well known, he could 'prove' that the actions of others were carried out according to her formulas. Emma had been arrested in 1901 as a suspected accomplice of Leon Czolgosz, the anarchist who bumped off President McKinley. Not only was she found to be innocent of the charge, but she had opposed the assassination. Nonetheless, eighteen years later, Palmer made the connection: '. . . Czolgosz's reason for assassinating President McKinley was that he didn't believe in this form of government. He stated that the same doctrines opposing this form of government were enunciated by Emma Goldman . . .' Two other anarchists, suspected of bombing the Los Angeles *Times* building, were shown to have known Emma Goldman personally. Also, three members of her own anarchist group blew themselves up in 1914, in a New York apartment, while apparently making bombs.

In June 1917 the State finally got her for obstructing the draft through the No-Conscription League she had organized. After a bit of collusion between government departments, Emma was stripped of her naturalization through a technicality involving a missing ex-husband she divorced decades before. Now Palmer was using her case to telegraph his plans for other radicals. In December 1919 Emma and 248 other alien subversives were deported to Russia on the S.S. *Buford*, dubbed the 'Soviet ark'.

Goldman was another dissenter-in-principle, exercising a vocal freedom that harked back to US founding doctrine and to Whitman. Her 'New Declaration of Economic Independence' demanded that 'the land shall be to him who cultivates it, the mine to the miner, the tool to him who uses it, the factories to those who work in them, and the common product to the whole people'. In her draft 'conspiracy' trial she told the jury the famous anecdote of Henry Thoreau telling Emerson that it was better to make a stand by going to jail when American liberty was in jeopardy.

But however subversive her politics may have been in 1919, that does not explain the hysteria that attended her lecture tours or the overwhelming effort of the Federal Government to break her. More likely, the ideas that did threaten to infect America derived from her guidelines for personal liberation. She defended prostitutes and their trade; described marriage as an 'economic arrangement' by which the man gains and the woman – his property – suffers; preached atheism; likened schools to prisons in which children were brain-washed to be obedient; taught birth-control techniques; believed in making love with anyone who wanted you in return, inside or outside wedlock.* This, combined with her willingness to express it all any time, any place, at any vocal pitch, made her the ideal choice for 'making an example'.

Emma's deportation meant that she could not attend the party thrown by A. Mitchell Palmer for some 3,000 US radicals on 2 January 1920. The series of raids which occurred on that night and the subsequent detention climaxed two years of preparation by the Attorney-General, who claimed only to be responding to the public outcry against leftist and alien atrocities.

For the occasion of May Day 1919, a batch of mail-bombs addressed to various radical-haters and notable capitalists had been discovered at a US post office; despite a concerted police hunt, the senders were never caught. A month later a wave of bombs had actually found a few targets, one of which was Palmer's house. The explosion was reported immediately by neighbours – a certain Mr and Mrs Franklin D. Roosevelt – but, again, no one was caught. There was one bomber found amidst the rubble (he was the only casualty), apparently having fallen on his own device in the great comic tradition of bungled blow-ups. Happily for Palmer, the terrorist could be identified from various bits (including some from his body) of evidence, including a subversive manifesto; he was found to be an Italian anarchist. One of the more provocative discoveries in this rebellious debris was *two* left legs! More fuel was added to Palmer's zeal when, in November 1919, a small-fry non-functioning 'Russian bomb laboratory' was found in New York.

But the anarchists were only the more ostentatious of trouble-

* By this time radicals had come to be associated, in popular myth, with sexual aberrations, and the Russian Revolution supposedly brought in a flood of these. The Bolsheviks had reportedly established a 'Bureau of Free Love', with which all women over 18 were forced to register. When Palmer issued his report to the Senate, it spoke of the 'nationalization' of women; a woman could choose any husband she wanted, and the man was not permitted to protest. In the New York *Times* version, it was the men who had all the fun, having no limit to the number of females they could consume, with the qualification that they could 'use one woman not oftener than three times a week for three hours'.

makers. 1919 had also seen some dynamic strikes and attendant police riots, notably in the crucial steel and coal industries; the IWW played a role in agitating these, and thus became another target for the Attorney-General. It was also no coincidence that the raids came just four months after the birth of the twin Communist parties; the possibility of a Bolshevik America became a guiding scare-theme.

The nature of Palmer's operation was determined by the absence of adequate legislation to deal with the situation. Whatever statutes existed focused on organizations; it was necessary to prove that a conspiracy had taken place. This made it difficult, for instance, to nail individual terrorists who somehow never bothered to register as a group. The only sedition laws related to a wartime situation; now some seventy congressional bills were pending, trying to define the character of peacetime treason. But even though Palmer urged the passage of such bills, he was content to act without them. This way he was able to move independently of Congress, using his own strategy and reaping all the accolades.

In August 1919 Palmer had established the General Intelligence Department (GID), administered under the Justice Department's Bureau of Investigation. With perhaps a divine gift of prophecy, the Attorney-General chose, to head the new office, a twenty-four-year-old bloodhound named John Edgar Hoover. The first assignment for the young chief was to gather info on domestic radical activities; he went at this with unparalleled enthusiasm, gathering, by 1923, 750,000 names on carefully filed index cards. Hoover also prepared numerous reports for Palmer, including the document on Emma Goldman. But the major contribution of the new office was the observation – in perfect accord with the views of the Comintern – that ninety per cent of US radicals were aliens and, if left to themselves, the native 10 per cent would collapse in revolutionary ignorance. Hoover also pointed out that the Left was gathering influence among normally acquiescent groups of workers and, more worrying, Negroes. All this was just what Palmer wanted to hear. He did not want to resort to costly trials which could get him into First-Amendment free-speech wrangles, and which might make martyrs of radicals. He went then for the

Alien Act of 1918 which provided for deportation without appeal. The trick was to make them disappear – and pronto – before the softy liberals had a chance to object.

After a couple of rehearsal raids in November and December, the G-Men hit 'em with the works on 2 January. Over 3,000 suspects were rounded up at night and arrested in thirty-three major US cities. Americans were separated out and sent off for prosecution by local authorities, while the immigrants were herded into detention centres. Many innocent foreigners were taken off the streets or out of pool rooms and social clubs, beaten and shoved into paddy wagons. Before the big day, those Feds who had already infiltrated the Communist ranks were instructed to make sure the Reds would be caught having Party meetings on 2 January; if no meeting was scheduled, they were to find an excuse to demand one so that the round-up could be more efficiently carried out. The raiding parties were told by a Justice Department official: 'I leave it entirely to your discretion as to the method by which you should gain access to such places.' Most agents took him at his word and did not obtain entry or arrest warrants. They merely kicked open doors (in the later Hollywood style) and told everyone to get 'up against the wall'. Others broke into printing shops and demolished the small presses that published leftist papers and leaflets. The Feds were often aided in their work by the local citizenry – ex-military men and vigilantes – who descended on IWW offices and foreign-language clubs, stomping on Reds and aliens. Because the raids ran well into the night it was often difficult to obtain legal help. But this hardly mattered; weeks before the event, Palmer and some officials in the Labor Department had reversed a part of the Alien Act which gave foreigners the right to consult counsel immediately, before deportation proceedings. Many could not speak English well and, when told they could not see lawyers, allowed themselves to 'confess', to stool-pigeon on others for better treatment or to be railroaded into deportation. Very high bail was asked in most cases, meaning that many low-wage earners would have to rot in prison up to five months without knowing their fate. Finally, no regard was given to families of detainees; their outlook was bleak if the prior S.S. *Buford* sailing was anything to judge by. In that instance, Hoover did not bother to inform wives or families that their men were no longer in jail, but somewhere out at sea.

The immediate effects of the raids were unsatisfactory for Palmer. He got a lot of negative feedback from liberal lawyers and concerned congressmen, got few convictions and less than a thousand aliens were ultimately deported. The anarchists were silenced, but only for a few months. In September a bomb took out a building on Wall Street, causing forty deaths; again, no one was caught. Since almost all the major Communist leaders were rounded-up, both organizations were driven underground. It was evident now – unlike in Europe – that becoming an American Communist was a clear-cut act of social deviance, eminently punishable. But the raids tended to strengthen at least the CP by frightening off its less-committed fringe.

Haphazard and inefficient as Palmer's operation proved to be, it nonetheless established groundrules for the future. His was the first significant *offensive* action against dissenters. It was planned chiefly in advance of, not in reaction to, any serious or immediate leftist threat. By 1919 the power of the IWW was waning. The Communists had almost no influence over the working class – despite Hoover's assertions – and they were hit even before they could properly organize themselves. When the raids came, they were out of all proportion to the facts.

Palmer was able to mount such a full-scale performance because the Federal Government had decided to take the Red-smashing business out of the hands of local law-enforcement agencies. But the outcome was not Federal legislation as Palmer promised (although the Immigrant Act of 1921 created a quota system for aliens); instead it brought in the prototype for a Federal police force which would soon solidify under Mr Hoover and his famous three initials. The FBI had its beginnings as a kind of Brain Police, what with Hoover's neat index, coordinating radical repression on a national scale – thereby force-feeding the myth of a Red *conspiracy*. The Bureau did not merely investigate actions, but ideas as well. In 1919 Palmer told the Senate he wanted to 'make sedition and seditious utterances a crime'.

The raids demonstrated that there were reputations to be made in the new free enterprise of chasing subversives. Palmer proved that the disunited Left was ripe for a career as slapstick straight-man for sadistic right-wing theatricals. Here was a pre-packaged syndrome which countless others could use to get votes, publicity or – irony of ironies – the power of influence in the political process. Immediately in 1920 bandwagon jumpers made themselves heard, one Senator even urging the deportation of *all* US radicals, native and foreign, to the penal dungeons on the American-owned island of Guam. A voice from the future, Calvin Coolidge, publicly endorsed all actions against dissident groups. His firm stand against 'Red' strikers while Governor of Massachusetts levered him to the Vice-Presidency in 1920 and, finally, to the Summit. Edgar Hoover was perhaps the main winner of the spoils and, whether or not he actually exploited the Palmer scare in order to build himself an FBI (as his enemies have suggested), he was never above using Red-baiting to achieve further power in later years.

But it was Palmer himself who set in motion the most interesting precedent – the fantasy that you could get to be President as a direct result of Red-baiting. (Another man, years later, would actually get there by that tortuous route.) It was his White House aspirations that moved him, even to the extent of obliterating the liberal reputation he had built up before the war. Now he carried his dream to excess and it swallowed him. Of radicals in general, he believed (that is, he *said*): 'Out of the sly and crafty eyes of many of them leap cupidity, cruelty, insanity and crime; from their lopsided faces, sloping brows, and misshapen features may be recognized the unmistakeable criminal type.' For Bolsheviks (and, by subtle implication, Jews) he had special sentiments. Their revolution was run by 'a small clique of outcasts from the East Side of New York ... Because a disreputable alien – Leon Bronstein, the man who now calls himself Trotsky – can inaugurate a reign of terror from his throne-room in the Kremlin; because the lowest of all types known to New York can sleep in the Tsar's bed ... should America be swayed by such doctrines?' He told the Senate it was not easy to round-up foreigners, because they act secretly and hide out in dark, spectral places 'not often visited by ordinary Americans'. His office asked Congress for two million dollars each fiscal year because that was the amount believed to be pouring into the US from Soviet Russia each *month*! Palmer even went above and beyond the call of duty (and legality) by giving the Justice Department a new role; it used part of its appropriation for sending articles and cartoons (free of charge) to newspapers and magazines, setting up the very Red Menace Palmer was about to stamp out, disseminating propaganda before and after the raids to build up his credibility and publicize his crusade. But his own zeal finished him. For May Day 1920, Palmer predicted the biggest Red uprising the US had ever known. Police were mobilized by the thousands and a great Red alert kept the citizens anxious. The day, however, proved to be the quietest, undemonstratingest 1 May for many a year – not a peep. Palmer didn't even get the Democratic nomination.

In years to come there would be many inheritors of the Palmer tradition, although methods would vary and sometimes even gain sophistication. One of these was a New York congressman named Hamilton Fish, who talked himself into the chairmanship of a specially appointed witch-hunt committee in 1930. Fish called some leading Reds to testify, hoping they might enlighten him as to this puzzle called communism (about which he knew next to nothing). Instead, he got responses that established the nature of dramatic repartees for such committees in future. The Communist witness, William Z. Foster, claimed righteously that the CP was only preparing workers to follow Jefferson's advice for overturning corrupt authority. He also scored the committee's work, telling them that, by their own logic, they would have to investigate 'those who died on the battlefields of the American Revolution'. Fish kept up these pointless hearings for six months and finally produced a report which recommended declaring the CP illegal; deporting alien Communists; an embargo on Russian trade; an end to the importing, specifically, of Russian timber; Federal laws to prevent Reds from spreading false rumours that might cause a run on banks! None of these suggestions was heeded and Fish never rose to power for his efforts, but his committee at least had the distinction of being the forerunner to the House Committee on Un-American Activities formed several years later.

The major recipient of Palmerism, however, was the American Left itself. Out of the Red-baiting came a defined future for its activities. Instead of provoking, it would spend a good portion of the next fifty years on the defensive, *responding* to the whims of entrenched power. It would seize upon the image of fearful midnight raiders, undercover informers and bogeyman inquisitors and give them supernatural status in anti-State fictions. Radical indignation would become the only refuge – at times – for the despair of the leftist plight. In 1947 a Party-oriented 'historical' report on the Palmer raids assigned a much more prominent and initiating role to Hoover than he actually played; by this time he had been advanced high up in the CP chamber-of-horrors index (everyone, in fact, had been pushed forward a notch after the murder of Trotsky). The report also told with dismay that G-Men had burst into peaceful working-class homes, ripped down pictures of Karl Marx from their frames and used them for face-masks as they cavorted drunkenly and obscenely about the room. Palmer had won a psychological victory he never imagined: the Left had accepted his scenario.

Palmer went out in 1921 when the Harding Administration took power, but his spirit continued to play a part in events to come. The most famous of these began in February 1920, when an anarchist named Andrea Salsedo was arrested in connection with the printing of the pamphlet found with the pieces of the bomber with two left legs who attacked Palmer's house the previous June. Instead of a prison-cell, Salsedo was put in the celebrity suite on the fourteenth floor of a Justice Department building in New York. According to J. Edgar Hoover's report, the man was there by his 'own choice' and was not being intimidated. Apparently he just enjoyed hanging out with the Feds for *eight weeks* of 'questioning'. After his visit he allegedly signed a statement confessing to having printed the pamphlet. Then, as Mr Hoover so succinctly put it, 'Salsedo put an end to his part of the arrangement by jumping from the fourteenth floor . . . upon the street . . .'

In April an Italian anarchist from Boston, Bartolomeo Vanzetti, came to New York to inquire into the fate of his friend Salsedo. But he did not learn of the latter's death until back in Massachusetts a week later. The Salsedo episode put the fear into Vanzetti's Boston group and they decided to destroy all their incriminating propaganda. On 5 May Vanzetti and Nicola Sacco were caught with the anarchist literature in hand and arrested; months later they were charged with having committed an earlier payroll robbery of $16,000 and having murdered two guards. They were subsequently sentenced to death, and a long series of appeals lasting until 1927 failed to save them.

Seven years after the arrest, the plight of Sacco and Vanzetti was a leftist legend, a part of popular drama, fiction and song. The essence of the radical argument was that the two were innocent of the robbery, but were being framed because they were anarchists. Overwhelming evidence exists to support the claim that this was a classic railroading, although there is no apparent reason why *these* anarchists, a shoemaker and a fish-peddler, should have been singled out. The importance of the case to the history of the Left, however, was not in its legal implications. It provided the much-needed impetus for drawing all the protesting elements together in cluster. Curiously, there was hardly a murmur out of the Left until near the end of the affair. The union defeats of the Coolidge era and the failure of the CP to win a mass base had weakened the protesting movement; now, at last, there was an emotion-packed cause to cling to. Liberal intellectuals, too, were frustrated with the 'Babbitry' and social anonymity of America, and searched for a road into the thicket of dissent. There was nothing to attract them in the factional muck of the CP, and much to fear – intellectually – from the implications of anarchism. It was the smell of death that juiced them into commitment; they could easily relate to a campaign that was abstract and symbolic. By 1927 nearly all the political meaning was drained out of the Sacco-Vanzetti case. Two free-thinkers were simply condemned to die for their ideas, and such a 'non-political' cause as saving their lives managed to unify the most disparate social groups.

Typically, the Party looked to reap the notoriety of the event. The Communists had been approached as early as 1920 to take part in the defence, but they declined, clearly because the case had no prominence at that time. But in 1925 the International Labor Defense, a Party front organization, raised money for the Italians, demanding at the same time to lead the Sacco-Vanzetti

Defense Committee. This was rejected by the liberal lawyers running the show, fearing the Party would turn it into a Communist propaganda festival. Still, in 1927, the CP did lead the protest on a world-wide basis, mounting an impressive fund-raising, speech-making campaign. This led Stalin to predict: 'We are on the threshold of new revolutionary events.'* Yet the camaraderie inspired by the situation did not last long. On the day of the execution the *Daily Worker* headline ran: 'The Socialist Party Betrayed Them.'

Like other great 'events' in American leftist history – as if some invisible chain of these events *was* that history – the Sacco-Vanzetti episode became politically important as it increased its heroic dynamic, its pretence to world-shaking implications, its limitless capacity for sentiment. But the real power of its effect on collective memory rests with the truly impressive character of Vanzetti, who won a leftist sainthood along with his martyrdom. His letters and speeches were packed with defiant dignity – offset by a shaky English – which gave them the full flavour of greatness in revolt. In one of his most famous statements, he touched a theme that could play upon the heartstrings of every generation of the American Left: 'If it had not been for these thing, I might have live out my life talking at street corners to scorning men. I might have to die, unmarked, unknown, a failure. Now we are not a failure. This is our career and our triumph.'

In saying that their lives were nothing and their deaths everything, Vanzetti was addressing himself, inadvertently, to the crux of the radical matter. He found futility in his political acts, but absolute personal achievement in his public role as victim of the State. If his body could not serve the cause, his *example* now would; his death would be his gift to tolerance, 'joostice . . . man's onderstanding of man . . .' The good-intentioned man who looked to change the system had turned a prison-cell and a death-

---

* The Soviet Union was in the process of eradicating its own anarchists, so the Party had to apply a bit of 'official reality' to its publicity. Sacco and Vanzetti became 'class-war victims' and their actual affiliations were never mentioned. In the opinion of the *Daily Worker* the 'big New England employers and the Department of Justice doomed them in order to frighten the foreign-born workers who were taking part in the big strikes of 1920'.

chamber into tools of struggle against injustice. No one will remember what Vanzetti stood for and worked for before 1920, but his self claims radical immortality.

The Sacco-Vanzetti case was by no means the last time the CP would exploit a highly emotional situation for political profit. If Americans were dim at maintaining a political through-line, they could be relied upon to fall for every thrill-packed dramatic 'issue' that achieved public prominence. One of the likeliest sources of perpetual outrage and sympathy was the Negro struggle.

This was an obvious stick with which to thrash the racist American establishment. Yet, in the early days of the Party, the black question was almost never raised. At best it was considered part of the general problem of working-class victimization. The CP had virtually no black membership until the thirties and – curiously – didn't try very hard to recruit any. In 1928 the Comintern (most of whose members had never seen an American Negro outside of one or two bourgeois delegates to the International) decided to support existing efforts for a separate Negro republic and 'self-determination'. In a resolution from its 1930 convention, the American CP admitted that 'to win for Communist leadership also the masses of Negro workers, the party must root out all traces of a formal approach . . . The influence of white chauvinism is still felt in the party . . . Negro workers and farmers persecuted on the basis of race discrimination must be accepted and treated as class-struggle victims.'

From this point on, the Party slowly worked up its rightful reputation as the chief defender of black liberties, with its famous cry of 'chauvinism' at the merest hint of racial bias. But it really got its appetite – and its largest influx of black members – from a hot event in Scottsboro, Alabama in 1931. Here, eight out of nine black boys were convicted and sentenced to the Electric Chair for allegedly raping two white girls on a train.* It was the biggest heart-throb frame-up since Sacco-Vanzetti, and this time

* The level of enlightenment under which the boys were tried is exemplified by the prosecution asking the examining doctor whether the semen found in the two girls came from white or black genitals.

the Communists did not waste a minute. They immediately took over the appeal and created a whirlwind fund-raising and rally-making operation which, after several years, helped to save the lives of the Scottsboro Boys. Naturally, the Party turned this into a working-class issue, claiming that blacks, along with immigrant workers, bore the brunt of the Government's attempt to divert attention from the Depression. The *Daily Worker* even went so far as to insist that most of the South's lynchings resulted not from blacks raping (or allegedly raping) white women, but from their demanding higher wages!

The Scottsboro affair presented a real chance for the CP to win vanguard status on the Left. But other groups were muscling in on the territory, and the Party fought with fury to keep the business all to itself. Foremost among these enemies was the National Association for the Advancement of Colored People (NAACP) which had the audacity to suggest this was not in fact a class issue; indeed, southern white *workers* were the chief nigger-lynchers, kept Negroes out of their unions and insisted that the Scottsboro boys be executed. The Party responded by sending its thugs to break up NAACP meetings or calling the cops when a Negro-led rally was organized. The major propaganda combat was over which group would get approval from the boys' parents, so that American mama-sentimentality might be milked. When the CP failed to win over all these elders, it simply invented them; occasionally, Negro women were hired to go around the country posing as Scottsboro mothers working on behalf of their sons for the Party. One of the *Daily Worker's* famous letters – it had a brilliant knack of receiving such letters – was from one of the mothers who said: 'I can't be treated any better than the Reds has treated me. And I am a Red too . . . Give all the Reds my love for I love them all.'

*

Sacco was the first to be strapped in the thing; the electrodes were placed, he cried 'viva l'anarchia!' and was stopped by the current. Vanzetti's turn came and he declared again his innocence. He forgave some who had done him injury, thanked his warden and generally reduced the proceedings to heartbreak with his dignified air. The switch was pushed, the lights dimmed, Vanzetti's frame fought in its leather straps. Ten seconds the buzz held; eased off; then they hit him again. The warden approached his corpse and spoke the words: 'Under the law I now pronounce you dead, the sentence of the court has been legally carried out.' Outside the prison a specially gathered riot squad stood with fixed bayonets and machine guns, while a police boat patrolled Boston Harbor expecting trouble.

It was ten years since the Bolsheviks had stormed the Winter Palace; American leftists were still preparing. In all that time a spirit of experiment reigned, an attempt to find a workable method for acts against the State. But leftist expression had not yet defined itself in the US; it changed tune as one political faction rose to prominence over another. This had made the young movement vulnerable to the will of the Federal Government – and now it was being ushered into a chamber where this instrument of death stood waiting. Of all the possible persecutions that came with being a leftist – broken heads, jail, fines, deportations, chain-gangs, witch-hunts – none ever loomed up so fearsome as this Electric Chair. The crackle of authoritarian electricity seemed to say that there was no more time for experiment. Few radicals would actually die in this Chair, but the terrible symbolism of the thing could bring the protest voice to a gasp. It would not deter political activism in years to come so much as give it shape, an end to which you might rise – and fall in a simple charge. It left no doubt at all where the Power was.

The Leftist Hero Exposes his Front

In the early months of 1924 members of the Moscow Art Theatre, led by the great acting master Stanislavsky, visited the White House for a courtesy audience with President Calvin Coolidge. After a long wait and a demeaning set of instructions forbidding them to speak to the Chief Executive (these were the first Soviet passport-bearers ever received at the White House), they were ushered into his office. 'Honest Cal', the lowest of low profiles, shook hands all round and mumbled, 'How do you do'. It is reported that he had no idea who these people were; this was not unusual since his reputed custom was to greet everyone *without trace of interest, much less flourish. There followed a deadly pause, during which Stanislavsky must have recognized in the Chief the plight of the actor stricken with vocal cramp. But before the Master could bend the paralytic moment to relaxation – one of his enduring gifts to his profession – the troupe was hastily led out and made to leave the building by the back door.*

In this brief, uneventful episode two psychological compulsions presented themselves in silent combat. Coolidge embodied the idea of revealing nothing of your inner self, cooling your passions so that the business of America could carry on without distraction. In the jargon of the Russian players, he would have represented the 'stencil', the duplicated personality without distinguishing attributes, precisely the effect an interesting actor sought to avoid. The Stanislavskian actor, on the contrary, had to follow his impulses at all times and never fall back on cliché gestures of body or soul. Keeping alert was more vital than keeping 'cool' (e.g. with Coolidge). Stanislavsky's American visit marked the beginning of 'Russian subversion' in American acting style, affecting, in subtle ways, even the leftist life-actor's heroic quest for public impact. American cultural entertainments would never be the same again, and it would be another forty years or so before blandness again became a virtue in personality. Thoroughly underwhelmed by the President, the Russian departed from his non-audience, leaving behind him a small, unspoken prophecy, as if the Trans-Siberian Express had come roaring through a railway graveyard in Middle America.

1

With its first real glimpse of danger – harassment, raids, committees – the Left was again faced with re-defining its role in American life. Its morale was already dampened, and only the coming of the Depression seemed to breathe new hope into the movement. This might just be the long-awaited pre-revolutionary brink, and the Party rose to it with an ultra-militant spirit, working overtime to find a working-class following. The political value of every strike and hunger march was exaggerated to give the impression of impending victory for communism. Party workers had quotas for recruiting new members, tactical meetings were held at every available hour, people worked to exhaustion. It was not for want of trying that there was little to show, even in the first years of the thirties, in terms of organizational strengthening. The Party tried to demonstrate that the Depression signalled the death of capitalism; but it had cried that particular 'wolf' so many times already that few paid attention. The organization just did not have sufficient tools with which to help the tottering system bang itself to pieces.

Faced with its inability to activate labour to rebellious pitch, the Party slowed to a style which better suited its American temperament. Inevitably, throughout the thirties, it came to play an increasingly propagandistic role, and here scored its biggest successes. Its accent was on building a bridgehead to Communist consciousness within the culture and becoming *popular* with Americans. This could not be achieved openly because of the CP's already blighted reputation, so instead the use of the front-group technique was escalated. The most vital work of the thousand-and-one fronts was to lure potential converts who wanted to change the world without going through Stalinist discipline. In the 1930s, such 'fellow-travellers' came to out-number card-carrying members by ten to one.

The Party was finding its niche in the blossoming American enterprise of public relations; and, like any good advertising agency, it often had to down principle in order to titillate. At the same time, the leftist spell could not continue to rely on drama-tizing 'one-off' events like Scottsboro. A broad theatre of opera-tions was needed to attract the masses. This was not easy as the thirties wore on. Roosevelt's New Deal – with its sops to the working class – began to entrench itself, and the CP suffered from the unwillingness of most people to break traditional political habits. The Party line – despite a new credibility in some unions and among blacks – could not catch fire.

It was an irony of history that did the trick. By 1935 Hitler's militarism put the fear into the Russian bear, and the guiding concern of the Comintern was to protect the Soviet Union from attack. The forces of international Communism were now marshalled into creation of a Popular Front, a propaganda vehicle designed to drum up political support for the USSR within western countries. The already existing principle of whitewashing the 'dirty Red' image turned to obsession in the course of the five 'popular' years between 1935-9. The American CP dis-covered that it had to reverse or subdue any previous position which might offend the US Government. The Party was no longer the vanguard against capitalism, but rather against fascism. The class struggle was replaced by the safer 'fight for democracy'. Where the New Deal was scored as 'fascization' before 1935, the administration was now called middle-of-the-road, a stopgap against the fascists; by 1937 Roosevelt was a leftist saint. The Party opened its doors wider than ever to every breed of dis-affected humanity. It sought a 'united front' with New Deal groups, with the 'progressive' (the best-selling catch-phrase of the era) tendencies in the Democratic Party and with socialists. Even the arch-enemy Catholic Church was well spoken of at rallies. By 1939 just about every colour of character including, in the words of Party chief Earl Browder, 'progressive capitalists' and 'stockbrokers', was considered a brother in struggle. The only exception – natch! – were the Trotskyites, for whom there was not even the merest hint of room at the inn.

These years were the strongest, most prestigious the Left ever enjoyed in America. 'American nature'-lovers achieved comfort at last within the organization; they could finally come out into the open and be themselves. It was an exhilarating experience for most of the rank and file. Upstairs, however, all was not 'up-front'; for Party professionals it was an elaborate bluff. Of course, protecting the Soviet Union was a glorious objective; if communism were crushed there it would take the fire out of the international movement. At the same time the USSR did not hesitate to sacrifice whatever small advances the Americans had made in theoretical-revolutionary consciousness, just to suit its own political-military needs.

It was the Comintern's directives on everything from president-ial elections to Party picnics that most influenced the still-developing character of leftist expression during the Popular Front. All of this was based on the lovely 'patriotic' ploy that 'Communism is Twentieth-Century Americanism'; it was carried to ingratiating excess. The founding fathers and principles sud-denly found their way into every Party speech or tract. On 4 July 1935 the *Daily Worker* printed pictures of Lenin and George Washington side by side, and also reprinted the Declaration of Independence. 'The Star-Spangled Banner' was sung with 'The Internationale' and the American flag waved with the Red one over CP rallies and meetings. Earl Browder said the Party believed in 'American democracy, in the spirit of the frontier, the covered wagon, Buffalo Bill, Steve Brody, Casey Jones and other heroic figures in our nation's copybook past'. Just 'plain folks' were the new fun people, and the endless string of guitar-plucking folk-moaners conjuring chain-gangs and dribbling Americana down the generations of the Left can be blamed on the requirements of the era. To top it all off, the Party sponsored an 'I like America' essay contest.

Aside from these symbolic gestures the CP adopted practical measures to help its stylistic overhaul. It now stressed the use of neighbourhood clubs – usually named after one American patriot or another – for dances, bazaars, socializing. This was to give the impression that Communists could even relax and enjoy themselves. One directive talked about 'the kick one gets from doing party work. We always play up the gloomy side of life with hardly any relief in sight before the social revolution; yet our party has picnics, outings, affairs and such things.'

Above all, there was to be little mention of revolution or anything that might upset the citizenry.

A major field of operations was the popular media. Here the Party hoped to infiltrate movies, the stage, literature in order to spread Marxist teachings without necessarily identifying them as such. It was a matter of finding the appropriate style for getting across the political message, while at the same time appealing to purely American instincts and taste. Also, the media provided a ready-made fund of 'names' the CP might recruit or exploit for the purposes of publicity or achieving social respectability by association. For many of these actors, writers, intellectuals, 'stars', the Depression signalled the end of bland Coolidgeism and the subtle Grand Design to obliterate individuality. The capitalist landscape that bred such robotism appeared to be in trouble; at that time, it looked as if the Communist Party could provide a programme of free-thinking values. Best of all, they had the luxury of not actually joining up, but standing instead as fellow-travellers or frequenting front groups.*

During the Depression, many of the pillars of American writing – Odets, Dreiser, Dos Passos, Hemingway – began to contribute to Party magazines and newspapers. In 1935 the first Writers' Congress was held in which many famous authors sang 'The Internationale' and spoke of the need to align themselves with the workers' cause. At a second conference in 1937 there was an even

---

*The Party had paved the way for this turn of events in 1927, when it moved its headquarters from Chicago to New York. Chicago could boast a tradition of tough industrial union action, but stopped intellectually short of Al Capone. The New York move symbolized the initial failure to engage mass labour strength, and impelled the CP to accept a lower-middle-class, more literate, considerably Jewish following.

larger turnout of 'names', many of whom came into the Communist sphere because of the Soviet Union's support for the Loyalists in Spain (only this time – the heart of the Popular Front – there was no 'Internationale' and little talk of revolution, demonstrating clearly that it was a CP-run affair).

Yet the new intellectual romance with Communism brought with it a built-in conflict of interest. Many writers, already flirting with a measure of public success, hoped now to play out their *own* revolutionary script against the broader background of class struggle. The Communists needed the skills these men had to offer, but also wanted to exert some influence over their output. Few writers actually went along with the tougher aspects of the Party Line, but the literature and drama of the period were significantly affected by the conceptual demands of Marxism, and also, to some extent, the political demands of Stalinism. Most of the authors were of middle-class origin, and the Party hoped this fact would enable them to reach bourgeois readers more easily. At the same time, if the future belonged to the working class, then this fact had to be reflected in the literature. Some of the writers who came out of a privileged background swallowed this central notion to the point of self-deprecation, swayed by the 'guilt' implicit in being intellectuals. They knew they were not entirely trusted by the workers or the Party (as traditional fence-sitters never were), and much of their effort was spent in trying to assimilate socialist premises. One delegate to the 1935 Writer's Convention claimed that an author's task was 'to vivify the daily struggles, the aspirations, triumphs, despairs of the future masters of life – the workers'. So powerful was this specific image of the artist's destiny that a delegate in 1937 was severely reprimanded for suggesting a verbal change from 'the workers' to 'the people'. No idea would ever mesmerize the American intellectual Left like the deification of the proletariat. (Even in the late 1960s when union reactionaries were pummelling them in the streets, young leftists often mouthed the traditional adoration of labour.) In the famous cartoons of Party newspapers, the worker always appeared as a looming tower of manhood, his sledgehammer a-poundin' down those bank vaults, his sexual potency written in his mammoth thighs, his historic victory imprinted subliminally in the very globe of his iron bicep.

And now the sons of the bourgeoisie were made to feel the pressure of such propaganda, the implication that *their* day was finished; if they did not begin to serve the glorious working class, they would be swept away with the rest of the capitalist rubble. So that they might properly depict the class struggle, the Party provided them with the theory of 'proletcult' (proletarian culture), which prescribed, among other things, a new concept of heroism based on reason rather than emotion. This un-cynical Communist hero had to be able to overwhelm the social forces that overwhelm everyone else. He had to resist oppression instead of knuckling under or giving way to despair. He could not allow himself to be victimized or mystified by those who sought to gain power over him. He spoke the language of the revolutionary proletariat and could stand up under the severest discipline. He was tough and could exist well enough without women or family if necessary. Finally, he never indulged in any sort of opportunism and understood the historical imperative which drove the working class on to victory. In short, he was a *winner* – to show him in any other light was tantamount to admitting the continued dominion of the bourgeoisie. His strength could appeal to American-manhood fantasies of tough power gained toughly. One writer at the 1937 congress talked of wanting to rewrite *An American Tragedy* along such lines so that Clyde Griffiths could stand up to social pressure with a new conscious will-power.

Those who did work to this formula usually failed to provide any flesh and blood for their characters. Others who tried and failed were criticized for rendering 'a subconscious sense of inferiority to the bourgeois world'.* The new demi-god just did not sit right with many writers, and they tended to interpret the spirit of proletcult according to a less cardboard pattern. The Com-

---

*This idea later spread in Marxist literary criticism to embrace the charge of a 'fascist unconscious' operating in some writers. These deluded intellectuals were simply not aware that their failure to cope with unimpeachable Communist facts testified to the secret lure of fascism working in them and confusing them.

munist hero, for them, would also have to be a modern American hero, and this fact made him more vulnerable and less perfectly mannered than the desired brand. It was simply out of the question for most post-Freud American writers to deliver a hero who was not, in some small degree, neurotic. The diminished hero had first to rid himself of the loom of the family and a sense of inferiority. Freud claimed, in his idea of the 'pleasure principle', that the aim of most instinctive human drives was the discharge of psychological energy. If this discharge produces an action, the drive is said to be 'satisfied'. (Otherwise it can be pent up in the form of 'wish fulfilment', in fantasies and dreams built up in lieu of actual release of tension.) It was this basic yearning for *satisfaction* of desire that had already become rooted in American fictions of the twenties. It all seemed like cheap thrills compared with the well-developed proletarian hero – who, by implication, already *had* everything he could possibly need, short of the final socialist paradise; and he wasn't about to demean that by *longing* for it! The Marxist winner could kick down all the barriers; his fight was fixed and there could only be one possible outcome. But he would never be a victim to his confused feelings, would never have to overcome *himself* to find his place.

Yet, despite the subtle pressures of official Party culture, the bulk of 1930s heroes floundered in despair and hunger for gratification. They may have paid lip service to the class struggle, even called themselves Communists. But their 'American nature' intervened at the Marxist brink; it turned our guy back to his endless soul-searching. Behind his drive was not the prize of proletarian revolution as much as *relief*, discharge, pure and not-so-simple, from a sense of alienation and dread.

2

The American theatre of the thirties gave the developing leftist hero his broadest field of exposure. The stage was a cunning public platform which could accommodate a call to arms, symbolically express a social act, inform just as well as a Party meeting (and be more entertaining), serve the needs of publicity-making and even make it seem like the world outside was aflame with revolution. In this decade the cross-breeding between Communism and the dramatic professions was at its height. The concept of the 'front' worked well with such potentially 'naked' media as the stage and the movie screen. Behind the elaborate mask of public entertainment might lurk a whole network of political revelations.

Yet the leftist message failed to make a substantial impact. The growing tradition of post-Freud American drama pointed towards the supremacy of a single character over the broader view of the play. The splendid cardboard Communist working towards a third-act Utopia could not hope to contend with the inner drama of personality in turmoil.

There was a more serious obstacle to the infiltration of politics; the only propaganda acceptable in the American theatre was that delivered by the *actor*, on behalf of himself. No stage hero could ever rise up to social influence in the public eye like the glamorous hero that was the actor. Nowhere could emotions repressed to boiling-point be so powerfully and unashamedly spilled as in his performance. Nowhere would a man be so much *himself*, and achieve relief from the tensions of personal want. Even for the leftist actors of the thirties, the desire to work with Marxist tools for character – even to perform in dramas of Marxist tone and circumstance – had to be channelled first through the American impulse for self-expression. Because of this, the Communist paragon was destined to get some new contours.

Out of this unhappy union of proletcult and the pleasure principle came a curious mutation looking a lot like John Garfield. Garfield, a tough but sensitive leftist actor, arrived in Hollywood in 1937, when the film industry was looking for a way to cash in on the new romance of the working class. He was immediately typecast as a proletarian hero, and retained this image throughout the forties. He was always Depression's child, the tough guy who no longer expected a piece of the pie. He was just a punk from Nowhere, but he didn't take crap from nobody. If he had been blind to the rottenness of the system, he wasn't a-gonna take it no more. He knew something Clyde Griffiths didn't: to usurp the bank account means you inherit all the hang-ups that go with it – sexual frustration, table manners, correct speech, all the dead-weight of the stuck-up brigade. Look instead at the freedom of being unaffected, no high-falutin' jazz, a guy could drink beer out of the can just as good as from a swanky glass. No, John Garfield he had on that tee-shirt and the greasy jacket slung over his shoulder by one finger – he announced his class origins with pride.

But that finger also indicated defiance. He was rebelling against middle-class taste – dropping his repressions like cigarette butts along the highway – but also rejecting authority, discipline and coercion. His stinking armpits would have offended Party bureaucrats as well as captains of industry. He may even have believed in the dictatorship of the proletariat, sure, why not? – but he didn't take crap from *nobody*. Mostly he was dissatisfied, angry at the whittling away of his humanity, the blunting of his identity; he was on the chase for his character. But he could not get satisfaction through the puritanical muscle of the proletcult saint. John Garfield's communism was the ferocity of revolt against oppression. He hadn't got the ascetic disposition to hang around for the Communist Big Finish; but he could (and would) make an irritant fuss in the Power's eye.

John Garfield got his acting instructions by way of artful Moscow agents; their ringleader was the Russian provocateur, Konstantin Stanislavsky. Stanislavsky brought his Moscow Art Theatre troupe to the US in 1923, and had an effect on American theatricals similar to that of the Bolshevik Revolution on radicals.* He knew he had come to the right place for his particular propaganda: 'The people here are very charming, friendly, good-humoured, naïve, eager for knowledge, not at all stuck up, lacking European snobbery, looking you straight in the eyes and ready to accept everything that is new and real.' Soon after the Moscow

---

*When the Moscow Art Theatre first announced their visit in 1923, a letter appeared in the New York press, disseminated by the American National League, accusing the players of coming over for propaganda purposes. The letter charged that the Russians planned to send one third of their box-office receipts back to the USSR to pay for subversive activities.

Art Theatre tour, some of its leading members, along with pupils of Stanislavsky, emigrated to America and established the first generation in a chain of acting schools teaching the Russian system; some worked in Hollywood, making films or training many well-known players and quietly laying the groundwork for the future of American acting.

Stanislavsky's initial theatrical impulses came out of a time when traditional roles and stereotypes were breaking down – along with class distinctions – in turn-of-the-century Tsarist Russia. Out of the pre-revolutionary atmosphere he conceived of a new total man – represented by the actor – who might learn to exhibit a new kind of emotional 'truth' in his daily life. There are strong elements of social therapy in the acting system, and it is meant to give broad scope to the idea of honest *performance* as a road to character-building on and off stage.

Yet Stanislavsky's political views were élitist; he hated theatre whose end was social action. Only after the Revolution did he even vaguely acknowledge the significance of politics in the life of the artist, but he still kept to an emotional view of the theatre's function: 'Political passions are the same as other passions . . . and to express them, one should be able to use the same techniques, with simplicity and sincerity . . . It is necessary for the actor to be imbued with these passions . . . for politics to become a component part of his consciousness . . .' In the early years of Soviet Russia Stanislavsky boldly continued to denounce activist plays, and was in turn slammed by Marxist critics as a bourgeois concerned only with the actor's subconscious. In spite of this, his system was given more or less official blessing by the Soviet Government after the Stalinist purge of more 'formalist' theatre experimenters in the late twenties.

The Stanislavsky system divides into two major segments: the actor's work on himself, and on his role, the one being preparatory to the other. A player is meant – through a series of exercises leading to maximum concentration – to free himself from his previous conditioning and break down his stereotyped gestures and actions before he can properly perform. Then, when he begins to transform himself into a stage character, he uses essentially the tools of his own personality. Stanislavsky had come to conclusions similar to Freud's, realizing that the subconscious was a potential fund of wonders for anyone working at self-expression. Material locked in the subconscious – for one reason or another – has an inherent dramatic power when released. Along this line Stanislavsky developed the idea of 'emotion memory', in which an actor uses the recollection of a past emotional reality as a reference for his work on a role. He cannot pretend to know the character's emotions as well as he knows his own, so he chooses instances out of his own life which most closely resemble the emotional events of the play.

The first American troupe to take the system seriously was the Group Theatre (1931–41), which likewise had the distinction of being the first important left-wing theatre in the US. Its intention was to produce plays of social protest, without resorting to the use of 'stars'. (Its more famous members, including Jules – later 'John' – Garfield, had to make their reputations in Hollywood.) Some of the Group's members joined the CP, and several others, at one time or another, hovered in fellow traveldom. Despite this, the company chose an acting style that resisted politicizing. But for them it did not seem inconsistent with the revolutionary impulses of the early thirties and the accent on liberation of personality and emotional candour. It meant that left-wing views were only as important as the man who held them – and, in this context, that was the actor. Stanislavsky had provided a new romanticism of acting, had given the player heroic status in himself, had allowed great scope for personal impulse and, above all, improvisation. For the leftist actor now swayed by this impressive system, political action would have to be a matter for powerful feelings. But so it had been in his personal life, and Stanislavsky's was only a revelation back to front. For with the lack of true political effect in the American Left, much 'action' had been only 'acting' after all. To the real-life leftist hero political acts had always required the presence of *audience* to make them worthwhile; the life's work of making a protest stand could yield little satisfaction without the reward of witness and, hopefully, applause.

The failure of the Group Theatre to move anyone to social activity can be attributed to their accent on introspection. The leaders of the company, Harold Clurman and Lee Strasberg, took Stanislavsky beyond the original premises and moved down a wholly American road.* Where the Russian had used the subconscious to find material to solve dilemmas of role-playing and character development, the Americans stuck with the actor's need to reveal himself honestly. Because of their post-Freud fascination with techniques of self-discovery, the Group often lost sight of the fact that the system was primarily designed for fiction, not reality. Stanislavsky did not expect the player to act himself out on stage; he plays a character's needs and whims *as if* they were real for him. But this presupposes a desire, first and foremost, to perform a play. The Group's intention came to look more like therapy. Said a European director, Michel Saint-Denis, who saw their work: 'I have seen this introspection pushed to the point of psychoanalysis, to what is called the Moment of Truth, when total sincerity is demanded of the young actor who, ignoring shame and self-consciousness, must bring back from the inner depths of his psyche the most secret revelations.'

Like Freud, Stanislavsky tried to loosen the grip of a man's critical faculty so that a stream of previously repressed material would flow freely. But when he said it was necessary for an actor to take himself apart to find out what makes him tick, he meant for the man to put himself back together again. The goal of the psychoanalytic couch may be a cure, but the stage always demands concrete action. Stanislavsky originally wanted to lead his troupe to 'communion' with each other, through an early form of 'sensory awareness'. A group had to imagine, for example, a circle in which they all stood, silently, sending out 'rays' of communication, chiefly through the honest office of the eyeball. The rest of the body – and the 'soul' – would follow through if the concentration were intense enough. Said the Master on such

*The American publication of Stanislavsky's two major texts suggests a reason for confusion about the system in the US. *An Actor Prepares* appeared in 1936 and dealt almost exclusively with the emotional honesty an actor must develop before he can go forward. The second, *Building a Character* (never intended as a separate work), was translated and published in 1949; this told how to apply the earlier work to the *role*, and came as a shock reminder – thirteen years later – that there was actually a *context* for all the preparation American actors had done.

occasions: 'I want to reach through the tip of my finger – to God – or, later on, my partner. I believe in my inner energy and I give it out – I spread it.' This was ultimately abandoned as unnecessary mysticism; Stanislavsky noticed that many of his emotion-inducing exercises produced only unwanted tension. Instead, he emphasized action and objective, saying that the actor ought not to concentrate on what he feels, but rather what he *wants*; feeling will come tagging along if the objective is clear. The 'political' lesson of this was thoroughly lost on the Americans.

The Stanislavsky system was perfectly suited for the plays left-wing Americans wanted to write (and watch). The clearest example of this is the work of the Group Theatre's leading playwright, Clifford Odets. Odets wrote his legendary *Waiting for Lefty* around the same time as he joined the Party in 1934, and the work reflects, to some degree, his decision for organizational commitment. It concerns a New York taxi strike and extends the form of the traditional labour play. The setting is a strike meeting where a paid informer is ritually unmasked. It builds to a rocking crescendo of agreement to 'Strike', with the audience urged to join in the decision. For an American audience, the style of the play seemed revolutionary, but nothing in it could upset anybody, nor did it move anyone to action in the streets. It was not the Marxism of the play which made it a Red-hot hit overnight, but rather the clever way in which Odets introduced flashback scenes of melodramatic anguish, and tailored the play's pitch so that the seduced audience could break sweat. Still, it demonstrated a very American way of making leftist drama exciting, and held great promise for more to come from both Odets and others.

It was not to be. *Lefty* was the first and last attempt Odets ever made at approximating Communist drama. This reflected the instant disillusion he felt with the more organized aspects of the movement; he could not bend to the discipline. When he headed a group going to Cuba to investigate labour conditions there, he discovered he was not in fact the leader – he had been chosen for his 'name' alone – and that the real object of the voyage was for them to be arrested on the island for publicity purposes. Odets felt he had been taken for a ride by Party professionals, and he burned badly in the deviousness of it. After only a brief affair, the innocent left the Party in 1935.

He remained loyal to the cause, though, and tried to serve it as he knew how. But his preoccupation now was with his own most private experiences against a landscape of class struggle. His characters were anything but tough hopeful Communists; they were Reds with the blues. Years later Odets himself admitted that if he 'were moved by certain situations of poverty, this would be because my mother worked in a stocking factory in Philadelphia at the age of eleven and died a broken woman . . . at the age of forty-eight. I did not learn my hatred of poverty . . . out of Communism.' When he tried to express this hatred in his play *Awake and Sing* (1935), he was denounced by the Party press. Here, the young hero (played by John Garfield) breaks out of his social trap by standing up to his Jewish mother and insisting on making his own decisions. Odets was attacked for writing a mystical conversion for the character, rather than a Marxist one. But it was the Communist playwright, Brecht, who best put the conceptual finger on Odets in criticizing a later play, *Paradise Lost* (1936). Brecht slammed the writer's overbearing sympathy for *everyone* who has fallen into disgrace, including those who have been guilty of capitalist exploitation – pity for the businessman, the hustler, the betrayer.

It was pity that reduced the leftist hero down to pint-size, and prevented Odets from delivering a truly Marxist play. This reached a climax in *Golden Boy* (1937), which he wrote with John Garfield in mind. Hollywood was then in the process of duplicating Garfield again and again in his own image: the bum with a gleam in his eye. But his good friend Odets preferred the more sensitive face, the poor boy from the Bronx squirting out an identity as he barrels down that highway. Golden Boy wants to be a boxer but his old man wants him to play the violin. Because the family has had its spine cracked under the brutality of the capitalist order, the boy feels the need to restore its dignity; the way to do this, he decides, is by promoting himself. It isn't the dough he's after as much as the glory. 'You could build a city with his ambition to be somebody,' says his girlfriend. Still, he can't quite achieve lift-off, even though he gets to be the Champ. He was born a nobody, and he can't seem to find satisfaction. He vents his frustration not on the social order, but on his father, his girl-friend, his opponents.

Most of all he suffers. Oh how he loves to suffer! His anger can never be directed to political purpose because he takes his social persecution with a heavy dose of self-pity: 'I've been running around in circles. Now I'm smashed! That's the truth. Yes, I was a real sparrow, and I wanted to be a false eagle! But now I'm hung up by my finger tips – I'm no good – my feet are off the earth!' Not at all a position for starting a revolution. The personal drama ends at such finger tips, and the pathos granted the hung-up hero brings only solace for his failure as a social changer.

Because the Left chose to express political passion, it could never really reason with its audience. Various innovations for using media as public social education appeared concurrently with the acceptance of Stanislavsky; but the American heart just wasn't in them.

The idea of using the stage as a propaganda vehicle did not blossom in America until the early 1930s. There had been union entertainments of a political nature, but these showed no concern for the development of a useful *form* for spreading the message. The American distrust of theory worked against the earliest attempts at didactic theatre. Even Emma Goldman (a drama critic in between jail sentences) found propagandistic theatre inadequate and lobbied for a drama of social dissatisfaction: one whose function was to tear down the social pretence and expose the canker beneath. She claimed that 'the modern drama . . . affecting as it does both mind and heart, is the strongest force in developing social discontent, swelling the powerful tide of unrest . . .' But Emma's dream theatre could only move the spectators to feelings of social guilt, lasting the length of the play and its lingering memory. For it to have political purpose it would have to lift an audience to the edge of *real action*, which would then be carried out – theoretically – beyond the theatre building.

In this light, the Communist Party toyed with the theatrical form known as 'agit-prop' (agitation-propaganda). Since these plays were aimed specifically at educating workers, they were simple and relied on the proletcult theory of character – one-dimensional, assured, thoroughly un-neurotic. Normally, these were strike dramas which followed a more or less set formula, ending with the conversion of a previously neutral worker to the cause of revolution. After a concluding call to action, the audience usually responded with some set expression of allegiance to the Party or to the Soviet Union. In 1932 the CP tried to collect several amateur agit-prop groups under its wing by establishing one of many entertainment fronts called the League of Workers' Theatres. Its stated purpose was 'to spread the idea of the class struggle, to participate actively in the class struggle by raising funds for campaigns and for the revolutionary press, and by recruiting workers into the revolutionary unions and mass organizations, and especially to arouse the workers for the defense of the Soviet Union, against the coming imperialist attack'.

The drawback of the agit-prop as practised by the CP was that it had no appeal outside Communist circles. The wooden humans, the sloganizing and lack of suspense could not attract anyone who wasn't already committed to the message of the exercise. As early as 1932 the Party realized it would also have to sway the bourgeoisie to its position by allowing a bit of razzmatazz; the agit-prop was maintained, but the Party agreed to sanction Broadway plays that had some political content.

Ironically, it was the CP's own Popular Front that killed off any hope for a Communist theatre in America. In bowing to the thrills-and-spills desires of an American audience, the Communists were admitting (if only inadvertently) that more native forms of expression – chiefly the American melodrama which had filtered down from the previous century – would best serve the interests of leftist publicity. What little formal experiment there was now found itself the victim of a frontal attack by boy-meets-girl or boy-wants-to-be-a-man dramas. The leftist dramatist was asked to oppose social evils where possible, but to avoid the 'public platform and political manual'. Political plays would now have to come through a screen – according to the new Party directive – of 'love, ambition, fear and hope'. This would have the effect, supposedly, of awakening the middle classes to 'new horizons of living'.

The Party's dramatic critics believed that any play which did not accept the capitalist system was therefore a play for social change. They did not take into account that a natural American theatre – even one run by leftists – would more than likely fall back on nostalgia, Freudian memory syndromes, misery and the endless probing of self, which quickly eats up your three acts and leaves no time for hustling up Utopias. The keynote of most leftist drama remained the same: 'the only way out of this crisis is revolution'. But there were no means for getting beyond the simple *wishing* of it; so deep now was the fear of *demonstrating* social change that the Party even came to reject the most important Communist playwright it ever had, Bertolt Brecht.

Brecht's 'epic theatre' style was a redemptive acid that could reduce drama to the bone. It pared away sentiment and demanded that unharnessed tension be turned to concrete political battle. The playwright called for 'detachment' or 'alienation' in which the spectator has no illusions about the performance being real. He knows he is in a theatre building and that he is not meant to get lost in the murky psychological forests of the play or the actors' egos. He is there to make critical judgements about what he sees, so that he may determine the course of his social actions. In this sense, Brecht woke the audience up, denying them their traditional mysticism and withdrawal: 'Only the man who is free of illusions, who compels the exploiter to reveal himself without justification, can direct his own life.'

Brecht understood that fascism could easily be reinforced in a sentimental theatre. His initial conception of 'epic theatre' was in part influenced by Nazi taste in his native Germany in the thirties. The goose-steppers revered the romantic German traditions which often subdued audiences through tear-jerking melodrama. Brecht believed those tears in the eye obscured political vision and made the spectator vulnerable to the subtle calls for loyalty to Father-land and Führer. Opposed to this staged brainwashing, a Marxist theatre should have enlightenment as its goal. But it could not achieve this while using the old theatrical forms. Brecht called instead for propagandistic effects – placards, slides, slogans, a more demonstrative, less hallucinatory style of acting – to summon the intellectual collusion of his audience.

Like many before him, Brecht hoped for a public platform in the US. He was drawn to the growing anti-fascism in America, and imagined that 'epic theatre' could play its part in helping to raise working-class consciousness. Before he ever set foot on the American continent, he had written several plays about Chicago. His vision of the place was distorted by the gangster films he loved, but he showed that 'character' there was basically a factor of economic considerations. Money was the force that either famed you or lamed you, your fate delivered dramatically by the dollar. Because capitalism held a certain fascination for him, Brecht never showed the typical righteousness of American authors who felt their individuality threatened by it. He could appreciate the material reality of America, the prosperity, the machines, the reduction of social relationships to strategies of finance. Although he vigorously opposed the system, the nature of his characters was reflected in it. He was a loyal non-Party Communist all his life, but he could not subscribe to the formula for the proletarian hero. If Brecht's characters ever 'win' they do so slyly and without a shred of dignity; they are masters of the comic subterfuge, never leftist saints. This, combined with his 'formalist' tendencies led to a closed-door policy on his work in the Soviet Union; his theory of dispassionate acting jarred with Stanislavsky's, and was regarded with deep suspicion by the Soviet cultural authorities. His only recourse – since he was in exile from the Nazis – was America.

Brecht arrived in 1935 to oversee a production of one of his plays at New York's Theatre Union – a leading socialist theatre. Instead of the Depression-weathered leftist heavyweights he hoped for, he found a den of Broadway weepers, left-wing movie-star hopefuls pumping for sympathy in the great gusher oilwell of audience emotion. When he tried to steer the production on to a political course, he was rebuffed. This was one of his most rock-hard, materialist, un-sentimental plays – a perfect explication of 'epic theatre' that glorified the Party – but unfortunately it was called *The Mother*, and there was only one possible interpretation New York actors could give such a title. To top off the play's American début, the Party slammed it for being 'experimental'.

A similar fate befell Erwin Piscator, the German theatre director whose revolutionary stage techniques prompted Brecht's theory of 'epic theatre'. Piscator – also in exile – worked in the New York theatre for several years, and stumbled upon *An American Tragedy*; in 1936 he produced a wholly 'epic' version called *The Case of Clyde Griffiths*. Here the stage was divided into three areas, the upper crust, the lower depths and Clyde in the middle of the two economic worlds. A Speaker/Narrator was employed to keep the audience's attention on the meaning of the play, not allowing them time to identify with the actors or reach for the proverbial handkerchief. They were told that the answer to theirs and Clyde's problem lay in a Marxist overhaul of society. The Speaker cried out: 'This is the crisis; Fate marches on relentlessly. Fate. You shudder at the word. It signifies a masked unknown. But we have torn the mask from his face . . . and have given him a name. We call him the Law of Economics, that inexorably and without compassion controls the destiny of mankind.'

Harold Clurman, head of the Group Theatre, who produced *The Case of Clyde Griffiths*, said it 'definitely went against the American grain'. Another critic likened Piscator to a 'travelling quack' who gathers the village idiots around an improvised stage to sell them a bogus panacea. Even Dreiser, now gung ho for Communism, could not endorse Piscator's onslaught. For the Party press it was a total disaster; they resented the experimentation of it, especially the use of the Speaker who interfered with the 'emotions' of the play.

So a truly Marxist theatre failed not only with the American public, but with the American Left as well.* The theatre of sym-

---

*In 1934 the Scottsboro case found its way into a play by John Wexley called *They Shall Not Die*. Since the appeals were not yet concluded, the drama had a real chance to achieve political ends. Instead it opted for absolutely realistic detail and probed psychological motives. It played upon the humanity of the Scottsboro boys and did not suggest any way in which the audience might aid the defence. The CP's only objection was not to the form, but the way in which its own role was minimized in the play.

The primary Sacco-Vanzetti play, *Winterset* (1935), by Maxwell Anderson, displays the leftist hero in a state of extreme self-consciousness and impotence. He is meant to be the son of an executed anarchist, wandering about, years later, with the guilt of his innocent father's name. He wants to get to

pathy came to serve the Soviet Union's ends because it told audiences what they wanted to hear in the way they wanted to hear it. But there is no doubt the leftist theatre would have taken this route anyway, since US radicals could not escape their bourgeois roots and themes, even on stage.

3

The Popular Front brought the Party impressive gains in labour including a strong foothold in the CIO (Congress of Industrial Organizations), and also helped put civil rights matters into public consciousness. But, for the most part, the Front remained locked in its own cage of publicity-mongering, having to be extremely cautious about rising to physical action. For a while it began to look like pure theatre, a pageant full of flamboyant gestures, speeches and pretence to political relevance. Soon enough, however, theoretical anti-fascism had its first explosive testing-ground. At last, the romantic drama of American protest might play itself out on the reality-stages of Spain.

For the European Communist parties the Spanish Civil War in 1936 was the logical outcome of years of ideological bantering. It was a show of strength between the Popular Front and the growing forces of fascism. Men from most European countries joined the International Brigades, including many adventurers, fellow-travellers and intellectuals, as well as Party personnel. For most of these, it was a matter of Hitler being on their very doorstep; unless Spain could be made the 'tomb of fascism', all of Europe would be in jeopardy. Americans, however, possessed little ideological background for understanding the complex web of the

---

the bottom of the (Sacco-Vanzetti) business, to scrape away the social lies and expose the frame-up. But the actual politics of the case do not consume him as much as the spectre of his father that haunts him night and day. He feels the need to become a *man* and break free of his self-pity. This unburdening comes not from the relief of an achieved political action, but through falling in love with the sister of a man involved in the killing for which his old man got the Chair. A melodramatic stage death redeems him at last from his overwhelming terror of social rebellion.

Spanish conflict; nor did it seem so *immediately* crucial for them. The general mood of isolationism in the US also touched the Left, and Europe was as mythologically far away as ever.

If Americans could not say with the same assurance as Europeans that the Spanish Loyalists were fighting 'our fight', they were sure enough that Spain was the long-awaited excuse for belting out their own radical war-chant. The Spanish struggle appeared to them to be clearly divided into baddies and goodies, it was a fascist uprising against a democratically elected leftist Republic. This made the cause a breeding-ground for Left righteousness and drew together even the hangers-on under the moral imperative of taking sides. While it lasted, no conscience-stricken soul could avoid the issue of Spain. A questionnaire published as *Writers Take Sides* – with a very CP tinge to it – intimidated intellectuals with the loaded questions, 'Are you for, or against, Franco and Fascism?' and 'Are you for, or against, the legal government and the People of Republican Spain?' Nearly every major American writer answered *of course the Republic* and, as intended, the combined cheers of Dreiser, Lewis, Hemingway, Falkner, Dos Passos, etc. made a lovely propaganda package. One of the few who was not impressed was Ezra Pound: 'Questionnaire an escape mechanism for young fools who are too cowardly to think; too lazy to investigate the nature of money, its mode of issue, the control of such issue by the Banque de France and the stank of England. You are all had. Spain is an emotional luxury to a gang of sap-headed dilettantes.'

Despite his usual monetary raving, Pound had a point. Spain was, among other things, a balm for creaky unemployed social consciences. Fund-raising and speech-making, whether on behalf of milk for Spanish children or arms for the Loyalists, abounded in the most unlikely circles – high society, Hollywood, Broadway – providing an early dose of what has come to be known as 'radical chic'. There was a good excuse for internal concern – the US Government's position on the conflict – and liberals could get involved in that without being *too* radical or courting danger. In 1937 Congress established an embargo against selling arms to the Spanish Government, as expression of American 'neutrality'. Hitler and Mussolini, on the other hand, were arming Franco to the teeth (often with American weapons supplied to Germany). Men of good will felt that the US was simply allowing the fascists to walk over democracy, which would in any case lead to a wider war. In March 1938 Franco began his offensive against Aragon, with the intention of taking Barcelona. With the certainty of Republican defeat looming up ahead, the leftist campaign to end the embargo reached its peak. Roosevelt was pressured by liberals to the point where he even considered changing course and allowing supplies of arms. His failure to do so demonstrates that even the strong propaganda machine of the Popular Front could not muster enough voice to overrule the reactionaries. It was the zeal of the American Catholic clergy that put paid to leftist efforts. Clearly the Church was on the side of Franco against the nun-raping, priest-buggering, collection-box-robbing Reds. The Catholic influence over American voters was more substantial, in Roosevelt's view, than that of the Left. The last word in the business was had by a leading US Catholic who virtually talked Roosevelt out of lifting the embargo, thereby ensuring Franco's victory. This was the US Ambassador to England, Joseph Kennedy, father of the team who years later continued the fight against the godless at the Bay of Pigs in Cuba.

For action-hungry leftists, Spain provided more than just a nominal taking of sides. In the first few months of the war several hundred Americans went to fight in the International Brigades, under the Popular Front-ish name of the Abraham Lincoln Battalion. Eventually, about 3000 US volunteers passed through Spain, some of them joining a tank unit called the John Brown Company, and others the Tom Mooney Battalion (named after a famous jailed labour leader), which was soon changed to the George Washington Battalion. (After many of the first Americans were wiped out at the battle of Brunete, the survivors merged together to form the Lincoln-Washington Battalion.) The US Government tried to stop the flow of men to Spain by declaring passports invalid for that country, and making it clear that it was illegal to be recruited into the army of another nation. Both of these pressures were circumvented. By the end of the conflict some 2,000 American volunteers had perished.

Most of the men in the battalions were Communists or fellow-travellers. Party propaganda played a large part in stirring the boys to battle, and the actual recruiting was handled clandestinely by various front organizations. The CP hoped to create in Spain politically conscious soldiers for an efficient mini-Red Army. For this purpose each unit had its own 'commissar' whose job it was to unite (at least for battle purposes) the varying leftist factions and see to their political education. This was to ensure that Spain would not become a stage for 'adventurism' – as the Party referred to individualistic actions taken outside its consent – but would serve the long-range interests of international Communism. It had such an effect on the Communist writer, Alvah Bessie (later to become one of the 'Hollywood Ten'), who had volunteered: 'I knew, about myself, that the historical event of Spain had coincided with a long-felt compulsion to complete the destruction of the training I had received all through my youth . . . It was necessary for me . . . to submerge myself in that mass, seeking neither distinction nor preferment (the reverse of my activities for the past several years) and in this way to achieve self-discipline, patience and unselfishness . . .'

But, as was the case with its own membership, the CP could not recruit only politically aware men. There were others more than willing to go, many of whom were simply professional heroes; it was hoped that Spain would turn them into good Party men. But many did see an opportunity for 'distinction' here. Men hoped the experience of Spain would be something more than just another series of meetings, factions and slogans. Nearly two decades had stretched away from the early impulse pivot of the Bolshevik Revolution. The vanguard Left was at the height of its popularity. It showed an understanding at last of the 'American nature' and its moods. But the long-range ideals of the movement seemed as long-range as ever. The Depression had come and nearly gone without the expected death of capitalism. If big business could survive pneumonia in its money-bags it could certainly stand up to flea bites from the Left. To all but the very blind, the pretence of a Bolshevik spectacular in the US was cancelled. In the face of this historical defeat and the now smoothly running bureaucracy of international Communism, the hope of real fireworks for the leftist hero was dimmed.

Spain, at least, brought back the spell of 1917. Here at last was something *tangible* to fight for, instead of demands which fell on deaf ears, pickets which walked you round in circles and pointless half-hearted half-actions. The adventure of Spain promised the return of dramatic tension and *personal* release from years of political impotence.

In the dozens of left-wing autobiographies published after the Popular Front period, Spain was always the educational fulcrum, the climax to revolutionary enthusiasm in which a man became perhaps a full-bodied Communist but, more often, just a *man*. Many of the volunteers were pacifists and had to learn what killing was all about (always a dilemma for the American Left). Others could shine up their soap opera with the old refrain of 'dying for an ideal'. For politically conscious comrades like Alvah Bessie there was the sentiment of fighting the great fight in the name of history and 'the people': '. . . the men in the train started to sing, spontaneously – "Arise, ye prisoners of starvation!" and the people on the platform lifted their arms, clenched their fists . . . Little babies in their mothers' arms held their tiny fists aloft . . . Our hearts were full . . .'

But the crescendo of such throbbing violins quickly faded as the scenario ran down to military fact. Unlike the European briga-diers, the Americans were chiefly students; they had neither war experience nor any of the compulsory military training nearly every European teenager underwent at the time. The first Ameri-cans were supposed to receive three months of training before entering the fray. But this was not possible in all cases since men were often needed prematurely, whether or not they could hold a rifle. Subsequently, the first months of American involvement were filled with gruesome mishaps and excessive casualties. Our heroes, first of all, did not know how to take cover, so that when Hitler's Luftwaffe hit, the effect was devastating. In the very first Lincoln Battalion battle 120 were killed and 175 wounded out of 450 men. It was reported that the American boys, in later battles, constantly asked, 'Where's the front?' In a skirmish inside a town where the enemy was known to be lurking, 'one of the Americans made the mistake of entering an open door before throwing a grenade through it. In a few seconds he staggered out, blood flowing from a deep bayonet wound. This was the battalion's first lesson in street fighting.' At the front itself this reached vaudeville heights: 'A whip cracked overhead and we ducked. We looked at our section-leader and said, "What's that?" "That", said Dick, "was a bullet . . ."'

The military inexperience of the Lincoln-Washington Battalion reflected a larger political and social naïvety. They complained at first about the bad guns, rotten cigarettes, oily Spanish food, the lack of proper bathing facilities and the notorious Spanish postal service. There was some friction between the Americans and the Spaniards who formed part of each battalion, due primarily to American snobbism and inability to learn the Spanish language. The fact that the boys kept to themselves in the first months, refusing to mingle with the European brigades, attests to the idea that they could not understand the international significance of the event. Said one correspondent, none 'of the Internationals are so conscious of their nationality' as the Americans.

Soon this passed into a more disciplined phase in which the rudiments of militarism, like saluting officers (at which many balked), were introduced. But by the time the Lincolns looked anything like a proper army, it was too late. Many were fled or dead and Franco was in command of the field.

Spain was only one disappointment in a series which threatened to reduce significantly the CP's prestige. The first of these had come in 1937 with the Moscow purge trials, in which former leading Soviet Communists were made to confess their 'crimes' against the Russian State. This did not go down well with some Party members and many fellow-travellers, and these either defected to Trotskyism or disappeared from the Communist camp altogether.*

* Many loyal fans, however, still showed their support for the Soviets in order to maintain the 'progressive democracy' drive in the US. In April 1938 a list of stars and 'names' appeared in the *Daily Worker* expressing agreement with the Moscow trials – among these were members of the Group Theatre including Harold Clurman and John Garfield. The tone of intellectual accommodation was set by Theodore Dreiser who said the trials 'seem characteristic of what might be called the Russian temperament . . . a real triumph of the spirit of self-abnegation'.

In August 1939 came the Hitler–Stalin pact which wiped out the Popular Front overnight. Suddenly, the entire thrust of the American Party was to keep the US out of a big war at all costs. Dozens of peace fronts, led by 'names' like Dreiser, sprang up to pump out isolationist propaganda. Almost all Popular Front positions were abandoned or reversed. As quickly as he had become a saint, Roosevelt was now vehemently damned. But Hitler spoiled all this by invading Russia in 1941. Once again the poles were reversed; now it was 'to arms!'* Again Roosevelt was an OK guy, American culture was all the rage, patriotism was stressed so that the US might come to the aid of the Soviets. Mention of class struggle or revolution was suppressed as before. Hard-core Party members who knew the knack of swaying in such Moscow breezes could handle the schizophrenia; others could not, and broke away in droves.

Perhaps just as devastating for some Party members were the long-range implications of Spain. Powerful illusions had gone into the Spanish effort; now the collapse of the Republican Government in March 1939 was an emotional catastrophe for the Left. Politically, it meant that the Popular Front had failed to break the strangle-grip of western 'neutrality'; it showed that the Red Menace was still more feared than the Brown Shirt.

Also, the issues in Spain had not been as black and white as some originally believed. The Soviet Union was the first to come to the aid of the Republic, but there was a price to be paid for Russian arms and services. The Communists wanted control of the Government's propaganda machine as well as the freedom to maintain its own secret police there. In this way Stalin could succeed in crushing the considerable leftist opposition in the Loyalist camp. The Trotskyites, who formed a significant part of the Spanish battalions, were accused of being 'agents of Franco' and of playing football (literally) with the fascists. A more threatening force were the Spanish anarchists whom the Party referred to as 'uncontrollables'. In May 1937 an 'uprising' of anarchists

---

*One CP journal got caught in the crush. A vigorously isolationist article had already gone to print when the sudden news of the invasion arrived; it was forced to run the piece side by side with the new and absolutely contradictory pro-war Party line.

and Trots in Barcelona was neatly arranged, as was a Stalinist massacre in reaction to it.

Few of these international intrigues had serious repercussions for the Americans. But some serious doubts were cast on life inside the brigades and on the accounts of blissful comraderie published in the Communist press. Because the CP had such a small following among the Spanish Loyalists, it was necessary to get in on the ground floor of the recruiting drive and thereby take control of the Internationals. This led naturally to factions and caucuses and power trips within the political structure of the battalions. Since it was easier to rise in rank here than in a normal army, many small-fry authoritarians came to power as commissars, causing friction amongst the men; these were also blamed for sending in troops before they knew how to fight.*

Yet the Party's unflagging energy in rallying support for the Loyalists and against the embargo could not be disputed. No other leftist group could challenge its perfectly operating publicity machine, nor match its gorgeous Popular Front accent on Spain. Americans were told to think of the conflict as if it were 1776, there in the 'snows of Valley Forge'. The Comintern issued a manifesto which demanded a 'policy of bridling the fascist violators of universal peace, a policy worthy of the traditions of Lincoln and Washington'. Naturally no parallels were drawn between events in Spain and the Revolution of 1917. At the same time Party propaganda played a negative role. It talked constantly of victory and hardly mentioned casualties. Relatives of the dead were not informed until months after the fact. An ex-commissar, on his return to New York in 1938, was greeted by a sign lauding the 'conquering heroes of the revolutionary working class who slew the ugly beast of fascism'.

But Spain was not the 'tomb of fascism' as promised. Bravado-boys stung by the thrill of the episode shouted 'They shall not pass!' but pass the fascists certainly did. One American fighter

---

* Party intrigues also made use of the deaths of some soldiers. The men had been made to hand in their passports upon arrival in Spain. Hundreds of these passports later turned up in the Soviet Union for purposes of overseas travel (to the US, primarily) by Russian agents. One of these was Ramon Mercader, the assassin of Trotsky.

pilot shot down a German plane and proclaimed: '. . . I saw neither plane nor pilot falling. I saw fascism itself crashing to earth.' Some men had come to Spain to act out a projected adventure, but were met only by dark, anti-heroic suggestions from the future. If the battalion men were politically conscious, they still could not defeat the cold steel of modern warfare. In Spain Hitler tested his new saturation bombing techniques, his anti-tank defence, and threw sophisticated artillery and planes against men with rifles that jammed when they got too hot.

The implications of this went far beyond Spain. Clearly this was preparation for the Second World War, and Germany, the US and the USSR were bound to come away from the earlier battle racing against each other in technological expansion. The Nazis may have systematically destroyed the Spanish countryside, but the Soviet Union's plans to socialize, industrialize and modernize Spain upon winning the Civil War would have had a similar effect. And this same sweeping mechanization of power, derived from authoritarian instincts, soon would proceed to crush the last vestiges of leftist romanticism that had blossomed again in Spain.*
The European battalions might now fall back on the stability of ideology or throw themselves into the immediate battle with fascism right in their midst. For the Lincoln-Washington boys it was not at all Valley Forge, merely the end of revolutionary experience as they had dreamed it.

Yet such American dreaming as this could not simply go away.

---

*Ernest Hemingway's (non-combatant) presence in Spain remained, in most personal accounts, expressive of the very spirit of 'adventurism' the Party admonished. In his play, *The Fifth Column* (1937), the hero – a Loyalist counter-espionage agent – acts not out of politics or ideals, but rather the Hemingway-ish notion that a man must do what he has to do. The character is not a leftist saint; he likes his booze and his broads as well as his work – to the chagrin of his Party superior. The non-fictional CP didn't care for either the character or the play. It was not produced until November 1939, during the Hitler–Stalin pact; its militancy proved embarrassing for the isolationist moment. Aside from that, Marxist critics, including Alvah Bessie, roasted Hemingway because his hero did not exemplify the marvellous role played by the Soviet Union's agents in Spain. He was too individualistic and flawed in ways that Marxists should not be. In his introduction, Hemingway said that if the play 'has a moral it is that people who work for certain organizations have very little time for home life'.

A group called the Veterans of the Lincoln Brigade continued to propagandize the Spanish issue years after the fact. They produced their own publications, worked for the Party line (first against war, then for it, between 1939 and 1945), and in 1947 were awarded a place of honour on the Justice Department's famous list of subversive groups. After one of their conventions, an observer wrote: 'It was good to see them in assembly again, these soldiers of Brunete and Teruel and the Sierra Pandols . . . Today the boys carry on in the newer, more difficult warfare . . . of getting the truth to America . . . They are warriors for the people, and they shall never give up the sword . . .' This was only 1940 – just two years later – and already the future seemed mapped out for rocking chairs. A tinge of the ideal would always persist – despite Party efforts to use the aura of the Civil War for current propaganda value – but only through lovely nostalgia. Many of the Lincolns went off to fight Hitler, but never again would they fight so passionately on behalf of the American Left. All that was left them was what might now be called their 'Chiang Kai-Shek complex', the dream of someday storming back 'there' in force – Spanish peasants waiting tearfully for them beneath the olive groves – to take what once they lost. It was a summing-up for many more than just those who fought in the Civil War. In or out of Spain, it conjured up latter-day Don Quixotes still struggling with windmills.

4

The Left proved that its strength lay in publicity rather than decisive action towards social change, and so the reaction against its only decade of real prominence in America was directed at its more 'famous' successes. The massive advertising campaign of the Popular Front provided a ready-made complex of targets. Where the Party had sought 'names' and stars to give it public recognition, Red-baiters and witch-hunters went after 'names' and stars to prove conspiracy. Where the CP had tossed up fronts and ideal causes, the reactionaries tried to get behind the front and find the cynical 'realities' beneath the ideals. The decade and more of Red Scare that followed the thirties was a blatant unmaking of leftist respectability. And, in this process, the right wing used similar methods, established, in effect, its own 'Popular Front' in which it could pretend a galloping patriotism as a smoke-screen to its dirty businesses, conservative propaganda and publicity-mongering.

The major channel for most right-winging in the Scare was the House Committee on Un-American Activities, referred to by clever leftists as the House Un-American Activities Committee or HUAC. It was here that actors, clowns, ambitious politicians and Communist superstars paraded their wares on a well-worn public platform. Major political careers were launched here and countless radical ones decimated. The Committee opened shop in August 1938, in the heart of the Popular Front. Its purpose, at that time, was to investigate Nazis and Commies, but also to have a few whacks at Roosevelt and the New Deal. The first chairman, Martin Dies, solemnly swore at the first hearing that this would be 'no three-ringed circus . . .' nor the 'old kind of investigation that would go after somebody only for cheap publicity'. But this was precisely the chairman's measure as well as that of most subsequent Committee kingpins. According to Dies, the Reds had put a 'Trojan Horse' in America in an attempt to destroy the nation from within; it was his mission to show up that lovely horse for what it really was – a Red dragon with a nasty sting in its tail. He looked for Communist infiltration in the CIO, in the Spanish Civil War, in the theatre and the cinema. He was also one of the first to point out that Communists had got into high-ranking government positions; although he did not pursue this to any great extent, it was a major theme in post-War years for other famous inquisitors.

By popularizing his Red-baiting and avoiding theory and sophistication (of which he was thoroughly devoid anyway), Dies could ensure the complicity of the mass media and the folks back home. His hearings provided daily anecdotes and sensations and, like the CP, he was not above using themes from popular culture to make his effect: 'Capone's racket, compared to Stalin's . . . was not predicated upon the premise of any Utopia. On the whole it was devoid of pretense and masquerade . . . Stalin's racket . . . confuses ideals with crime. Capone wanted only our loose pocket change. Stalin wants our entire national income.' He was myth-making, giving the Committee a niche in public consciousness, providing a sadistic form of entertainment. It turned the Silent Majority on and made the Left more sanctimonious – soon everyone was hopping to the Committee's tune.

One of the side-shows Dies provided was a further attempt to sour the experience of Spain. (This process was already in effect; several congressional resolutions urged stripping Lincoln Battalion men of their citizenship.) Dies brought the first wave of ex-leftist stool-pigeons before the Committee and elicited Spanish atrocity tales from them. Two former brigade members testified that they had 'escaped' from the Loyalist camp, and that ninety per cent of the men wanted to return home but were prevented by the Reds. Another witness told how the Party recruited secretly in American universities and arranged a kind of 'underground railway' that took men to France and then Spain. Two years later Dies suggested that the FBI look into these recruiting fronts; the G-Men responded with a series of raids in Detroit, but the leftists were released soon after.*

One of Dies's major successes was in helping to kill the Federal Theatre Project under the Government's Works Progress Administration. The point of this project was to give work to actors and theatre people during the Depression, as well as providing cheap mass entertainment. But the nature of the times also dictated that this would be a more or less leftist theatre (although a good part of its repertoire consisted of wholly non-political melodramas, musicals and children's shows). The major innovation of the project was the theatrical form called the Living Newspaper, perhaps the closest the American theatre has ever come to its own 'epic' style. This would probe or expose immediate social

---

* Never one to be daunted, J. Edgar Hoover kept up his own abuse against the Lincolns. His particular fantasy of recruitment was, as usual for him, a sexual one: 'An enlistee might be promised a lucrative position in Spain, cash rewards, or travel accommodations. A young girl would entice unsuspecting men; in return for her favors they would promise to enlist.'

problems in the hope of educating and alerting the audience. The methods were anything but realistic – projections, public announcements, use of film clips – extending the notion of the agit-prop. The CP's view of the Living Newspaper (and of the theatre project in general) was typically ambivalent; although the plays could serve the cause, they could also prove highly embarrassing during the Popular Front. The fact that such agitational work was done anyway attests to the Party's very small influence over the Federal Theatre Project. This did not, however, stop Dies from seeing it as a conspiracy to create class consciousness in America. His drift was to confront FDR with the fact that he had been the impresario for 'putrid plays spewed from the gutters of the Kremlin'.*

Communist influence in the popular arts was hardly profound, but the Committee's saying it was seemed to make it so. The domineering role the Party hoped to play in the theatre and cinema – which it failed to achieve – was now flatteringly attributed to it by the inquisitors. This was uppermost in the public mind when the HUAC decided to liberate the great fortress of American reality in southern California. Both the Party and the witch-hunters knew that to control Hollywood was to win a major battle for consciousness. The silver screen was the most popular 'front' of all, and it was against this landscape that the Committee made its first all-out, no-holds-barred strike against leftist infiltration.

From its beginnings, Hollywood seemed the least likely place *any* outsider could penetrate. It was quick to establish its own groundrules and mythologies, one of which was a mystique of impregnability. The code for any possible political content was expressed candidly by Will Hays, President of the Motion Picture Producers and Distributors of America and chief arbiter of public taste: 'The industry has resisted and must continue to resist the lure of propaganda in that sinister sense persistently

---

*One of the 'putrid' plays cited by the Chairman was W. H. Auden's *Dance of Death*, which celebrates the 'decline of a class'. In the drama-ballet, factories are seized by the workers and, at the death of the capitalist, the shadow of Karl Marx appears on a backdrop announcing: 'The instruments of production have been too much for him. He is liquidated.'

urged upon it by extremist groups . . . most pictures reflect no higher purpose than to entertain, with "escapist" entertainment if you please.'

One of the first Communists to be told to keep his social significance out of Hollywood was the great Russian director, Sergei Eisenstein. Curiously, he was hired by Paramount in 1930 to make a film in America, and he chose to have a go at *An American Tragedy*. Eisenstein saw the novel as a story of failed American bourgeois ideals. His script, approved by Dreiser, was faithful to the original, conveying the stark social background of industrial America. Clyde Griffiths was important chiefly as a representative of his class.* Paramount wanted only a simple 'whodunit'; Eisenstein was un-American enough to insist that the film have a 'world attitude'. Which meant, in dollars and cents, no sentiment and no stars; indeed, he didn't even want to use professional actors, but preferred to look around California gas stations for a possible Clyde. To make Paramount's life even more difficult, Eisenstein stumbled upon his very own witch-hunt, giving him a taste of the sun-stroked right-wing fanatic fringe of southern California. A certain citizen, Major Paese, feared the 'Jewish Bolshevik' would inject his Soviet poison into American movies, and hounded Eisenstein wherever he went. This ball was soon picked up on a national scale by the Hamilton Fish Committee; Paramount cancelled its contract with the Russian.

An American Tragedy did finally get made, but it had been rendered quite safe.† The job went to Joseph von Sternberg, a European who had learned to give Hollywood what it expected. Here the entire first section of the novel, that which gives it social determination through Clyde's background, was simply omitted,

---

*Dreiser had carried on an ideological dispute with Eisenstein when the two met in the Soviet Union in 1928. The Russian stressed the need for collective thinking, but the American stuck to his pre-Communist guns: 'I said to Eisenstein that I still considered the drama of the individual to come first – his personal trials, terrors and delights – since only through the individual could the mass and its dreams be sensed and interpreted.'

† A later safe version was made by George Stevens in 1951, called *A Place in the Sun*, with Montgomery Clift as a 'method' Clyde. It paid homage to the frightened fifties, concentrating fully on the love story and steering miles clear of social comment.

along with the final death-house sequences that round out the character. The emphasis was on Clyde's sexual nature; it ended with the sentencing in the courtroom, playing upon the American love for trial dramas. This version brought a lawsuit and scowls of rage from Dreiser: 'If an earthquake or any other catastrophe happened, much less an economic depression, they (Hollywood) would still be employing their magnificent brains out there on the right length of a kiss, or "the impatient virgin".'

The Party reacted to the vulgarity of Hollywood by virtually ignoring it throughout the early thirties. Since it was so thoroughly a big business dedicated to preserving bourgeois values, there was little hope of getting across a class message. At best, Marxist critics could console themselves by righteously believing that the Hollywood ethic marked the demise of capitalism. One of them went so far as to say that in Mae West 'we possess a lady who could assume her position now as the Statue of Liberty and who so obviously represents bourgeois culture at its apex that she will enter history as a complete treatise on decay'.

During the Popular Front, however, there was no choice but to cheer such an all-American wonder as the film industry. Suddenly the Party was praising the worst crap B-movies because they were in the democratic tradition. By 1937 the *Worker* could proclaim that 'Hollywood has become the West Coast center of progressivism.' Party members were polled, and decided their favourite film stars were Gary Cooper and Claudette Colbert. In Communist movie criticism the good guys and bad guys were described as the 'progressives' and the 'reactionaries'. Slowly, too, a social conscience began to seep into the Hollywood foundations. Successful leftist playwrights, like Odets, were too hot a commercial property on Broadway for Hollywood producers to ignore any longer. The importation of such men to the West Coast was bound to affect the intellectual environment, if not the movies themselves.

Surprisingly, the Hollywood community responded to the call. There was a certain snob appeal in the concept of the Popular Front, and much of the industry became conscience-stricken overnight. Innumerable meetings and rallies were held, and Hollywood fund-raising events were staggeringly effective, considering the class of funds that could be raised there. A front called the Hollywood Anti-Nazi League gathered 4,000 members. (After the Hitler–Stalin pact the name of the organization was changed to the Hollywood League for Democratic Action, demonstrating CP influence.) Local unions, like the Screen Writers Guild, usually cautious, began talking of affiliating with the CIO or building a combined union of stage, screen, radio and (later) television artists. (Party infiltration into the industry's unions was one of the prime motivations for the Hollywood investigations of 1947.)

The biggest boost to conscience was – naturally – Spain. Nowhere was the glamour of the faraway conflict felt as it was in the land of dreams on the Pacific. Some few small-time actors were recruited into the brigades; but the main task of the Hollywood Left was to collect money for the cause, donate cars and ambulances and generally to build popular sympathy for the Loyalists. The most unlikely stars were turned on by the romance of the Civil War. Among these was the stripper Gypsy Rose Lee who, ironically, was given the job of collecting clothes for Spanish children. At one mass meeting she announced: 'I have not come to lift my skirts, but to lift the embargo on Spain.'

Despite this activity, the CP still found the actual celluloid of the place impenetrable. It could not get its message into films, mostly because of the structure of the industry and the involvement of so many different people on a single project. In 1937 John Howard Lawson (one of the 'Hollywood Ten') was asked to script a film called *Blockade*, about the Spanish Civil War.* In the film, an unnamed, but clearly Loyalist, village is cut off from its food supply and bombed by an unnamed, but very Franco-looking, army. The inside story was pure melodrama which the author had to adapt to fit the particular screen images of two Hollywood stars, one of whom played the Spanish conflict, in Lawson's words, with 'glycerine tears'. Nonetheless, the Catholic press and the Legion of Decency had a fit, putting pressure on distributors and cinema managers not to show it. The shape of charges to

*Lawson had been called in to undo the work done by Clifford Odets on the script. Odets's version was, according to Lawson, 'an inept melodrama . . . having no bearing on the events in Europe'.

come was telegraphed when one Jesuit paper called the politically harmless *Blockade* the 'first picture to raise the question of propaganda issuing from Leftist brains in Hollywood'.

Naturally, then, Martin Dies was ready, in 1938, to put his finger in the Hollywood pie and hope for a few Red plums on the upsweep. The Committee's chief investigator reported that 'evidence tends to show that all phases of radical and Communistic activities are rampant among the studios of Hollywood and although well known, is a matter which movie moguls desire to keep from the public.' By 1940 Dies was already playing a theme that a later Committee would take up with a vengeance – stars giving their money and their names for CP-organized causes, either knowingly or through the 'innocence' of the fronts. To prove his point, Dies went to Hollywood to pick off a few actors, including Frederic March, Franchot Tone (ex-Group Theatre), Luise Rainer (ex-Mrs Clifford Odets), Humphrey Bogart and James Cagney. Cagney himself appeared before Dies and vehemently denied that either he, Bogart or March had done anything wrong. Whether or not Dies thought it best to tussle no further with tough guys like Bogey and Cagney, he soon left the dream city to its own devices. Others, seven years on, would not give up so easily.

The Committee's 1947 Hollywood investigations brought a swift end to the Party's brief encounter with the movie colony. Where Dies had made only threatening overtures, the new 'Cold War' Committee under the direction of J. Parnell Thomas could actually force the industry to 'clean house' and establish a blacklist against Communists. In the course of the hearings the CP's penetration of Hollywood was shown to be a fairly well-coordinated complex involving unions and front groups. But such information was incidental; what the Committee hammered home was the idea that the Party's message had wormed its way into the movies. There was no evidence of Red propaganda produced, but the Committee was determined to find it there because of all the Communists working in the industry. One of their 'friendly' witnesses, the actor Adolphe Menjou, told them that a Communist actor could inject subversion in a film 'by a look, by an inflection, by a change of voice'. Others carried the theme further. In Clifford Odets's film, *Humoresque* (1947), John Garfield plays a working-class violinist who falls for a hoity-toity dame (Joan Crawford). She finds their love impossible and ultimately jumps in the sea for the whole length of time it takes Garfield to play the 'Liebestod' from *Tristan Und Isolde* in the background. Yet what seemed like B-melodrama took up the testimony of J. L. Warner (of the Brothers): 'John Garfield . . . was mad at Joan Crawford for romantic reasons and said, "Your father is a banker." He was alluding to the fact that she was rich and had all of the money. He said, "My father lives over a grocery store." That is very, very subtle, but if you see the film with these lines in it you will see the reason for it. But it is not in the film. I eliminated it from the script.'* This was not merely right-wing fantasy, but the sort of caution bred by the Popular Front/Trojan Horse idea. Chairman Thomas also spoke of the 'Rip Van Vinkle opinion' of those who thought he was looking for bogus Commies; it was precisely because the industry had gone to sleep on the job that it was now so full of treasonable cancer.

Yet the Committee's intentions were far from honourable, nor was it simply misguided as to the extent of propaganda in films. It clearly hoped to exert its own pressure, not merely on the hiring and firing of personnel, but on the very content of films. The inquisitors pointed out that there were not enough anti-Communist movies made; they insisted that more films should depict the benefits of the free enterprise system. Moreover they endorsed the criteria set down by the reactionary novelist, Ayn Rand, in her 'Screen Guide for Americans'; films should not, according to Rand, smear free enterprise, industrialists or success, nor should they glorify the 'common man', the collective or failure.

The witch-hunters could not resist the urge to steal some of the thunder from the movie stars. In these and in subsequent 'show trials' Committee members often fought amongst themselves to determine who would go to Hollywood to investigate or hold

---

* Odets himself was not above playing the opposite side of this theme. In the film script Garfield argues with his orchestra conductor over cutting part of a concerto. The *maestro*'s assumption, because of this, is that the violinist must be a Communist!

preliminary hearings. Also, their 'performances' in front of television cameras were far in excess of their subdued questioning at closed sessions. They knew that the folks back home were watching only to see the stars on trial, but this meant there was a captive audience from which they might benefit as well – either for the sake of votes or simple notoriety. In his 'friendly' testimony the movie mogul, Louis B. Mayer, compared the 'personalities' of the Hollywood colony to the British Royal Family. They served the same social functions, set examples of behaviour and work for the good of the nation. Behind this, although unstated, was the idea that actors were also high priests of social morality, mesmerizing the populace into being silent model citizens. Their conditioning function – through sheer glamour – was bound to cause a measure of envy in men bent on the manipulation of power.*

Many were quick to notice that bashing Reds in public had a real glitter. 'Friendly' witnesses like Robert Taylor, Gary Cooper, George Murphy and Walt Disney now came forward with atrocity tales and 'evidence' of film propaganda. Reputations were made here; Ronald Reagan, actor: 'Our Red foes even went so far as to threaten to throw acid in the faces of myself and some other stars, so that we "never would appear on the screen again". I packed a gun for some time . . .' John Wayne led a posse called the Motion Picture Alliance for the Preservation of American Ideals which vowed to wipe out not only the Commies, but also 'the so-called intellectual superiors they have helped to import from Europe and Asia'. Gary Cooper said he disliked Communism because 'it isn't on the level'. More vigilant was Leo Carillo, the actor who blazed the old West trails as the Cisco Kid: 'Communist rattlesnakes are bent on inoculating the mind of American youth. Clean out the rats.'

*In 1946 an ex-naval officer and product of a southern California upbringing was elected to Congress in a district not far from Hollywood. On the strength of the Red-baiting smear campaign he ran against his opponent, he was assigned, in his freshman year, to the Committee cleaning out the vermin in – Hollywood. One year later he was demonstrating his acting talents by pulling secret documents from pumpkins on TV, five years later conjuring soap opera puppies and weeping his way to power. Twenty-five years later his obsession with actors continued unabated.

If the right wing had such lions, the Left rose to the challenge with a multitude of Christians. Of the nineteen 'unfriendly' witnesses, only eleven were called to testify. Of these, ten insisted on their First Amendment rights and refused to answer questions about their Party affiliations. These were all writers, directors and producers, but there was no chance to question them about film content. They were determined not to cooperate with the Committee, a fact which angered the more liberal representatives of the industry who had been prepared to back them. All these were cited for Contempt of Congress and sent to prison, gaining their place in radical folklore as the 'Hollywood Ten'.

But the Ten were far from tight-lipped. They performed even better than the witch-hunters, slinging verbal abuse and contempt for almost every question. Each had a prepared statement, which only a few were permitted to read. The statements expressed horror at the proceedings, called the Committee un-American, invoked the spectre of Nazi Germany and generally played on the leftist heritage of martyrdom – stung at the challenge to their patriotism – filling the platform with impressive, but pointless, rhetoric. John Howard Lawson tried to turn the treason back at the Committee, lashing out with a sanctimonious panorama of their reactionary traits. He claimed the purpose of the HUAC was to 'cut living standards, introduce an economy of poverty, wipe out labor's rights, attack Negroes, Jews and other minorities, drive us into a disastrous and unnecessary war'. None of the familiar clichés of the leftist theatrical repertoire were lost in the stormy 1947 hearings, including that most arrogant of all American assurances, 'the whole world is watching'.*

As the second front against Hollywood Reds opened in 1951, the Left was at the brink of its most infamous nervous breakdown. The proud moral stance of the 'Hollywood Ten' was now dispersed over a series of events which had occurred since 1947, and

*One of the Ten, Alvah Bessie, years later expressed the presumptuous leftist notion – echoed by others throughout the Committee's years – that the HUAC and its members would be rendered insignificant by public opinion: 'On the rostrum, the Committee is seated and . . . there are McDowell of Pennsylvania, Vail of Illinois, Nixon of California and others who will later sidle or fight their way into political oblivion.'

it stretched away to a cowardly dread on the part of some witnesses. The Korean War had put a scare into many liberal sympathizers, and ex-Communists who now came up for investigation found themselves no longer heroes, but untouchables. China was 'lost', and this one was laid again at the doorstep of Popular Front-ism and its cunning infiltration of the US Government, primarily the State Department; this was the most useful tool right-wing witch-hunters had yet been given for stirring up the public and, in a hurry to ride the anti-Red wave, some turned again to the movie-star sweepstakes.

The behaviour of the witnesses was also affected by the change in political climate. The Smith Act (1940) had been upheld by the Supreme Court, making it illegal 'to knowingly or wilfully advocate, abet, advise, or teach the duty, necessity, desirability, or propriety of overthrowing or destroying any government in the United States by force or violence'. Hence it was no longer useful to invoke the First Amendment (as had the first wave of Hollywood witnesses) because *advocacy* of Communism was now a punishable offence and – apparently – not constitutionally guaranteed. Witnesses after 1951 had to rely on the non-self-incrimination factor of the Fifth Amendment if they wanted to keep silent about their affiliations. But this course of action was tantamount to not working again in Hollywood. After 1947 right-wing pressures and the fears of financial backers forced the film industry to adopt a blacklist of ex-Communists and fellow-travellers considered too risky – publicity-wise – to hire. Some directors and writers went into the black market, and sold their talents under pseudonyms; this, of course, was impossible for actors, whose faces told their story. Those who wanted to work openly, or work again after years of unemployment, could not possibly invoke the Fifth Amendment; silence now, in America, was taken as a presumption of guilt. Many who were summoned did in fact call upon their constitutional privilege and were duly made *persona non grata* in the industry. But most of the witnesses called between 1951 and 1954 were either voluntary repenters or were made to 'see the light' when called. Some of the most well-known names in Hollywood gave evidence of personal experience as well as the names of CP members; once the floodgates were opened, they fell over each other to testify. Even one of the original Ten, Edward Dmytryk, recanted and spilled his beans.

The Committee, too, had changed with the times. It had streamlined its effort, and lost most of the haphazard quality of earlier investigations. It knew what it was after in the 1951 trials and chased it with a fearsome virulence. The new research director of the Committee chided the 1947 witch-hunters for concentrating on the content of films, which he considered 'the weakest argument' against Hollywood. Far more significant was the amount of publicity and finance the Reds had got out of the movie colony; this was the real damage that still had to be undone. Thus the Committee was not satisfied with merely helpful information. If actors had given their names for Party propaganda, they were now expected to do no less for the HUAC, to serve *its* ends. A strong confession of anti-Communism was required; without this minimum, a man could still be in danger of the blacklist. Lawyers now got rich on obtaining 'clearances' for many performers. 'Letters of explanation' were publicly circulated to show that a certain star or director had not only seen the error of his ways, but actively joined the fight against the Red Menace. In this, too, the Committee enjoyed a new measure of power – given it by sheer default of witnesses who feared for their livelihoods. This allowed the witch-hunters a new measure of sadism, where they could watch stars – the most famous household names in America, including some classical tough guys – grovelling before them in embarrassment and humiliation, reciting prepared rituals of exorcism. So Edward G. Robinson called his inquisitive Committee 'the only tribunal where an American citizen can come and ask for relief from smears, false accusations and innuendoes'. The actor, Larry Parks, begged to be allowed to tell what he knew without naming names; the Committee admitted it already had these names, but forced Parks to become an informer in the public record just to show it could break him, or anyone else it wanted to break. Nor did it stop short of blackmail to bring people round. One famous choreographer-director was threatened with revelations of his homosexual activities unless he gave names to the Committee; fearing such exposure, he chose the 'lesser' slur on his reputation and complied.

By 1951, however, it was hardly necessary to *force* some leftist film people to recant. Given the shaky foundation on which they had staked their political claims, their lack of staying power was inevitable. Almost none of the witnesses called in the new hearings were, or had been, hard-core Communists. Many had gone through the Party mechanism and out the other side in under a year. Some had anticipated cut-price Utopia and lost interest when it was not forthcoming; others were simply attracted by the Popular Front. There was no point now in maintaining a stand which worked against self-interest.

Yet the Committee was not even content with simple renunciation of past affiliations and beliefs. The witch-hunters were just as eager to demystify the strong sense of personality assertion that had been an adjunct to leftist politics, and they applied a psychic brutality even to some who came along willingly. It was obvious, most of the time, that the investigators knew in advance the answers to their questions, had all the names a witness could possibly give and realized that the only 'political' benefit of the event was in obtaining the *submission* of public figures. They did not want answers as much as the witness's complicity in the very questioning. In many of the testimonies now this was given more than willingly. For those who had spent a lifetime chasing an identity, the crisis hour had come. Your character had been 'assassinated' and your compulsion was to clear your 'name'. To get this, you had to submit to the curious public psychoanalysis practised by the Committee. Years after an event or person had passed into the subconscious, it was probed, brought to the surface so that 'dangerous' symptoms could be eliminated. Many witnesses welcomed the opportunity to divest themselves of their 'free associations'. Testimony had to follow a jingoistic formula, but the amount of subconscious material yielded up often demonstrated a feeling of personal release more than anything else. Freud can help us out here: 'In Confession the sinner tells what he knows; in analysis the neurotic has to tell more.' Years of repressed anxieties about leftist involvement and failure came spilling up over the psychic edge. Tough guy Lee J. Cobb admitted that being able to testify afforded him 'subjective relief'.

But some testimonies went beyond cooperation and broke

through the therapeutic barrier. If it was a simple matter of confessing, the whole business might have been done with and everyone could get back to work. But whole lives and reputations were in the balance; when you took the stand you had to tell 'more' than you knew about that stand you once took. You had to correct the course of your wayward life, and bring it back to the warm hearth of the American Way.*

For American actors, the new Committee hearings had a special irony. The vanguard of the profession had long since given up the pretence to getting across a political message through performance. Once out of the thirties, they were free of the political imperative that governed their acts, and now acting style could develop in a way the actors really always wanted, unhindered by conscience. In the 1940s and 1950s dozens of post-Stanislavsky acting schools were established, oriented more towards training and technique than actually producing plays. The most important of these was the Actors Studio, founded in 1947 by Lee Strasberg, and its famous acting style came to be known as the 'method'. Strasberg had never been part of the serious leftist wing of the old Group Theatre, and was responsible for much of the non-political emphasis of the troupe. Now, in the 'post-Communist' era, Strasberg could carry the psychoanalytic approach even further, emphasizing always the undercurrents of personality that had to be probed. The end was not character development, only powerful exposure. Every consideration was secondary to the ultra-reality of the actor's experience, his digging for pure, un-phoney emotion. One of Strasberg's most famous exercises was called the 'private moment', in which an actor was made to recall an intense

---

* Psychoanalysis played a very *specific* role in the later hearings. The actor Sterling Hayden had gone to the FBI and finally to the Committee to obtain his 'clearance'; several years later, in his autobiography, he renounced his act and laid the blame on his analyst: 'Sonofabitch, Doc . . . I don't ask for any miracles, but I would like to get just a little relief . . . I'm thinking of quitting analysis . . . If you would only hold out some hope to me, then it might be different . . . I'll say this too, that if it hadn't been for you I wouldn't have turned stoolie for J. Edgar Hoover.' Another Hollywood analyst, whose clients made up a fair proportion of the film élite, simply ignored professional ethics and turned his files over to the Committee.

past emotion under the scrutiny of other members of the Studio. All thoughts of restraint and 'privacy' were banished, and the actor strained to deliver his rawest self. In such moments Strasberg himself was often described as playing an 'inquisitorial' role, pulling truths out of reluctant players with fanatic determination. He was the first to admit, however, that he never gave the exercise to people with deep psychological problems for fear of inducing neurosis. (Although rumours abounded of doctors being rushed in to treat actors in shock.)

Strasberg's goal was to cut away personality barriers so that actors could express *themselves* with total freedom and absence of shame. In this he presumed to be following the example of the Russian master: 'The simplest examples of Stanislavsky's ideas are actors such as Gary Cooper, John Wayne and Spencer Tracy. They try not to act but to be themselves, to respond or react. They refuse to say or do anything they feel not to be consonant with their own characters.' This was Strasberg's conclusion much more than Stanislavsky's, and it demonstrated the extent to which he had veered off the original course. For out of his desire for honest performances he created a phalanx of stars, most intent on being stars, projecting only themselves at the public eye.* What had begun in the Group as an attempt to use the Stanislavsky system as a vehicle for social expression passed quickly into a hunger for revealing the subconscious. The American theatre had strayed into the electrifying territory of psychodrama. And, in this 'method', actors gained a power over their audience which Stanislavsky would never have imagined possible. The relation was thoroughly intimate now, tearful ecstatic fantasies could be shared as you watched a man in the psychologically painful throes of becoming *somebody* in public.

The total emphasis on the projection of self made actors even more vulnerable to the Committee's bullying of personality. For an actor under the threat of the blacklist everything was at stake, not merely livelihood but a whole life's work of building an image

---

*Strasberg's influence on American popular culture and archetypes is immense. Out of the Actors Studio alone came Marlon Brando, James Dean, Marilyn Monroe, Paul Newman, Jane Fonda, Rod Steiger, Sidney Poitier, Steve McQueen, Montgomery Clift, Anne Bancroft – the list is endless.

bridge to fame. Those who could not work were deprived of their public platform; could not, in effect, be themselves.

Some of the leading lights of the Group Theatre – many of whom had become Hollywood stars – appeared at the sessions between 1951–4 and were made to speak of their old political commitments. These ex-dramatic rebels, whose style was once akin to speaking their minds, now came squealing their grief. It was 'method' testimony now, a far cry from the bombastic performances of 1947, and slotted in perfectly with the Committee's psychodramatic intentions.

It was only a matter of time, then, before an inquisitor would ask, 'Who was Stanislavsky and what was his method of acting?' This came during the voluntary appearance of Lee J. Cobb, an ex-Group Theatre 'method' actor. Two years earlier (1951) the Committee had questioned another volunteer, Jose Ferrer,* about sending a telegram to the Moscow Art Theatre on its fiftieth anniversary. By the time Cobb's turn came around, the influence of this suspicious Ruskie and his outfit must have come up dozens of times in the Committee's research. Cobb insisted that the Russian master was 'above political questions', but the interrogators were not convinced:

Mr Wheeler: Was it possible that an actor can portray in any way the Communist Party line through the method of acting? Can he get over a political line or thought?

Mr Cobb: No. I don't think that was at all possible. However, a project was undertaken, led by John Howard Lawson, to re-write the precepts of Stanislavsky's method on acting, to try as far as possible to color it by the prevailing Communist ideologies. The project failed miserably because the moment we departed from the text . . . we destroyed the most important aspect of it . . .

The most famous and successful of all 'method' directors, Elia Kazan (who had started as a Group Theatre actor), passed before the HUAC in 1952 and demonstrated the vital link between his work and political reality. He appeared first in closed session – refusing to give names – but then changed his mind and testified

---

*Ferrer was in a hurry to clear himself before the Committee so that he might win an Academy Award for his role as Cyrano de Bergerac.

publicly. He now said he wanted to name names because secrecy only served the Communist cause. To this end he provided the Committee with a lengthy affidavit, full of the names of ex-Communists, and the next day he put a paid advertisement in the New York *Times* explaining his position. He admitted to being a Party member between 1934–6, but soon quit and absented himself even from front activities after that time. One of the reasons for his defection concerned the Party's petty tribunals and censorious meetings: 'The last straw came when I was invited to go through a typical Communist scene of crawling and apologizing and admitting the errors of my ways. [A Communist functionary] made a vituperative analysis of my conduct in refusing to fall in with the Party line and plan for the Group Theatre, and he invited my repentance.'

Kazan, more than any other witness, danced to the Committee's tune and told them 'more' than he knew. He claimed patriotic motives, but giving the names of people who were active eighteen years before – names the Committee already had – could serve no cause but Kazan's. The comprehensive curriculum vitae he produced as part of his testimony far outstretched the required expression of loyalty. It was spectacular self-publicity and self-congratulations. On this investigative stage he could eradicate all traces of ugly memory and catapult his cleansed name back up in lights. He even felt the need to call his film about the Mexican Revolution, *Viva Zapata*, an anti-Communist work – which it most certainly was not – and wrote a lengthy article afterwards saying so again.

Clearly his experience haunted Kazan long after – as it did many others. Once cleared, he directed *On the Waterfront* in 1954 which involved Lee J. Cobb as well as another Committee informer, the writer Budd Schulberg. The film concerns a young hero who eventually squeals on a corrupt union boss in order to keep his self-respect; in many ways, it reflected the investigative experience. Hollywood was very happy with the film (and its point of view) and showered it with Academy Awards. Afterwards Kazan made a point of hiring at least one blacklisted actor for every film or play he directed. In one instance, a blacklistee was having trouble getting into a role that required him to express hatred. Kazan, 'methodically' famous for using the most intimate psychological facts of an actor's private life to get an effect on stage, told the player to think of him – Kazan – and what he had done, a fund of all the hatred he needed.

When Kazan directed Arthur Miller's play, *After the Fall*, in 1964, the process was more or less complete. Miller had been up before the Committee in 1956, told of his own leftist activities but, unlike Kazan, refused to implicate any other person: 'I want you to understand that I am not protecting the Communists or the Communist Party. I am trying to, and I will, protect my sense of myself.' Miller got no contracts for his response, only Contempt of Congress. By the time he wrote *After the Fall*, however, he had come to grips with the lingering trauma of the Committee, and could accommodate and forgive even characters who had informed. The play is a staged psychoanalysis, taking place in the 'mind, thought and memory' of the lawyer-hero. Two of his friends are summoned before the Committee, only one of whom actually gets there. After he squeals, he tries to blame it all on the Party: 'I think we *were* swindled; they took our lust for the right and used it for Russian purposes . . . What I propose – is that we try to separate our love for one another from this political morass.' The other victim holds on to his Communist faith although he recognizes he's been a stooge for Stalin. He is torn by the lies he has kept inside and by his apology for Soviet Russia. He wants to repent, but he cannot play the turncoat and retain his self-respect. Instead, he drops his subpoenaed ego in front of a speeding train.

The hero's guilt at the friend's suicide rounds out the slow dying of his own political involvement. Earlier in the play he asks: '. . . is it altogether good to be not guilty for what another does?' Yet, at the crunch, when he is asked to serve as legal counsel for his frightened friend, he freezes; he knows that to defend someone before the Committee is tantamount to staking his own career: 'I wanted out, to be a good American again, kosher again . . .'

Clifford Odets was yet another who wanted to be made kosher

again; in 1952 he awoke to sing for the Committee. By this time he was already a political shipwreck and, as for many others, it was just a matter of making it official. His play, *The Big Knife* (1949), falls between the two sets of interrogations, and there is certainly prophecy here of Odets' later capitulation. The hero (played by John Garfield) is a successful movie star whose earlier political ideals have been destroyed by his Hollywood years. He cries: 'Don't they murder the highest dreams and hopes of a whole great people with the movies they make? This whole movie thing is a murder of the people.' Here was a stunning irony. While the witch-hunters were looking for paltry evidence of Communism in films to demonstrate a national disease, it was only those who had come West to spread a radical message that were finally contaminated. Communism had brought no chaos to Hollywood, but the industry drove its leftists to collapse, to further analysis, even to suicide. Men who once hoped to inform the public with Utopian visions were now informers of a different ilk.

Characters in *The Big Knife* talk about the promise unfulfilled, the Revolution that never was. They had flunked the class struggle. The Odets hero finds life unbearable now without the dynamic of social change and chooses to put a stop to it. For Odets the man, it was a death of the spirit. He could now tell the Committee what it wanted to hear, how the Party had duped him, had tried to influence his playwriting then attacked him when he became a renegade. He said now that he left the Party because he wanted to write plays for average Americans in an American idiom. In the years ahead – now that he could work without fear – this would reflect the American theatre's total retreat into the subconscious, the apolitical, the dream state. Odets's last effort before he died in 1963 was a screenplay for Elvis Presley.

If there were witnesses who lived constantly with the ghost of protest past, there were others who tried to make it disappear. John Garfield was subpoenaed on 23 April 1951 and came to the experience denying everything. He claimed to have been an anti-Communist, was merely a liberal dupe whose famous name and prestige had been exploited. He emphatically denied membership in the Party and declared the organization should be outlawed. He even said he knew nothing at all about Communists until he watched them 'capture' Henry Wallace's presidential campaign in 1947. 'My life is an open book,' declared Golden Boy. But the Committee was mystified by his performance, indeed, found it difficult to suspend its disbelief. Here was a leading light in the Group Theatre, the living archetype of the popular proletarian hero, a crusader against the Committee's 1947 investigations protesting he never saw Red until 1948. No one seemed to believe him, and there was talk of summoning him a second time.

Garfield was one of the worst casualties of the inquisition. Like Odets, Hollywood had already drained him of his famous fire. Odets clearly saw Garfield himself when he wrote, in *The Big Knife*: 'You used to take sides . . . You used to grab your theatre parts and eat 'em like a tiger. Now you act with droopy eyes . . .' Hollywood had twisted the actor to its own dimensions and kept him in his place by perpetuating his image. When he asked to play the part of George Gershwin in the film *Rhapsody in Blue* he was told he 'wouldn't look right in a full-dress suit'.

Now the leftist hero did not come swaggering before the Committee; he came crawling, full of anxiety and doubt, repentant and hungering to be wholly American again. It was not in our tough guy's nature to lose his nerve; yet he staged his own humiliation and appealed to the HUAC to help 'protect people like me' from the Red Menace. He was taking crap not only from a sceptical Committee, but heaping it on himself as well. He was even at work on an anti-Communist pamphlet, 'I Was a Sucker for a Left Hook', when, at age thirty-nine, Golden Boy's heart attacked him for the third and last time.

*

There was an eleventh 'unfriendly' witness at the 1947 hearings, but his testimony sounded like nothing that had come before or would come later. He did not refuse to answer questions like the 'Hollywood Ten', yet he told the Committee nothing. Even though he was a German citizen and hadn't a constitutional leg to stand on, he could have told the witch-hunters to 'stuff it' and then puff out full of libertarian wrath. But this would not have been in keeping with the character style he had developed in his work, one designed to deflate emergencies in order to calmly manipulate political situations.

This witness, Bertolt Brecht, had just seen his play, Galileo, *performed in the US. In it, a worshipping admirer derides the ageing scientist for recanting his beliefs before his inquisitors. Galileo responds by claiming a dread of physical pain and points out, later in the play, that he has been able to finish his work secretly because he has remained alive. But he admonishes his admirer: 'Pity the country that needs heroes.' Now Brecht faced his own inquisitors and twisted them to his amusement. He managed to apply a Brechtian smile, an undercover cynicism, to the moment; he saw no need to make a fuss. The Committee allowed him to smoke his famous cigar, and he later claimed he used it to create pauses in his testimony. This was not the 'star pause' of the 'method' theatre, in which an actor rests and gears up for high explosive penetration in the next action. Nor was it the pregnant silence of cowardice in the face of interrogation. It was a smokescreen.*

Phoneys and Revolutionary Puritans

In his New York Daily Mirror *scandal column, on Independence Day 1951, Walter Winchell wrote: 'Julius Rosenberg, the atomic spy now in the death house, told guards: "If I could last two or three years, I'd be rescued by Soviet airmen."' Rosenberg, who had been convicted (along with his wife Ethel) of conspiracy to pass bomb secrets to the Russians, waxed indignant. He wrote to the warden of Sing Sing Prison, complaining of this attempt to further defame him and link him to Moscow. The warden insisted no information had been given to the press from his office and, as far as he knew, the prisoner had made no such statement. This was poor solace for the already victimized and paranoid Rosenberg. He felt it was unthinkable that such a campaign of lies could be waged against him while he was still appealing his conviction.*

Rosenberg, of course, was awaiting execution, and the comic absurdity of Winchell's gag did not strike him as funny in the least. But this showed him to be out of step with the new and thoroughly B-movie era in which he was jailed. His better memories lay back in the thirties and early forties where humanitarian-leftist ideals got popular play. Now he was being tortured by the rumour-ridden fifties in its dungeons quickly filling with political prisoners. All around him the language and culture were subjected to dynamic twistings and stretchings, bogeys and demons sprang up from the grave of logic. Rosenberg would not be the only leftist whose trial – full of secrecy, perjury, fabrication and frame-up – would haunt the conscience of the Left in later eras. Great patches of doubt would linger after the political trials of the fifties, the testimony of super-star informers, the great spy fantasies conceived perhaps in lonely toilets at the FBI. Political reputations rested on secrets pulled from pumpkins, jello boxes cut in half for espionage purposes, the Red Army crossing the Polar Region to invade North America via Alaska, yes, even Russian paratroopers falling from the skies over Sing Sing, playing Mission Impossible for the greater glory of the Kremlin. To doubt or question it was to fall foul of the historical moment. Here was a parade for Reds and rednecks marching in step on the opposite sides of a common grotesquerie. Those who couldn't laugh would pay with their names, their minds, their jobs, sometimes their lives. They had insisted on credibility in the hour of its demise and renounced their claim to a piece of the fun at the Asylum Ball.

1

It was not witch-hunting alone that brought the Left to collapse in the Dark Ages of the 1950s. Further internal dramas in the Communist Party and a startling new cowardice in the face of repression combined to weaken the movement at the source and render it even more vulnerable to attack. In this time the Party lost not merely numbers, but also the vital prestige it had won. Most of the achievements of the Popular Front were nullified, and the Left would never again come so close to obtaining a mass base in America.

During the Second World War the CP had seen its sharpest rise in membership. It had been able to whip up sympathy for the Soviet Union and publicize the image of the heroic Red Army in its battle against the fascist hordes. As an extension to Popular Front thinking the war had been interpreted as a 'people's war' rather than the usual shoot-out between capitalist factions. The Party caused no trouble during these years, vigorously opposing strikes, Negro demonstrations, anything that might tend to diminish the military struggle. In this way, the organization climbed in public acceptance even to the point where it was to able win small electoral victories. The new respectability led a fluctuator like Theodore Dreiser to declare, 'The name of Stalin is one beloved by the free peoples of the earth' – and put his name down at last:

These historic years have deepened my conviction that widespread membership in the Communist movement will greatly strengthen the American people . . . Belief in the greatness and dignity of Man has been the guiding principle of my life and work. The logic of my life and work leads me therefore to apply for membership in the Communist Party.

It is inconceivable that a man so riveted in the 'American nature' as Dreiser would have joined the Party in 1945 if the fear of Kremlin encroachment was still strong in popular myth. The Americanization process had done its job, the Jefferson-Washington-Paine palaver even connected well with the natural patriotism of the war effort. 'Clyde Griffiths' found organizational shelter at last in – of all places – the Communist Party.

But it was precisely at its finest hour that the American CP began to pull itself to pieces. With the end of the war the alliance between the US and the USSR was shown to be little more than a marriage of convenience. The idea of the Soviet Union scratching backs with the world's ultra-capitalists was not only repugnant, but no longer politically expedient. Once again a major change of Party line was in the works, and this naturally affected American Communists more than most. Most of the overtures to Americanism had to be retracted, all talk of coexistence minimized; as early as 1946 the Party press described the US as well on the road to fascism.

The chief victim of the demolition of the Popular Front was Earl Browder, head of the Party from the mid-thirties to the end of the war. The idolatry of Browder rose to fever pitch in the early forties, his American pioneer ancestry was played up and he was heralded as a great champion of the 'people'. His basic line in the war years was that the fight against fascism was making big business more responsive to the needs of the working class. This was partly to allay capitalist fears about the ultimate intentions of the Soviet Union; but Browder also hoped somehow to reconcile the two economic systems on a permanent coexistent basis. In 1944 he even dissolved the CP and established the less 'fearsome' Communist Political Association. Browder had carried his conviction to the point where the original enemy of communism could not be distinguished, and by 1945 this 'Browderism' was a source of ideological embarrassment to Moscow – even though the Russians had given it their blessing for years. In July 1945 he was toppled from power and replaced by William Z. Foster; the old Communist Party was reconstituted. Overnight Browder was stripped of his heroic stature and became an enemy of the Party. He was denounced for having lost faith in the 'people' and for placating capitalist swine; in 1946 he was expelled altogether, his achievements written out of Communist histories. 'Browderite' now became a latter-day form of abuse – not quite as heinous as 'Trotskyite' – to signal the crime of revisionism. The Party, too, was overdue for one of its ritual exorcisms, and those who had maintained the Browder line were made to answer for it. A series of 'I was a symp for the turncoat Browder' confessions followed, in which Party leaders – under no physical compulsion – admitted, *mea culpa*, to unthinkable sins against the organization and the 'people'.

With this new 'Cold War' face the CP's American fortunes began to decline steadily. It suffered a slow loss of membership, which gained momentum once the Party declared renewed war on creeping American fascism and the creeping fascists, in turn, stepped up their persecution of the creeping Red Menace. Both Right and Left in America began to attribute the breakdown of US–Soviet relations to an internal conspiracy by the other.

Seriously weakened, but with a renewed sense of Communist purpose, the Party made its last major bid for political power by encouraging and manipulating Henry Wallace's presidential campaign from 1946–8. Involvement in the electoral process had again become part of CP style. Aside from electing its only Communist Congressman, Vito Marcantonio of New York, the Party began to throw its support behind candidates it hoped to influence.* The idea of a third national party, led by a well-known progressive, had a special appeal. For one thing, the international Communist publicity machine could point to the development of a mass leftist party as evidence of great social unrest in America. Also, here was another chance to ride the back of a 'name' and win respectability by contagion. Wallace had been one of the more

---

*In 1946 the CP backed the Wisconsin senatorial bid of a budding unknown named Joseph Raymond McCarthy.

ardent supporters of the Soviet Union while serving as FDR's Vice-President; at the very least, he would take a 'soft' line on Communism. He had a fairly substantial liberal following to exploit, and it was only natural that some of the silver stardust from Saint Roosevelt's hair would have fallen on Wallace's lapels. The Party had few illusions about him or its ability to control the man; nor did it entertain the absurd possibility of his winning (although many misguided rank and file expected victory). The CP wanted, minimally, a clear five million votes out of its effort; this would attest to post-war Communist strength and serve as impetus for a new drive on membership.

The CP played an aggressive, if often backhanded, role in the formation of Wallace's new Progressive Party. The campaign attracted many hesitant liberals and revived post-Browder spirits – which had been depressed – in Party members. Publicity turned the quite ordinary Wallace into a demi-god (so much so that rank and file were forever being 'disillusioned' by his more non-Communist, often anti-Soviet, remarks). Wallace helped this image by stressing a campaign theme no sincere leftist could resist: '. . . the People's Peace will usher in the Century of the Common Man'. Even the dormant Communist youth movement perked up at the sight of such an attractive father-figure, and thousands of students worked overtime in an aura of new idealism.*

But nearly all strategies backfired in the Wallace campaign. For the early part of the business the CP managed to keep itself on the sidelines without making its influence too conspicuous. But at the 1948 founding convention it brought along its own cheering section (having requested members to give up their summer vacations) as well as its most famous one-man entertainment fronts, Pete Seeger and Paul Robeson. The Progressive Party platform was so designed to serve Soviet propaganda needs that it soon became clear who was running the show. Wallace, however, refused to repudiate Communist support and, subsequently, many non-Communist Wallaceites defected. It was the first clear indication since the Popular Front swept them in, that liberals and non-

---

*An observer who walked the floor of the Progressive Party Convention would be the recipient of a parallel grass-roots movements in later days of false leftist optimism – George McGovern of South Dakota.

committed intellectuals wanted out of the 'one big happy family of the Left' image projected by the Party. But the greatest loss of the Wallace campaign was the CP's bulwark of working-class support. The unions felt, for the most part, that, while backing Wallace might benefit the Soviet Union and the international movement, it would be harmful to the immediate needs of American labour. The traditional union links to the Democratic Party had reached a peak in the New Deal years, and it was feared that Wallace would draw vital votes away from the Democrats, thereby ensuring a Republican victory. This would mean an acceleration of the anti-union legislation already gathering reactionary momentum in Congress. All this was not worth the few symbolic advantages that might be gained from joining a Wallace bandwagon. The Party was warned well in advance, by many union leaders, of the probable consequences of its adventure; these went unheeded. The CIO backed Truman, labour helped to elect him with a large turnout and Wallace got little more than a paltry million, primarily middle-class votes. All the advances made in the 1930s that gave the Party a measure of real influence over the workers were quickly disappearing. Soon after, the Communist-dominated unions were expelled from the powerful CIO and, by 1950, the Party controlled less than five per cent of organized labour in the US. With its lack of sensitivity to political facts in America, the CP could do nothing now to prevent an inevitable situation – years later – when workers would take for their hero Wallace, *George*, oblivious to or contemptuous of the traditions that spawned Wallace, *Henry*.

The Wallace defeat did not actually crush the Communist Party, but it came at a crucial moment during a mounting crisis of confidence. A more severe blow had come earlier that summer when eleven Party leaders were indicted under the Smith Act. This occurred only two intimidating days before the founding convention of the Progressive Party; it was Truman jumping the anti-Red steamroller in a bid for votes.

It was an important moment for the Left, heralding a new era in American social history as well as a major shift in CP strategy. The 1947 Hollywood investigations had given a hint of things to come, but the new indictments did more (if less ostentatiously) to show the legal temper of the times. The Smith Act became law in 1940 and had hung around virtually unused for eight years.* The Government now argued that when the Popular Front existed, its aims were not in fundamental opposition to US security. But when Browder was deposed and the Party reconstituted in 1945, it revived – allegedly – its original intent to teach and advocate the overthrow of the Government by 'force and violence'. The Government's operation had been slowly building since the war in an effort to cut off all circuits of the Left. The Smith Act was the easiest vehicle since no actual *act* of insurrection had to be proved; advocacy was enough. It had the advantage over congressional investigations of tying the Party up in the courts as well as securing substantial fines and jail sentences.

The resulting trial of the CP's top brass in 1949 exposed the considerable network of Federal agents that had been working in the Party for some time. (One of these was the famous Herbert – I Led Three Lives – Philbrick.) A major witness, too, was the ex-Managing Editor of the *Daily Worker*, Louis Budenz, who ushered in (along with Whittaker Chambers in the Alger Hiss trial) the first wave of renegades to star for the prosecution in major trials against former friends and colleagues. All these informers were considered 'experts' on the subject of Communism; they testified to the *real* meaning of the Communist classics, claiming that Marx and his followers had developed a sinister 'special jargon' that only Communist Party members could decipher. Behind their mask of social humanism they really dropped a series of coded messages teaching nothing less than – surprise! – force and violence against capitalist governments. High-minded passages were, according to Budenz, 'merely window-dressing asserted for protective purposes, the Aesopian language of V. I. Lenin'. All this showed that the eleven were being tried for the words and ideas of others – some written exactly one hundred

---

*In 1941–2 members of a Socialist Workers Party in Minnesota – a Trotskyite group – were prosecuted under the Smith Act. Naturally, the CP supported the Government's case. Said the *Daily Worker*: 'The American people can find no objection to the destruction of the Fifth Column in this country.'

years before – as interpreted by paid stooges. The presiding judge called it an 'ordinary criminal case', but it was a railroad job in the great tradition.

The Party chose to play a propagandistic role in the courtroom, trying to drum up sympathy for the Communist cause on a ready-made public platform. They set out to expose 'Wall Street's "cold war" . . . its "get tough with Russia policy" . . . its colossal arms race . . . its atomic bomb diplomacy . . . its preparations to launch another world war'. This strategy failed miserably, as it only could have in a 1949 American court. If the Communists had chosen to ignore public sentiment and concentrate on the constitutional issues involved, they might at least have swayed the Supreme Court in their appeal. As it was, they preferred an ideological side-show – ignoring the American public's new distaste for Reds – and paid for it with five years each in the slams.

If the Smith Act wasn't enough of a front against Reds, a whole series of congressional bills, designed to outlaw or cripple the Party, now made their appearance. Out of the same impulse that produced the Hollywood investigations came the short-lived Nixon-Mundt bill, which required the Communist Party and its fronts to register with the US Government. This eventually became the McCarren or Internal Security Act of 1950, which claimed that American Communists 'repudiate their allegiance to the United States, and in effect transfer their allegiance to the country in which is vested the direction and control of the world Communist movement'. The registration procedures under this act proved to be cumbersome to institute, and it was succeeded in 1954 by the Communist Control Act, fathered by Senator Hubert Humphrey. This tried to outlaw the CP by saying it was not a political organization, but an agent of a conspiratorial power which wanted to overthrow the US by force and violence.

Just in case the Reds and their symps didn't get the message of right-wing legislation, then good old American muscle could help to ram it home. In 1949, at Peekskill, New York, a violent flare-up of anti-Communism brought the Silent Majority directly into the drama. The occasion was a scheduled Paul Robeson concert, and this brought leftists to the open-air sight in great numbers – as only the great Red black man could. Robeson had been giving concerts without major incident since the thirties, but now his pro-Soviet stand helped to trigger off a massive riot tolerated – if not organized – by local police and the FBI. The first concert never got off the ground, as thousands of local vigilantes closed the area, thrashing the handful of spectators who had got in. Some weeks later the event actually took place, with a self-appointed phalanx of movement men surrounding the area. But this only delayed the action. Cars and buses leaving the grounds were stoned, blacks were billy-clubbed, whites were roughed-up, the cops looked on in amusement.

Peekskill was another reverberating trauma for the movement. The Left certainly had a history of street fighting, cops and union men trading punches in the early days, rednecks pounding radicals everywhere. But here was a crowd of middle-class, mild-tempered folks, the pacifist contingent running afoul of WASP America and getting its nose bloodied. It was only natural that Left right-eousness would make this a key moment in American radical history, that it would be seen as evidence that Hitler was alive and well in Upstate New York. Said the Communist writer, Howard Fast: 'The *Peekskill* affair was an important step in the prepara-tion for the fascization of America and for the creation of recep-tive soil for the promulgation of World War III.' Fast also claimed it was a concerted effort by the reactionaries to employ *lumpen* elements – against their own class interests – to fight the Com-munists. But Peekskill was not the onset of jackboot-ism in America as the Left predicted. In the years ahead, the goon squads were hardly needed again. The point had been well taken, and radicals were fast clamming up.

The Party's response to the massive increase in right-wing in-itiative was perhaps logical and practical, but equally self-defeat-ing. After the Smith Act convictions (upheld by the Supreme Court in 1951) had tied up the Party's top brass,* a new vigilance against infiltration of the CP came into effect. The loyalty of every member was double-checked and many were expelled upon the slightest suspicion. New members were subject to incredible

* Four of the convicted leaders became fugitives from 'justice' at this time, but were caught years later and jailed.

scrutiny. All membership lists and Party cards were ordered destroyed. The Communist 'clubs' broke down into groups of from three to five members for reasons of security. Second-string Party leaders who were not well known to the public changed their names and left their homes to go underground, soon becoming known as 'unavailables'. The entire operation, down to details, resembled the days following the Palmer raids in 1920.

In its new defensive militancy the Party naturally purged heretics and malcontents as well as suspected FBI agents wherever it could. But it also began a systematic reduction of the rank and file down to an efficient minimum. Many loyal members were dropped simply because they could not dedicate enough time and energy, or because they cramped the streamlining of the new operation. Those members allowed to remain were ordered to enrol in the Party's own courses in Marxist theory; almost as an afterthought to years of recruiting anyone and everyone who showed the slightest interest in the cause, the Party suddenly discovered it was full of people who knew next to nothing about communism. Now, in order to separate the wheat from the chaff, the organization renounced, in effect, its freewheeling 'American nature', purged some of its sentimental, non-theoretical fringe and tried at last to become a revolutionary striking-force.

The Party could make no headway, however, without first obliterating, once and for all, the American preoccupation with personality. A theoretical battle was now mounted against bourgeois psychology and, in particular, Freudianism. Freudian thinking was, of course, contradictory to most fundamental tenets of Marxism. Communists were supposed to believe that psychology reflects the specific social conditions of any given society. The development of a child depends almost entirely on the nature of the social milieu; a child born into a bourgeois background expresses, for the most part, the values of his class. Freud himself discovered a fairly common set of understandings which he believed to be true for all classes and societies without essential distinction. Classical Marxists saw in his work an attempt to divert the blame for repression and social distress from the society to the family. Freudian psychology could also explain away fascist power by concentrating on its sado-masochistic tendencies, thereby diminishing the historical-economic factors which gave rise to it.

Given this bias, it was easy for the Party to interpret psycho-analysis as a Wall Street plot against the working class. Many analysts treated any attempt to change the social setup as a form of neurosis; a radical was often considered maladjusted because he could not accept and integrate with society as it was. The task of the analyst, in such cases, was to 'cure' the rebel and send him back into the world bereft of his unhealthy desire to stir up trouble. All this, the CP felt, was propagandized in popular culture – in films, in plays, in the press – creating, at the same time, the 'illusion' that life's critical decisions depended on individual choice.

Such a Marxist critique was nothing new, but it had been thoroughly buried under two decades of the Party's flirtation with Americana. The CP itself had been deflected from a hard theoretical line and now it was striking a blow for a sense of materialist or collective thinking. What few writers remained in the Communist camp were attacked for indulging in 'Freudian mystifications', i.e. their heroes made personal choices without necessary reference to class. Psychoanalysis was discouraged for members because it provided false hopes for a better personal life. (Behind this was the very real fear, in days of Inquisition, that Party members would reveal political secrets to their analysts.) In the Soviet Union, it was pointed out, mental anguish had been all but eliminated with the inception of a Communist society. For analysis-obsessed America, then, the alternative was to work full speed ahead for the Party so that it could swiftly bring about a socialist United States. This position was cunningly stated in a leftist scientific journal, during the anti-Freudian onslaught: 'To put loyalty to one's cause above all lesser loyalties is the best preventive of psychosomatic disturbance. By providing adequate outlets for love and hate, faith lessens the danger of exclusive self-assertion . . .'

This came too late; self-assertion was the cornerstone of American leftist experience and could not be unlearned, even with the weight of a Party directive behind it. The effect was to reduce the ranks even beyond the desired losses.

2

The Party's new belligerence only helped to bring on the heavier artillery of reaction. The heightened secrecy of the organization gave weight to the charge that dirty businesses were transpiring behind the scenes. The clandestine image played a major role in the winning of Smith Act convictions; the decision to go underground afterwards was a final gauntlet thrown down. Necessary as it may have been, it only tended to make the inquisitors more inquisitive. What better excuse for rooting out Reds than their own 'admission' of guilt through secrecy and hiding? Had the Party chosen to fight openly, risking all – even its security – it might have weathered the storm. Instead, its 'complicity' in establishing its own negative image allowed the witch-hunters to demolish previous leftist achievements under the pretext of their having been got by 'conspiracy'.

People for whom the CP had been little more than a *kaffee klatch* now discovered they had been consorting with 'traitors'. Fellow-travellers who had given their names and their money, through the fronts, were suddenly contaminated. A liberal might manage to distinguish himself from the hard-core Communist but, more often than not, the inquisitors would not give him the benefit of their doubt. Even if a man were ultimately absolved of actual guilt, the investigative experience disarmed him – which of course was the intended effect. Anyone with half an ear to the ground knew that the Party was seriously damaged by 1950, and that its influence was negligible. The real purpose of the Red Scare was to ensure that no shade of leftist conceit would ever gain a foothold in the American *future*. The only way to do this was to frighten off the fence-sitters and those concerned citizens whose tendency had been to flirt with the romantic idea of political revolution.

With the Party's edifice cracked beyond repair, the hatchet men came along in force to finish off the job. Official laxity (so it was argued) had resulted in the Communist infiltration of the Government. China had fallen to the Reds and this could be laid at the door of the State Department, rife with vermin who had advocated friendly relations with Mao Tse-tung. China was a major turning point, providing the perfect excuse for cracking down on Reds, levering a new generation of Grand Inquisitors into prominence (backed by the wealthy and powerful China Lobby which played a major part in American foreign policy for two decades). But the drift was not merely to root out treason or to alert pinkos to the dangers of free association; it was equally to prevent the more attractive side of Communism's long arm from reaching into places like Omaha, Nebraska. After years of Red filth, the witch-hunters had in mind a long-range purification of the American landscape, a continuation of the original unspoken Grand Design to mould a truly complacent Silent Majority in America.

The key to success here was again to make Red-baiting a popular sport, appealing to sadistic and prurient public fantasies. In 1949 the HUAC attempted to play its hand in alerting the populace by issuing a series of pamphlets under the general title of *100 Things You Should Know About Communism in the USA*. They were designed for even dumbos to understand, taking the authoritarian form of the catechism:

What is Communism?
A system by which one small group seeks to rule the world.

Is it aimed at me?
Right between your eyes.

What is the difference in fact between a Communist and a Fascist?
None worth noticing.

Was Marx Crazy?
Perhaps. But Marx was not the first evil and crazy man to start a terrible world upheaval, nor was he the last. Hitler was like that, too, but look at what he did.

In selling the era to their audience, the witch-hunters had to perfect their dramatic skills. There were lessons to be learned from the fact that no one had taken much notice of the Committee until it started thrashing movie stars; suddenly there was a lustre about the boring operations of boring men. But the investigations demonstrated, too, that the Inquisition would need to cultivate its own heroes.

Top of the list of top bananas, at least until 1951, was Edgar Hoover, along with his trusty crew of G-Men. This is because the Bureau played heavily on a theme that was rapidly becoming top cultural fantasy – espionage. Without the master equation of Communist = spy, the entire anti-Red show might have quickly exhausted itself. Surely the interest could not be maintained through boring theoretical trials or even lengthy congressional investigations. Instead, it was revealed that American Communists had not been working for the downtrodden Negro or the sweating labourer or even the American CP, but for – whether many knew it or not – the Russian Secret Police! It followed that only the FBI could get at the Reds where they were – underground.*

The glamour of the FBI's tight, cool machismo appealed so to public appetite that it was quickly carried into profiteering and marketing overkill. In 1954 Attorney-General Brownell was forced to introduce legislation in the Senate against taking the name of the Bureau in vain. Advertisers were discovered to be using the initials to promote wholly unrelated products. '*Investigate* before you buy' ran a typical ad, followed by 'FBI' propaganda for Floyd Brothers Irons or Ford Business Insurance or Frozen Beans Incorporated. There was also a flood of films and TV shows which told the 'inside' story of the FBI. Brownell charged that such publicity mocked the serious purpose of the G-Men and provided blueprints for criminals: '. . . the Bureau enjoys a most enviable reputation for efficiency and for the qualities of "Fidelity, Bravery and Integrity" as emblazoned on its insignia . . . Too often . . exploitation is accomplished in a manner which must necessarily lead to humiliation and loss of public confidence in the Federal Bureau of Investigation.'

With the FBI stealing all the thunder, Congress fought hard to rise above the dull impact of mere legislation. In 1949 the

---

* When the HUAC was considering anti-Communist legislation, it was Hoover who warned it to make the Party register, but not to drive the Reds underground. Nonetheless, it was Hoover, more than anyone else, who led the Party to its decision. By 1950 the CP was crawling with provocateurs and informers and this not only fed paranoia of the outside world but created inter-factional suspicions as well.

Committee issued a new pamphlet called *Spotlight on Spies*; at least this had some life in it as it set out to expose devious Red procedures:

Can you name some of these?
Tiny photographic films, containing secret messages, are soaked in a solution to make them flexible as cloth. Then this soft film is tightly rolled up, put into a small cylinder, and inserted into a tube of tooth-paste.

Any other methods?
Sometimes the film is softened in the same way and cut up and sewed inside the lining of neckties . . . Messages have also been placed in hollow parts of toys and in the hollow handles of safety razors.

There was also some 'Hooveristic' arithmetic in this pamphlet, the disclosure that there were 74,000 members of the American CP and, for every one of them (so the FBI calculated), there were ten symps and front-groupers ready to do the Party's bidding. This meant that in time of national emergency there were 740,000 Soviet followers prepared to do spy work in the US.

It failed to grab. The Congress, as a rule, was too lumbered with procedure to turn that spotlight in on itself. The American people would never have looked to the legislature for its Commie kicks were it not for the arrival of a superstar amongst the zombies.

Joe.
If it had become legal and respectable practice to hunt sub-versives and frighten liberals, there was at least one man in it just for the scuffle. Where even the young Representative (later Senator) from California, Mr Nixon, might be accused – in a generous moment – of having some integrity, there was still another witch-hunter who enjoyed the simple thug delights of victim-bashing. If Nixon was precise, insidious, a plotter who could snigger implications that would last decades, McCarthy was an improviser, wrong on nearly every hunch. But if Nixon's crypto-fascist style proved to be the more lasting and expedient, it was Joe who did more to popularize his own era, to give it his stamp and his name. Joe's actual achievements were few. He never introduced any congressional bills, and almost never found

actual evidence of Red activity (although many lost their jobs simply because *he* had questioned them). He looked for Reds in government, Reds in the military, Reds in university positions; he managed to scare two US presidents. Still, his reputation is overblown, and the fact that his name and 'ism' could cause the severest attack in the leftist heart attests more to the cowardice of the movement than to his actual power. He could, of course bark louder and command more attention than any other inquisitor. But this showed him to be little more than the most successful example of creating self-propaganda through the medium of political activity. No, something in his *character* touched an exposed nerve in the Left, and there was a frightening familiarity about much of his style. Everything once held dear in leftist mythology, the common, speak-your-mind, tell-it-like-it-is, 'people's-man' image, the sexy actor hamming his way at the expense of repressed establishment figures, the hatred of the big shots – this was Joe, a fascist John Garfield punchin' his way through the 'phoneys'.

Above all, he hated a punk. He had come upon the Communist Party in its hour of withdrawal, of – in street-fighting terms – chicken-heartedness. He had no ideological reason for chasing Reds; he merely wanted to get himself known. But once he started he went at it with a bully's glee. Harvey Matusow, ex-Communist witness, then part of the Senator's entourage, claimed that Joe was enraged by the new secretiveness of the Communist Party. He is reported to have had great admiration for Earl Browder because the ex-CP boss stood up to him instead of cringing behind the Fifth Amendment. Joe told Matusow: 'If the Communists all had guts like Earl Browder I wouldn't be involved in the Communist issue. I'd be talking about farm parity.' Naturally, there is a large measure of Joe's hokum in this statement, but it is true that the victimized posture of the Left only incited him further.

The biggest faker of the era, he chased fakes and phoneys out of their hiding places. A mammoth liar, he insisted on the old American honesty factor. He knew, better than anyone, the technique for playing on the needs of the Silent Majority. So he described Dean Acheson, Secretary of State: '. . . this pompous diplomat in striped pants, with a phoney British accent proclaimed to the American people that Christ on the Mount endorsed communism, high treason, and betrayal of a sacred trust . . .' This delivered up many social masks at once, appealing to the popular distrust of 'class' and status, the hatred for dissembling, the traditional Anglophobia of the middle-American mentality and the Puritan scorn for effeminacy. With such an armoury of well-oiled weapons at the ready, Joe could erase anyone's credibility – no matter what the politics of the situation.

His sadism extended even to driving 'sex deviates' out of the State Department because of their supposed vulnerability to blackmail and because homosexuals tend to attract 'other perverts' into government positions. In this, Joe was employing Hooveristic tactics, summoning up traditional notions of leftists and liberals having 'free love' attitudes and a certain tolerance of homosexuals in the ranks.*

If Joe was not a born State-smasher he nonetheless recoiled at concepts of morality and order. His use of language was anarchic, causing words to be torn up by the roots from their dictionary meanings, all for the *effect* they might have when used. He played on the American love of 'facts', especially when he had none, convincing people he had foundation for his allegations. He was a backwoods medicine-man and juggler, master of double-talk and double-think. His style was bound to cause trouble and embarrassment for the Power. The chaos he wrought even did some good for the ailing CP. His attacks, said Herbert Philbrick, 'add greatly to the confusion, putting up a smokescreen for the party and making it more difficult than ever for people to discern just who is a Communist and who is not'. When the true holders of right-wing power sensed he had gone too far, so far he might

---

* The Senator's frankness and sexual aggressiveness carried over into his own life. Harvey Matusow: During the '52 campaign, I'd go up and knock on the door and he'd be in bed with another girl every day. He might have played with boys, as some people say, but I only know he played with girls . . . He was like a pop star. He had his groupies . . . right-wing Republican groupies.'

even blow their cover, so far that he might even try to win the presidential nomination in 1956, they cut off his life-lines to publicity, censured and broke him in the Senate. Leading Republican figures, including the then Vice-President, Richard Nixon, rebuked him publicly when he tried to uncover evidence of Red conspiracy in the US Army. By 1954 he was powerless and, at last, without credibility.

Yet, even then, he continued to strike traumatic gongs in the radical subconscious. At the height of his early fifties fame, much of the Left had already run for the cover of bourgeois respectability. The leftist hero had donned at last his grey-flannel suit. In this manner he could confront his inquisitors and plead his innocence or beg forgiveness. Joe was a reminder of the unwashed proletarian past. The scatology, the dirty jokes, his unpressed clothes, his biting sense of humour, his disruptiveness and moral corruption – innocent of purpose or logic – constituted an attack, first and foremost, on middle-class manners. It was an affront that would be re-enacted by the sons of ex-Communists in the mid-sixties. Joe would have been right at home amongst the drug-stricken freaks who likewise waged war on phoneys; and they would have had great fun with him, this the first 'Yippie'. Had he appeared twelve years later, however, he could not have frightened anyone and would have had no power. He would have seemed just another funky ego-tripper doing a pointless number.

3

Nothing was quite so demoralizing for the already demoralized movement as the spectacle of one-time leftists ratting on old friends and colleagues. The Party never did take lightly to defection, and if the organization had one cardinal sin this was it. A turncoat was never talked back into the fold nor was his decision to leave debated with him; it was as if, in the very *idea* of breaking off one's commitment to membership, the act had been achieved. This hard, unbending attitude made for even more hostility between renegades and the CP, and tended to drive many of the simply 'disillusioned' into the waiting arms of the reactionaries.

Ironically, the overwhelming loss of Party membership in the Red Scare was, in many ways, a good riddance. It is of course true that many were genuinely disaffected when made aware of the CP's 'real' nature. But few had ever been prepared to take the consequences of their rebellious acts anyway. Others welcomed now an excuse for getting out; they could discard their shoddy political commitment and have the *Party* to blame for it. People could cry now that they had been 'duped', and no CP crime – not the Moscow Trials, not the Hitler–Stalin Pact, not the murder of Trotsky, none of which had driven these latter-day 'dupes' from the fold – could ever compare with the fact that the Party had been *dishonest*! And so great was this rage at being 'had' that a violent anti-Communism began to flourish among renegades and tearful liberals. As if to justify the failure of their personal experience, these leftists simply reversed course and struck out at the CP with a red, white and blue vengeance.

No doubt it was a strong sense of personal betrayal that led many to quit. Utopian hopes had been dashed because the Party was forced to toe the Moscow line. For some of the hurt ones, there was nothing to do but sink back into the American morass and forget. Others, with a keener eye to the political carnival, saw a career rising out of their despair, and came blustering forward now as lords and ladies of the Ex-Communist Racket. Informing seemed a ready-made syndrome for continuing the original drive towards self-publicity that brought some into the movement. If the Party could not yield up sufficient public exposure and a sense of personal achievement, there was more than enough to go around in the new open city of Commie-catching.

The actors, writers and directors who had come before the Committee were usually fighting to maintain or regain their jobs threatened by the blacklist. Often they were forced to inform to avoid sheer poverty. The new 'professional' ex-Reds were not usually worried about jobs; in many cases, squealing was a full-time (and lucrative) mode of employment. There had always been and would always be informers; but the new breed projected and paraded, allowed themselves to be publicized and over-exposed.

It wasn't just a question of one Committee hearing, blow the gaff and go home. They wrote autobiographies, gave lecture tours and were known all over America as celebrities. They were often on call to committees and grand juries, considered experts on the subject of spying and Communist infiltration. Their very names were meant to register in the collective ear as having the cut of authenticity. The Party had been shown to be closed and cryptic, working through hocus-pocus and secret codes; only these 'insiders' could claim to have the real dope.

Perhaps the king among witnesses was Whittaker Chambers, the man who put Richard Nixon on the map. In 1948 Chambers came before the Committee and acccused Alger Hiss, a leading light in the State Department, of having been a Communist agent and of passing confidential government documents to the Communist underground. After a long battle of wills between Chambers and Hiss, and the unflagging determination of Congressman Nixon to bust him, Hiss was convicted of having perjured himself before a grand jury; in 1953 he was jailed for five years.*

There is no doubt about why Nixon broke his back to get Hiss; his efforts made him Vice-President four years later. Chambers's contribution was more subtle. Whatever the truth of the Hiss case – and certainly *somebody* was lying – Chambers's entire life afterwards was devoted to a lengthy justification of his actions. Almost all the famous ex-Communist witnesses wrote their autobiographies during or just after the investigative circus. But Chambers's *Witness* is 800 pages long! Chambers saw his life as somehow symbolic of the spiritual crisis of modern man, of how he seeks a new faith in himself, in science, in materialism, in Communism and rejects God. But his sentiment and humanitarianism go even beyond the immediate plight. Chambers introduces his book as an explanation to his children, presumably to help them avoid the pitfalls of an amoral life. He tells them about the Ninth Symphony: 'I told you that that music was the moment at which Beethoven finally passed beyond the suffering of his life on earth and reached for the hand of God, as God reaches for the hand of Adam in Michelangelo's vision of the Creation . . .'

*To this day Hiss maintains his innocence, seeking a presidential pardon from Richard Nixon.

But the Suffering of Life on Earth is a cinemascope smoke-screen; it sugar-coats, with all the razzmatazz of Hollywood melodrama, a trial proceeding which had a public reputation for viciousness and smear. The operatic tremble of Chambers's voice is meant to put him among Beethoven, Michelangelo and Adam as one of the great sufferers. But the infinite care he takes with his autobiography and the literary pretensions of the thing leave the impression that he has brought his humanism with him into the famous Hiss case and that it existed even prior to the alleged espionage and his joining the Party in the early thirties. This gives his tale the quality of a divine Fall into Communism, almost as a test of his ultimate faith. His final return to God and Nixon is told with such exquisite memory and sparkling lingo that it shows up – in spite of itself – the desperate horror of a *natural* informer behind it all. His prose waxes purple when he writes about Reds; it swells to great myth and subsides to sanctimoniousness. It is a mammoth whitewash of the self, the pilgrim's progress of a stool-pigeon. The guilt is everywhere, showing the terrible rupture suffered by naïve leftists. Chambers loses his political virginity to the Red Menace – yet another! – and seeks absolution from some mystical conception of moral history. It takes the form of confession to his offspring: 'My children, as long as you live, the Shadow of the Hiss Case will brush you. In every pair of eyes that rests on you, you will see pass, like a cloud passing behind a woods in winter, the memory of your father – dissembled in friendly eyes, lurking in unfriendly eyes . . . you will ask yourselves the question: What was my father?'

This is wishful thinking for it grants him a place in history he has not really got; were it not for the fortunes of friend Nixon, no one would remember Chambers's name.* But his desire for historic fame shows us his reference point: the idea that a man can play witness to his times and hope for the testimony of his life to penetrate public consciousness. This was perhaps Chambers's reason for joining the Communist movement – but he found only

---

* Chambers and Nixon became very close after the Hiss case and had undying respect for one another. To Chambers's children, the Congressman became '"Nixie", the kind and the good, about whom they will tolerate no nonsense'.

de-personalization there, an underground existence. Now he had hit the headlines, but these could not deliver his truest self to the public. He wanted to be remembered as an example of right reason and good will, coming out of an era of moral corruption. His informing was an act of kindness which he left as a bequest to the nation.

It was Louis Budenz, ex-*Daily Worker* editor, who first brought informing into the field of private enterprise. After he left the Party in 1945, he made thirty-three separate appearances before committees, courts and grand juries; figured in investigations of Owen Lattimore (a China expert), Gerhart Eisler (alleged Comintern representative in the US) and Alger Hiss; gave lecture tours, taught courses, wrote articles and four books on Communism (including an autobiography). By 1953 he claimed to have made some $70,000 out of his efforts.

Yet his motives were not so base as the simple getting of filthy lucre. Budenz's particular gimmick was a powerful Catholic evangelism with which he added spiritual spice to his life story made public. As a young man he believes the salvation of America, and of the individual, lies in a national turn towards the Catholic tradition. On his autobiographical highway, however, he stumbles upon the working-class cause and gets socialistically sidetracked from his original faith. In 1935 he is seduced by the Popular Front, and enters now into worship of the Party, the Stalin and the Holy Comintern. Yet, this is the famous 'God that failed' many others, and equally it fails Budenz as he sees it revealed for the Moscow plot it really is. In 1941 he stumbles into St Patrick's Cathedral, a moment of holy illumination for his slow road back to the true path, and prays for a 'Catholic–Communist reconciliation'. But this cannot be, and he slowly inches his way towards the moment he will make his getaway. So intense is his struggle that he now keeps a rosary in his pocket and fingers it while writing *Daily Worker* editorials. In October 1945 he finally flees with his family to the sanctuary of Notre Dame University where, *two days later*, he becomes a professor. So swift is his conversion that the Reds only hear of it from his public announcement; his name has even remained in the staff box of the *Worker*.

Budenz made a vow to refrain from public life for one full year so that he could seek meditation and divine guidance. After that year he came back like an avenging angel, telling his story of Russia's design for the 'maiming of the American nation and the atomization of the American people'. He appeared now on radio and in the press, playing up always the angle of his own change of heart. He claimed to be acting out of 'Catholic charity' for those poor dupes still held psychological captive by the Reds. For them he would pray 'to the Mother of that God who cried out two thousand years ago- "Saul, Saul why persecutest thou Me?" – in the hope that they shall be granted the courage to break their chains and be restored to personal integrity'.

Budenz was another renegade reacting to a sense of hurt. Yet he could not let it simply fade, choosing instead to play the mission-ary, so that others might 'profit' by his lesson. In his ponderous autobiography, he claims to have been guided from childhood by awe and reverence for the 'Christ crowned with thorns'. The Party could not match it, even with its powerful guilt-making notion of 'sin' against the organization. There was no balm there to soothe his social ache, and certainly no Communist blessedness at the end of his pains. Communist Heaven seemed so far off, and could not offer to any soul a sense of himself. The beatification of Budenz would have to begin, rather, at the gates of the FBI.

Another well-paid witness was Elizabeth Bentley, the 'Red spy queen'. She referred to ex-Communism as a 'livelihood', giving lecture tours and writing articles about her life and loves as a Kremlin stooge. There is also no telling what income she received for her info delivered to the FBI.

Bentley's special number was love. She managed to give es-pionage a niche in the world of True Romance fables; although 'true' is hardly the right word for it. She was another ex-Red who claimed she could remember the most minute details fifteen years after the fact. She is reported, in an off-moment, to have called her memoirs 'fiction', although she later denied saying it. It hardly mattered either way. True or false, her story gave the spy game the slightly delicious ring of illicit sex and third-rate tragedy. (Even the title of her autobiography, *Out of Bondage*, breathes momentary promise of Moscow rubber fetishisms and Commie profligacies – none of which are revealed, however.) She expresses shock at what seems to be a full-scale operation of scarlet ladies turning tricks in the line of Party duty, or being expected to spread their legs for all and sundry comrades. She was a tame forerunner of the cheap paperback tradition in which broad-shanked G-Men slap around thick-breasted comradesses for info – 'Who stole the A-bomb formula, Natasha?'*

Bentley joins the Party out of emotional concern for mankind, though she soon learns the need for Stalinist self-criticism and discipline to bring about detachment and mastery of emotion. This theme is whipped to death by nearly all the ex-Communists to show the dreadful inhumanity of the Party, but here it serves to justify Bentley's defection.

The pivot is a man. Elizabeth agrees to do undercover work for the Party (checking out waste-paper baskets for secrets) and her contact turns out to be a Russian, Jacob Golos, who turns out (later in the story) to be a Russian Secret Police agent, who turns out to be plotting the assassination of Trotsky. But all these world-shaking events become incidental; soon, after a night of tough Party work: 'His hand touched mine, I looked at him, and then quite suddenly I found myself in his arms, his lips on mine . . . Time and space seemed to stand still . . .' On Spies' First Date they fall heavily, and the tragedy unfolds immediately. They agree to bed down, but must live apart so as not to blow their cover. As if to telegraph the necessary end of such a love, Golos feels a 'pain' after their famous first kiss. Ultimately this pain will kill him, but for now it is only his middle-class indigestion talking:

---

*There is a very real side to the sexual concerns of spy-catchers, as shown by recent disclosures of J. Edgar Hoover bugging leftist bedrooms (including Martin Luther King's) and feeding political scandal porn to LBJ for bed-time amusement reading. The ex-Communist, Harvey Matusow, claims the FBI sent women to seduce him on at least two occasions and, when he appeared before a grand jury in 1955, every woman he'd slept with for years was paraded before him and made to discuss his extra-curricular activities for the benefit of the court.

'It would be so very simple if only we were two ordinary Communists, moving in Party circles. Then we could live together as good comrades do. Perhaps, if you wished, we could even be married legally at City Hall in order to conform to bourgeois conventions . . . We are forbidden to form close friendships and, especially, to fall in love. You and I have no right, under Communist discipline, to feel the way we do about each other.'

Bentley's transformation comes – naturally – after the death of Golos in 1943. She has seen atrocity upon atrocity, discipline without end and she wants out. She blames it all on the Russians, pointing out that the Yanks never related to heavy Communism anyway. Even Earl Browder was a patsy and had been assigned a Russian wife – a former Secret Policewoman – to keep an eye on him.

Like Chambers and Budenz, Bentley has been in the muck and mire and is ready for cleansing. Where else will she find her course of action but in Budenz's miracle, taking refuge in the Catholic Church.* In her epiphany scene, she fumbles into a church: 'I caught my breath and held on to the back of the pew ahead of me; somehow a strange sense of peace came over me. And then, in the empty church, the voice of my conscience seemed to ring out loudly: You have no right here – yet. You know now that the way of life you have followed these last ten years was wrong; you have come back to where you belong. But first you must make amends! . . . go to the FBI . . .'

By late 1952 Bentley had spent all the money from her autobiography and her star-quality was fading. Harvey Matusow, comrade witness, remembered her as a lonely, sad ex-spyess after her testimony was exhausted and she had nothing more to give. In the great tradition of such soap-opera starlets, she was ripe for the junkheap. Yet in her short heyday, she gained public credibility. Although none of the people she accused directly were convicted, she supplied information – some of it undoubtedly useful – and

*There were other ex-Communists drawn into redemption by the late Red-baiter Cardinal Spellman and by the brothers Kennedy. These latter had been perpetual spectators at the Communist trials and were aids to Joe McCarthy (also a Catholic), always on the alert to see which way the wind was blowing.

played a part in the Rosenberg trial, claiming to know Julius as a spy (although she never met him) since 1942. It is doubtful, however, that the FBI fell for half of her tales – would the Russians employ a dame like her for important espionage work? – but America lapped up every bit.

The Bentley and Chambers objections to Communism arose out of a terrible moral fear which burned in them every time the Party shifted ground or became secretive. There is a feeling of tremendous breakage in these cases, a prelude to the general nervous collapse of the Left. The Party was being lashed and hounded from all sides, its fringe whittled away. If, in the past, its loss of membership demonstrated a dialogue in its survival, now it was learning how to die.

Harvey Matusow's case perfectly symbolizes this final crack-up of the Party. More than any other ex-Communist witness he spoke to the perverse 'fun' of the era and summed up its delicious insanity with his own perpetually shifting centre, and a conscience/consciousness so expanded truth couldn't contain it: 'The only way to keep to myself the things I treasure most – because I don't trust people, I've been hurt so many times – is to be in a three-ring circus all the time. Because when you're in a three-ring circus, nobody will ask you what you're doing.' Matusow turned rat for the FBI, worked for Joe McCarthy, played the professional ex-Red for money and for thrills until he denied his own accusations, wrote an autobiography exposing his own fraud and perjured himself. Later he would argue that he had been a self-appointed double-agent all along, working on behalf of progressivism to show up and destroy the informer system from within.*

Matusow came to Communism out of a lonely sub-nothing post-war Bronx tradition. He found a home in the Party, and related especially to its great events like the Wallace Campaign and Peekskill. But it was the Party's decision to go underground after the Smith Act indictments that first gave him pause. His extrovert temperament could not brook this instruction, and he refused to

---

* Matusow claims he could not reveal his double-agent role in 1955 because his recantation would not have been accepted and the trial decisions, in which his old testimony was instrumental, would not have been reversed.

comply. (He was not kicked out of the CP, however, until 1951, after it was discovered he had been working for the FBI for over a year.) The CP had ceased being a joy to him now that it had entered its faceless phase. He did not become truly anti-Communist, but he needed a taste of action. For him, the FBI had all the glamour. But he probably would have agented for the Left if it could have accepted his mad terms of reference: 'I just couldn't understand why the Communist Party accepted the tyranny of the Government's investigation and its use of paid informers without striking back . . . The Party was so moral, it refused to accept the morality of espionage.'

In his autobiography, *False Witness*, Matusow claims to have been motivated, in great part, by the showbiz side of informing (he was also a part-time actor): 'The dramatics of my testimony were all directed at the committee members. They were the backers of my show. And I knew that if I pleased them in my first reading, I'd open with my name in lights.' He describes his ego-trip in great detail, the gratification and public recognition quest for which he would (and did) go to any lengths of informing and witnessing. There is also indication that Matusow infiltrated group after group, committee upon committee, in order to receive the *affection* of his superiors. But all these motives wrap in too coherent a bundle. The fact is that witnessing had become his *addiction* – to plumb his reasons would be to render such a narcotic reasonable. He appeared in the moral armour of a crusader, but his crusade made no sense. It was not, as it was with Chambers and Budenz, a logical, religious extension to his life. It was more of 'a Walter Mitty insane fantasy', as he later admitted.

He was ripe for a link-up with Joe. Matusow joined McCarthy's staff and campaigned and smeared for him in the 1952 elections.* Matusow, too, understood how easy and delightful it was to terrorize the Left. He went after old comrades, not merely by informing, but by chasing and persecuting, lying and smearing. Aside from numerous lectures and articles on Communism, he

* Matusow was – and still is – a great admirer of the famous Senator – the 'most charming guy in the world . . . One of the most beautiful characters of the twentieth century' – although he disowns most of his actions and despises what he stood for.

worked for the blacklisting magazines, *Red Channels* and *Counterattack*. These were dedicated to keeping the media clean of Red influence, and Matusow assumed the role of headhunter. He would hound film companies and television stations, pretending to be an irate American (dozens of times, using his different acting voices), demanding they not put so-and-so on their show or in their movie because he was a Commie or a pinko. He was part of the team working on obtaining John Garfield's 'confession' in 1952, after *Counterattack* challenged the actor to come clean.

There is no gut to the Harvey Matusow saga. He shifted focus often, went through multiple stages of turning and turning again. He had got his notoriety, had become the 'somebody' he said he longed to be. It was not enough. Even after he made up his mind to expose the Ex-Communist Racket he continued to be a government witness. He always felt the guilt of his actions, yet performed them with confidence and expertise. During the height of his witness days he suffered acute constipation from nerves yet he could jauntily do his night-club act as a stand-up comedian – under one of many aliases – all on the same day.

Inevitably, he got involved with his own fakery. It is unlikely he had come to believe in the informing game, but the schizophrenia now began to torture him: 'I had to get into total character for protection.' He had run to danger point: 'If J. Edgar Hoover had been aware of what I was doing before I had a chance to make public my confession, I would have conveniently died.'

The prospect of literal insanity, the fear of the two Harveys disuniting beyond repair, moved him to choice. In 1953 he went to the *New York Times* with an affidavit claiming he had been a false witness. This might then and there have blown apart the informer system and even jeopardized the Army-McCarthy hearings which were about to begin. But the *Times* was afraid of the times, and sat on the story. He had to wait until 1955 for the case to break. His recantation paved the way for the demise of the witnessing racket (although it was nearly finished by that time and had lost its glitter). Matusow himself was jailed for perjury and served over four years.

When Matusow broke the news to the press that he had lied

not only before grand juries and defamed innocent people, but
had been false as well to Senator McCarthy, Joe (by this time a
washout himself) called him into his office:

'You must be very lonely now, Harvey.'
'Yeah, Joe. I'm lonely.'
'I understand.'
'I thought you would.'

'Comes now Harvey Matusow peddling his memories. Who
can buy them all?' said columnist Murray Kempton at the time of
the false-witness exposé.* Matusow's name alone had become
synonymous with the credibility dilemma of the era. But, because
he lived on the inside of every twist and turn of the times, he came
out a casualty on the other side. In one explosive character he
showed the nature of the Party's fall, the power of the inquisitors,
the hysterical pitch of the leftist personality under fire.

4

The atom was the icing on the spy cake. Nothing more earth-
shaking than this nuclear tool could ever be laid at the doorstep
of the Left. The judge sentencing Julius and Ethel Rosenberg in
1951 claimed that the bomb secrets they allegedly gave the Russians had caused '. . . the Communist aggression in Korea, with
the resultant casualties exceeding 50,000 and who knows but that
millions more of innocent people may pay the price of your
treason. Indeed, by your betrayal you undoubtedly have altered
the course of history to the disadvantage of our country.' In this,

---

*One person who would not now buy all his memories is Harvey Matu-
sow. He doesn't expect or want credibility – such a virtue has no place in his
private Bedlam. He sees himself as the Daniel Ellsberg of the fifties and his
own revelations as important, in some ways, as the Pentagon Papers. (The
parallel even extends to his pilfering documents from various committees
and rifling the files of *Counterattack*.) But he doesn't imagine many others
will see it this way, and accepts his reputation with a nostalgic bitterness. He
is still haunted by the fifties at every stage of his life and feels, melodramatic-
ally (though sincerely), that 'only in death will I find peace'.

the leftist couple were granted far more significance than they deserved – even assuming they had done the deed – and this was the Government's lever for executing them. They had been chosen to pay for the fall of humanism and the rise of atomism, for China, for Eastern Europe, even for the Popular Front. Their plight bore implication for countless others on the Left. Those who had looked for justice in American institutions felt betrayed; some who sought further justification to leave the Party found it here. The Government itself used their image to cause a rupture with the lingering Russian ideal and to justify the building of the H-Bomb and massive increases in military spending.

Neither the guilt nor innocence of the Rosenbergs has been proved beyond all doubt, despite massive legal tomes, numerous books pro and con, plays, novels, letters, stories, songs and a film on their case. They were convicted of 'conspiracy' – not with any particular act of espionage, only with *intent* to spy. The case hinged on the testimony of David Greenglass, Ethel's brother, who had supposedly given them a sketch and information while working on the A-Bomb project at Los Alamos. Greenglass testified that he had been brought into the spy ring by Julius; through his informing he received a much lighter sentence than the Rosenbergs. But the defendants' private lives were also dragged in as evidence. The claim was that the Rosenbergs had gone 'underground' in the early forties, had cut off most of their contacts, given up their subscription to the *Daily Worker*. Whether or not this was true, it brought in the essential spy element of hush-hush, and the defence did little to dispel the mystique. The couple refused to answer questions about their CP association – and rightly so, as this would have prejudiced the jury against them. On the other hand, silence was now as good as evidence and the Fifth Amendment, in 1951, was considered by the Silent Majority as something only Reds took. The jury was already against them, and the web of silent piety the Rosenbergs spun about themselves could only spell disaster.

Even if the Rosenbergs were guilty in some degree, the massive frame-up, railroading and sentencing they suffered was out of all proportion to their alleged spy operation. The idea that the Soviets would entrust a big-time network to such obvious small-fry as these taxes credibility. The A-Bomb sketches made by Greenglass and produced as damaging evidence were primitive and could not give any indication of the bomb's mechanism. Julius's use of two halves of a jello box to link agent to agent was a gesture of a thorough amateur. Also, the use of such highly emotional and often neurotic people as the Rosenbergs, Greenglass and his wife and the middleman, Harry Gold, to do the most important bit of espionage in the twentieth century is wholly incompatible with Russian methodology. Finally, master spies are rarely caught.

Still, the Government played the case to the full, pulling every melodramatic stop for effect. The kidnapping of the Rosenbergs' co-defendant, Morton Sobell, by Mexican agents who drove him across the border to the waiting arms of G-Men, was silly B-movie strategy. Revelations were staggered and arrest made upon arrest from smallest to largest spy, until it seemed like the Government would produce Mr Big himself. It was beautifully orchestrated, not merely by J. Edgar Hoover, but also by Roy Cohn, who was one of the prosecutors, had been chief legal adviser to McCarthy, was a pal of Nixon's and a brain behind the Smith Act trials. If the Rosenbergs were innocent, it was a master stroke to pick them out of a hat and manage to convict them. If they had done the deed – or even a lesser version of it – government propaganda turned them into remarkable demons. The Death Penalty was the final touch. It would achieve little strategically, would scare off no spies, but it would provide thrills for the general public and strengthen reaction's hand in fulfilling its Grand Design.

While it lasted, the shot of adrenalin the case gave to the movement brought it up out of retreat. In the two years between sentencing and execution in 1953, there was a huge eruption of sympathy for the couple. The Party now joined in the fight, although the *Worker* had kept strangely silent about the Rosenbergs until *after* the trial. The organization was suddenly reinvigorated, working overtime to promote its own Julius and Ethel Show. The leftist theatre used the Living Newspaper technique to inform people about the case; but Rosenberg Drama, given the nature of the affair, was destined to be one of sympathy.

At one fund-raising play the stage was set as a prison wall containing two barred windows. Behind the wall taped voices were heard – supposedly those of the Rosenbergs themselves – reading their letters to one another. As an HUAC informer described it: 'These letters, alleged to be reproductions of those written by the principals to each other while in prison, seemed to be designed to exploit Mother's Day, the date of the meeting.' Even after the executions, reported Herb Philbrick, the CP ordered a step-up in activities, including 'hard-back books, long-playing recordings, dramatization and songs'.

The entire campaign was painstakingly documented in an HUAC report on The National Committee to Secure Justice for the Rosenbergs and Morton Sobell: 'Gathered in . . . were the misfits who like to believe that they are handicapped by our political and economic system, and those prone to blame their failures on religious and minority prejudice instead of their own inadequacies.' The Government was now adding insult to injury, but there was a measure of accidental truth in such slander. The campaign was a maudlin business, inspired by emotional frustration rather than clear legal or political strategy. Its tendency was to obscure the actual questions raised at the trial by throwing in its own red herrings, primarily the charge of anti-Semitism. This was time-worn paranoia, the idea that persecution of a Communist who also happened to be a Jew necessarily indicated a pogrom. Even if it turned out to be the case – in a trial where the judge, prosecutor and a subsidiary member of the prosecuting team were Jews – it was no basis on which to fight. Also, the accent on drumming up international sympathy could only further alienate a government whose view of foreign opinion was guided by the arch-reactionary John Foster Dulles. All this energy might have been put to better use in collecting funds to gather a competent legal team and build a sound case for appeal.

One of the essential contributions of the campaign was the publication of the *Death House Letters* of the Rosenbergs. It has been suggested, by unfriendly critics, that the couple had no hand in authoring these. This suspicion comes from what the Committee called 'their pretentious, oracular style . . . intended . . . to stimulate . . . sympathizers'. While this is an accurate description of the style of the letters, the basic charge is wholly unfounded in the light of all the deeply personal material that appears in them. More likely, the Rosenbergs knew in advance a book would be published – in order to gain converts to their cause and to establish a trust fund for their children – and subsequently censored themselves and embellished at the same time. It is also true, however, that some of the letters were doctored by the Party for propaganda purposes years later, even after their death. One such letter, written by Julius in May 1951, expresses shock at the execution of a Negro, Willie McGee, on a rape charge, and expands briefly on the Southern practice of legal lynching. When it appeared on a CP campaign flyer two years later, it had gained the following passages not in the original: 'Mark my words, dearest, the harsh sentence passed on us is part of the atomic hysteria designed to brutalize the minds of the people . . . It serves the added nefarious purpose of establishing a fear paralysis among progressive Americans . . . The most important thing is that the camouflage has to be ripped away, the loud braying of jackals of hate has to be answered with reason and fact . . .'

Where the Rosenbergs are most apparent in the book is in the heavy emphasis on the children. They have been accused, unjustly, of having abandoned their kids for their principles; the letters give it the lie. They are full of deep concern for the children's education and upbringing, and clearly this was the major source of their distress in making their final decision not to talk. Still, the idea that 'red-diaper babies' had been cast adrift while the folks went off spying became a publicity weapon of right-wing critics. One of these, S. Andhill Fineberg, was led to write: 'If permitted to control the lives of the Rosenbergs' children, the Communists will have the two young orphans as their hostages. They could rear them as propagandists whose identity would stir deep emotions in susceptible audiences . . . Will the sins of the parents be repeated by the children?' This tends to show how much the future was a chief concern of the reactionaries. But it is true that the Rosenberg boys were occasionally exploited in order to build up emotional pressure on the Government. They were displayed at demonstrations and even made to deliver a tear-jerking letter to the White House. A campaign leaflet called for a 'happier holiday for the Rosenberg children'.

The entire matter of leftist families in Red Scare crisis was raised by the affair. David Greenglass had squealed on his sister and won a jail sentence instead of execution. Curiously, the letters hardly refer to Greenglass, as if his act implied such primal corrosion it had to be erased from consciousness. The Greenglass family, too, laid the blame with the Rosenbergs, claiming they had led the impressionable David astray. The most desperate moment of all came when Ethel's mother visited her in prison and urged her to talk:

Ethel: 'What, and take the blame for a crime I never committed, and allow my name, and my husband's, and children's to be slandered . . .?'

Mother: 'Even if it was a lie, you should have said it was true anyway! If you had agreed that what Davy said was so, even if it wasn't, you wouldn't have got this!'

The Rosenbergs appealed their conviction at the judicial level as well as petitioning Truman and, later, Eisenhower. They maintained their innocence fiercely. But the FBI wanted their co-operation. They needed the name of Mr Big, or at least the next rung up the spy ladder. But it was no go; the Rosenbergs might have saved their lives. Ethel's response to the offer of life for info was typical of the case: 'Our respect for truth, conscience, and human dignity is not for sale. Justice is not some bauble to be sold to the highest bidder.' At the eleventh hour there was even an attempt to play off one against the other. The rumour was that Ethel would be spared, and not Julius, the strategy being that his imminent death would force her to talk in order to save him. However: 'I shall not dishonor my marital vows and the felicity and integrity of the relationship we shared to play the role of harlot to political procurers.'

And that was that. It might be argued that if the Rosenbergs were convicted by a lie, they could have retaliated with a lie to save their skins. But that would have erased both dignity and credibility in one gesture. Instead they chose to assert American principle and humanitarian arrogance, calling upon a personal morality which seems ludicrous in the face of their era. The movement had always postured so, but now it was a matter of life and death. Still, the Rosenbergs' powerful stubbornness was evident throughout the entire affair. Their lack of legal manoeuvring, their appeal on little more than moral grounds, the constant invocation of the Fifth Amendment, the acceptance of their victimization – all this convicted them in a political climate that had come to adore the sheer sadism of bashing punks and scourging sufferers.

Worst of all, it gave the Left a dose of martyrdom like it never had before. Because the movement had suffered a massive loss of influence and had seen its edges worn away by crippling defections and noxious informers, it had little recourse but to retaliate with a sense of wounded honour and ingratiating virtue. Now, with the example of the Rosenbergs, this was carried to extremes. The couple was lifted into the Pantheon of Left Saints, where they stand perhaps at the core of American leftist collective memory. But the political heritage of the case was a disaster. The execution drove many people into fearful shelter for a decade, and those who remained could not profit from the experience. The Government had clouded the real issues by playing up the spying, but the movement further obscured them with sentiment. Because the Left had linked its emotional fate so closely with that of the Rosenbergs, it had no choice but to rise to the pitch of their sanctimoniousness and die equally without achievement.

'We are the first victims of American fascism.' These were the last words of Ethel Rosenberg as she walked down the corridor. They were, at any rate, the first husband and wife team to play the Chair, and the first American political prisoners (technically speaking) so erased.

The Chair was first used legally in 1888 and is deemed the most humane of all American modes of public execution. Unlike the primitive barbaric European devices, it is above all a testament to clean technology. No messy chopped heads and hanging tendons here. Indeed, if it weren't for the fact that the criminal pisses himself when the charge hits him – in addition to the skull frying like rancid bacon – it would be as clean and purifying as an American shower. It is electro-shock therapy writ large, designed to induce tranquillity in anti-social patients. From the time Sacco and Vanzetti fell to the switch in 1927, it was thought of as shock treatment-by-example for the radical movement. It was brilliantly conceived as Angel of Death to the American State, bearing in its wooden clutch more mythological potential than any other public weapon of individual annihilation.

Whatever had been rekindled of the movement's morale by 1953 was now extinguished in the Rosenberg roasting. Only Ethel's unflagging composure in the face of it served shining example to those who like their saints consistent. Julius had gone down before her in two minutes forty-five seconds, and there is some ghoulish speculation – he being the morally weaker – that he might have talked had he been last, but couldn't bear the thought of shaming his wife while she was alive. The charge of 2,000 volts of 60 cycle ac, at a range of from 4 to 8 amperes, rocked him three times in fairly rapid succession and his muscles convulsed in violent spasms. With the immediate autopsy he was pronounced dead, removed, and his piss mopped up so his wife wouldn't be sloshing in it.

Ethel's head had been shaved in preparation and, upon entering her last room, she performed a series of acts of grace, like kissing her matron and generally reducing the proceedings to hushed guilt. She was seated in the wooden Chair (which is meant to be a bad conductor of electrical current). The metal electrodes lined with moist sponge were attached to the back of her skull to let the current in, and to the left calf to let it out of the body. As the straps were tied round her head, arms, groin, legs and chest, she shifted politely to make it easier for the attendant to strap her in place. Her head was covered by a leather hood, which must have brought some solace to those in the room who had to face her. Now followed the first charge – the strongest, at 8 amps, meant to knock out the most hard-bitten, muscle-bound hoodlums in thirty seconds. A puff of smoke rose from the face mask – nothing special though, since the flesh naturally resists such a rocking current and the body temperature rises to 140 degrees Fahrenheit, causing a slight sizzling in the brain. After this, two more at 500 volts 4 amps, in order to reduce the heat and not broil the body. These last two are generally superfluous, since breathing is cut off with the first jolt, the heart pumping to swift denouement right behind. But somehow, this was not in keeping with the nature of the case. If Ethel had given the entire affair her Titanic Will, she was not about to stop now. The doctor applied his stethoscope and discovered she was still breathing. The switch-puller asked, 'Want another?' – and hit her twice more with all he had. It was some four minutes and thirty seconds before she yielded them any relief.

5

The Red Scare was just what the doctor ordered. It removed from the Left the terrible historical pressure of having to be a revolutionary force for social change. Ex-radicals would always have the luxury now of saying that Russian spying and secrecy seriously weakened the movement and that McCarthyism killed it; dedicated Communists could merely subscribe to the latter notion. And certainly these were major factors in the final collapse and retreat of the Left into liberalism or apathy. But many had also been clutching at excuses for putting an end to a political involvement they could no longer believe in. Also, no external excuse can erase the frightful timidity of the Left in this era, or explain why its fear persisted for upwards of five years after the political 'thaw' had begun in the late fifties.

During the Scare years, the remnants of the CP entered a necessary ideological phase. Its labour base was gone, it could have no *practical* impact of any kind on the American scene and, moreover, it was afraid to show its face. After the death of Stalin, in 1953, there were even some attempts to revive Browderism and make the Party an American Party again. But longing for the relaxed days of the Popular Front was little more than desperation. The CP might easily have gone on treading such theoretical water indefinitely had it not been shocked and rocked by two more major explosions in 1956. One was the brutal Soviet suppression of the Hungarian revolt – an event few would have questioned in the old days. Now it suddenly appeared that American reactionary allegations against the USSR had a ring of truth. But Hungary was nowhere near as devastating as the Khrushchev revelation that Stalin had been a rat all along. Such a blow of mammoth *ideological* import took from the Party everything it had left of purpose and even memory. The *Worker* reeked for months with *mea culpas*, apology upon apology for undemocratic transgressions in the name of – Stalin. Many used the revelations as a reason for quitting the CP, others found themselves a new ideological weapon – the crutch of *anti-Stalinism*. Now the reasons for leftist failure were clear – it had been Stalin's mess after all! But Khrushchev's critique had further implications. He accused Stalin of fostering a 'cult of personality' around himself, thereby betraying the notion of collective leadership. But it was precisely Stalin's personality that had led many into the Communist movement, and now it could just as easily be an object of scorn. A political involvement that relied on the worshipping of a hero was bound to dissipate when the hero was shown to be, after all, quite human, in this case even cruel. Now these leftists (and the Party itself) would reconstitute their politics on a foundation of berating Stalin and his 'ism', so that all *their* ills and misjudgements might somehow be possessed by his corpse and buried with him forever.

The Party was over. Even nostalgia for the days when the Party was a party, a harbour of political and cultural excitements, was gone. From now on it would be thought of as an anachronism, an example of lingering bourgeois sentiment in the Old Left. The CP continued now to await the rising of the proletariat, and even tried, at times, to relate to the whole new political spectrum that sprang up, years later, in its wake. By 1966 the 'New Program of the Communist Party, USA' spoke of urban blight and pollution, congested freeways, 'now'-concerns based on some small awakening inflicted by the new generation. But the Communist fate had been bound up with the ethics of industry and ever-increasing production, with conquering nature and poisoning field and stream and air. It could not catch up, hopelessly swept into the past, an old man's nostalgia trip. It even continued to rage against 'tendencies, which appear under "Left" banners and engage in revolutionary bombast to justify adventurism and, on occasion, the resort to provocative actions'. *Adventurism!* Memory of its own rough beginnings, its own glorious provocations, its own proletarian hopes was eradicated in this new middle-class severity. The new breed of State-smashers would come to judge the Party – if at all – by its conservatism, having no working knowledge of *adventures* long since past.

Once the thrill of the spy spectacle had diminished and the Party had given up the fight, there seemed little impetus or cultural hunger for witch-hunting. By the late fifties, the process of de-mystification had already begun. Joe had long been censured by the Senate and lately consigned to drink and death. In 1957 the Supreme Court, in effect, finished off the Smith Act in a case against some minor Party officials, declaring that no sufficient distinction had been made between 'abstract advocacy' and incitement to revolution. In June 1958 the Court ruled that the State Department could not deny passports to American citizens – as it had done to Communists like Paul Robeson – for reasons of 'beliefs and associations'. Another 1957 ruling even heralded the beginning of the end of the HUAC's effective power. This came in the case of a man named Watkins against the US Government. Watkins had refused to give names to the Committee, although he did testify in regard to his own Party activities. But he had also declined to use the constitutional protection of the Fifth Amendment. He was given Contempt of Congress, but this was overruled by the Court. This finally curbed the Committee's power of punishment without a witness getting a normal jury trial. It paved the way for a whole generation of future witnesses who could now tell the Committee to 'stuff it' without fear of legal reprisal. Chief Justice Earl Warren snuffed out the whole point of the past Inquisition: 'We have no doubt that there is no congressional power to expose for the sake of exposure.'

By 1960 the Committee's influence was severely diminished, but the children of the Left continued to take it seriously. In May of that year the first-ever wave of inquisitor-bashers descended on San Francisco, where an HUAC Subcommittee had come to investigate Commies in the teaching profession and the unions of the Bay Area. On the first assault demonstrators tried to get into the hearings and were either kept out or ejected. Some of the witnesses inside grabbed microphones and began singing the 'Star-Spangled Banner' while the Committeemen – resigned now to take crap on the orders of the Supreme Court – sat like victims. Subsequently, the riot squad made its entrance and the leftists were washed down the steps of City Hall, some clubbed and smashed. Girls were dragged bumpety-bump, and shocked movement spokesmen reported that their dresses leaped up over their heads, attesting to deliberate indecencies of the cops (this being prior to 'heavy days' when the dames learned to go to the demonstration in jeans). This incident has been described by radical reporters as the 'Odessa Steps' of the sixties, sparking off the new movement unto inevitable – revolution.

At the second confrontation with the Subcommittee, it was the decided purpose of the anti-HUAC campaign to appear more dignified than the witch-hunters. There was no violence, no shouting, no singing(!), no pushing or shoving, and leaders boasted of the military order of the pickets. It was all given the name – by the right wing – Operation Abolition, the first attempt on a mass scale, to force the vomit back down the Committee's throat. Strangely enough, only one *student* activist had been summoned in these hearings; the rest were older, hard-bitten CP members or front-groupers. The only relation the young protesters had here was with the *memory* of the HUAC. They had yet to learn that their particular fight was elsewhere, and they were serving in the employ – knowingly or otherwise – of an out-of-date Party.

The movement was not about to rise up like the phoenix. At best, it would re-emerge slowly and painfully, still draped in the dank sewage of the witch-hunt era. The hunted of the fifties had been badgered into accepting the 'reality' of espionage and their own inadvertent treason. This was not so much an admission of guilt as an acute awareness of contamination. If it was no longer necessary to resort to the Fifth Amendment, the fear of self-incrimination lingered on as a thick voluntary silence. Some who had been fiercely political ran into quiet cultural pursuits, and remained there after the shouting was over. Others lived with the idea that it *did* happen here, and folded inwards against the prospect of a second coming. Loyalty oaths, civil-defence drills, blacklists remained to lend a taste of the recent past. The fear of having your name smeared and the need to prepare a clean future prevailed.

Naturally, it was the young who would emerge committed. Their movement would, of historical necessity, live for a while in the shadow of the past. It was of course directly affected by the anti-Communism which was now part of the American blood-stream. Given the conditioning of the times, this was a safe posture in which to begin. Also, it was clear the Party had failed and, to many, this implied that communism could never make it in America. Finally, it was the spectre of the Party, even more than the inquisitors, that made the later movement *insist* on the free-dom of the individual. The merest hint of a return to Stalinism set leftist teeth on edge.

Subsequently, all the Party's achievements – the stress on solid organization, the get out and do it, hard materialist attitude of more successful CP days – were ignored along with its more bitter memories. The only heritage of the Old Left that was taken up – and this with a vengeance – was its fierce morality. The Red Scare had been steeped in corruption and slime – as in those cartoons that showed Nixon unshaven or McCarthy emerging from street-sewers – and the new movement would be clean at all costs. It was time for a leftist wash so as to put up a more superior front to reactionaries. No more tell-tale John Garfield armpits, no more insurrection by fist and gut. It was the first time in American radical history that labour was thoroughly out of the picture, and it had taken with it its natural grease and grime. The movement was now almost 100 per cent middle class (except for the black contingent), and would be appropriately well dressed, close cropped, high minded. The right-wing 'purifica-tion' had worked in ways it couldn't have imagined.

Because it was starting from a base of absolutely zero political power or cultural influence, the new movement was forced to accent *principle* above concrete action. The Inquisition had left behind, more than anything else, a fear of militant activity. Amer-ica was not yet ready to have its boat rocked again and would react violently to the merest suggestion of it. But, in many ways, this suited the new leftist disposition. It could rely now – as before – on pretence to revolt, could prance righteously and lay claim to wondrous ideals. All this led to a new bias for abstraction and symbolic gesture – an obvious moral substitute for concrete power. The new targets of its moral war would, of necessity, match the proportions of the movement's gigantic new *conscience*. But, accordingly, the achievements of the New Left would never be as *substantial* as those of the Old.

The witch-hunts and the Rosenberg case had succeeded in convincing progressives that their political lives were now forever linked with atomic warfare and nuclear fallout. This had a perverse appeal for latter-day leftists who now responded with their own Thermo-Nuclear theatre which giggled up death in abstract phantasm-bubbles. Death, in fact, was too devoted a comrade to leave the movement now, and when the new forces regrouped it was a natural consequence of the fifties that they would find themselves in the service of the Ultimate Commissar. Death fed up its hugest-ever beastie to the myth-hungry Left. This was *The* Bomb, a bomb to end all bombs, not the one the Rosenbergs gave the Russians, nor even the hydrogen or cobalt bomb. It was not even the bomb that filled the milk of babes with Strontium 90 or Caesium 137, turning a generation into radioactive lepers. No, it was *The* Bomb, against which civil defence was no defence, under whose mushroom cloud, as the 'Talking Atomic Blues' had it, 'all men may be cremated equal'. It was destined to replace even the FBI as chief chimera in leftist fairy tales. And how did it drop? Easy: *The* Button. Some zombie, some low-IQ yokel out of Middle America, sat poised over *The* Button that activated *The* Bomb. His eyes never left it, his finger hovered while other robots checked the radar to see if he needed the green light. But what if he fell on it or slipped? Worse, what if he were deranged? *The* End.

There was only so much one could do in the struggle with *The* Bomb – refuse to take part in civil-defence drills, picket nuclear missile sites and Polaris submarines, campaign against fallout shelters. But Death was pointing now towards a more accessible patch of ground; the new leftist right reason could more proudly blossom in the territory of capital punishment. There were some Rosenberg memories here, but somehow, in that case, the death penalty itself was never under protest. It was now in keeping with the shuffle towards principle that the movement would concern itself not with a specific crime but with *The* Punishment.The major test (indeed, the *only* one) came in 1960 with the death of Caryl Chessman in the San Quentin gas chamber. Chessman was not a political prisoner, but his moral dilemma managed to capture the imagination of political people. He had been convicted of many counts of armed robbery and two instances of kidnapping women and committing acts of sexual aggression in their mouths; it was for these latter crimes – resultant from kidnapping – that Chessman was sentenced to die under California law. But there was some doubt as to his involvement in the perversions, and on this doubt he won eight stays of execution over a period of twelve years. The eighth time around he was saved only by Latin American protests on his behalf; Eisenhower was due for a trip south of the border and the State Department wanted to avoid incidents like the stoning, some years before, of Richard Nixon's car in Caracas.

It was not until the leftist campaign to save Chessman got underway that the Power decide to wipe him out once and for all. It is true that his insistence on defending himself at his trial and his personal defiance of the rules condemned him in the eyes of the legal establishment. It is likely the case would have ended in execution anyway. But the Left was demonstrating again after all these years, now ringing San Quentin with its obnoxious pickets. In came the liberal theatricals, Marlon Brando, others who had been silent for eight years since the Hollywood investigations – all adding their names and fames to the cause. Into the folklore hit parade jumped 'The Ballad of Caryl Chessman'. Up until this point, the State had no *political* stake in erasing Chessman; he was then only part of the legal machine. Now the sudden surge to front and centre exacerbated the proceedings, and reactionary California was not about to lose face.

The Silent Majority, too, was still getting high on capital punishment.* It was not about to relinquish its claim to a sacrifice now and again, especially one who had gained the backing of symps and pinkos. Most of them had never even heard of Chessman before the fuss was kicked up, and those who did thought he was a murderer and a child molester. In any case, it never hurt to give somebody a whiff of cyanide in order to teach the others a lesson. Moreover, the death penalty was high on the list of culture-kicks now that spying had run down. In 1958 Barbara Graham had gone down gagging in a flurry of publicity as a result of allegedly pistol-whipping an old lady and spilling her brains helter-skelter. Barbara had hardly choked her final choke when Hollywood and Susan Hayward made public myth of her. The film version of her death, *I Want to Live*, took a stand for this dame because she'd had a tough life. It was gutsy stuff, first and foremost, designed to play upon the fantasies of gas-chamber groupies. The film did little to stir up sympathy against capital punishment because it chose to grovel in her past and in her emotional distress. The most it could do was to show the actual mechanism of the gas chamber, the cheesecloth bag containing cyanide pellets hanging under the chair, awaiting the lever pull that drops them into the pan of sulphuric acid below. For her pains, Susan Hayward got an Academy Award.

Chessman didn't. But he managed to play upon the publicity of his plight. He knocked out not one but *three* autobiographies and a novel from inside his cell. These works show a self-educated, deep-feeling man, and it was to his quasi-intellectual face that the Left came running. They had never bothered to defend ordinary killers under sentence of death, even where there was some doubt of guilt. Although Chessman – a self-confessed petty thief and hoodlum – had nothing in common with middle-class do-gooders, he was in the process of developing personal integrity and a 'political' eye on the world. His cheap paperback novel, *The Kid Was a Killer*, is full of *lumpen* attitudes towards killing gooks (Koreans in this instance) and stomping on liberal punks. But suddenly, as if by miracle, the mood changes to enlightenment at

*In 1972 the people of California voted two to one to kill a recent Supreme Court decision banning the death penalty.

the end of the book: 'In time we would substitute vision for vengeance. We would rise above our own fears and insecurity and senseless prejudices, and when we did we would build a better world, one whose architect was neither force nor violence, retribution nor suspicion. The alternative was increasing barbarism, the propagation of doubt, the loss of freedom and, ultimately, a nuclear Armageddon!'

These were the exact sentiments of the leftist hour and they rang bells in the heads of people who – at Chessman's moment of truth – were trying to bring coherence to questions of Right and Wrong which had got obscured and twisted in the decade just gone. But if their new image was thoroughly humane, there were still no available political tools to force the Power to react in kind. The pellets dropped in spite of all moral effort.

The new leftist hero that began to emerge in the era of principle was, indeed, a hero-in-principle. His chase after an identity was not so much a search for new vistas as a kind of moral rearmament, a pruning away of the recent heritage of repugnancy, indecency and cruelty. The acquired fear of demonstrating a *physically* militant character led him to see that his particular heroism now lay in acts of conscience. More than ever the leftist hero was his own man, unhampered by organization, ignorant of class, undetermined by anything but his own conscious choice. Yet this did not imply a freewheeling freedom without restraint; a rampaging sense of moral responsibility came with the territory. There was no Holy Comintern looking after business any longer or creating external ethical systems for all to abide by. Nor could there be any more John Garfield-style luxury of being your own man and devil-may-care what happens to everyone else. The new unwritten obligation was to revive the spiritual values of American doctrine and work towards the new Pure State to eliminate hunger, poverty, exploitation, along with unkindness, filth and – if it were only possible! – death.

One of the earliest prototypes for the new man of the early sixties was the character of Holden Caulfield in J. D. Salinger's novel, *The Catcher in the Rye*. Although written in 1950, numerous leftist writers and critics have interpreted this boy as the dropout rebel that would re-emerge in the mid-sixties; the book was one of the several gospels of the era of principle. Holden is a casualty of American education, declining a piece of ambition's pie, rootless and terror-stricken. He has no stake in any scheme, he breaks no cultural membrane. He is what used to be known, in his own time, as a 'goof-off'. Yet he is linked to the early sixties because he is looking for a road back into the arena of cultural acceptance. He hungers to be kosher, but he has no tools for action other than moral ones. The character has been cheered by leftists for his cynical attitude towards institutions. He is determined to cut away social lies and vents his verbal wrath on the pageant of untruthfuls parading in his path. He hates actors because they do not behave like real people. He also washes his soul clean of 'perverts', people who are 'conceited' and, above all, 'phoneys'.* He erases the 'fuck-you' graffiti from public walls and yearns for a time when the entire social landscape will be pure enough for children to avoid contamination. It was Holden Caulfield's naïvety that appealed especially to budding leftists in the early sixties. It was a nostalgic reminder of times long ago when America – presumably – was unpoisoned by wrath, by character assassination, by obscenity.

The new leftist hero took crap from everybody; but it was his crowning *virtue*.

After the Martin Luther King demonstrations began in the late fifties, it was clear that the new leadership in leftist tactics was going to come from the black community. Black demonstrators had evolved a new strategy of going limp under the billy-club, of not fighting back with fists against racists out to spill coon blood. In 1959, in Nashville, Tennessee, James Lawson set up some of the first workshops in strategic non-violent methods. And in Greensboro, North Carolina, the first of a rash of peaceful student

---

* As Marxists would say, it is *no accident* that Holden Caulfield chose, in 1950, the same word of ultimate contempt ('phoney') as Senator McCarthy. The word had special implications for Middle America, demonstrating the age-old hatred of social sham. Joe and Holden were equally avenging angels against 'taste' and they crisscross in that twilight zone where moral zeal and fascism often meet.

'sit-in' demonstrations occurred. But where turning the other cheek was a practical black tactic, it became a white *cause*. A natural pacifism had always existed in the Left, chiefly as a result of its middle-class values. But now that abstract thinking was the order of the day, it seemed a perfect choice to turn one's own fear of physical harm into a positive, lofty gesture. Nothing could better show up violent reactionaries for what they were, nor better exemplify the new post-Inquisition moral guidance the Left was determined to give America.

This new 'passive resistance' had a proud precedent in American culture. The Godfather of the new era was the nineteenth-century Yankee philosopher, Henry David Thoreau. Everyone was reading him, especially his famous work 'On The Duty of Civil Disobedience'. This tract influenced Ghandi's tactics and, naturally, Dr King's, infecting the growing civil-rights movement and lending the weight of historic example to a gesture of political expediency. Thoreau referred to the need to be a 'counter-friction' to the 'machine' of government when it grinds out injustice. He was against slavery and commercial war, mass government and interference on the individual, in perfect accord with the pacifist sentiment of the early sixties.* Thoreau wrote his essay in 1848, the year Europe was rife with revolution, the same year Marx and Engels put together the *Communist Manifesto*. But Thoreau nowhere reflects these events, insisting instead on an élitist *moral fibre* as proper response to exploitation and injustice: '. . . the State is not armed with superior wit or honesty, but with superior physical strength. I was not born to be forced. I will breathe after my own fashion. Let us see who is the strongest.'

The great Thoreauvian heritage for the Left was jail. The heart-throb anecdote that moved the new movement was told time and time again at demonstrations (just as Emma Goldman used it

---

*Thoreau would have another effect on the leftist fringe just a few years later. He had insisted on a Sensate Man, one who understood the complex design of nature, could live without material or physical accoutrements and respected the godliness of the ecology. His wanderings in anti-social paths and pure-breath natural surroundings (Walden Pond) would be interpreted as an early form of 'dropping out' and a logical extension of the pacifist impulse.

forty-three years earlier to justify her own civil disobedience): how Thoreau had spent his famous night in jail for tax evasion until Ralph Waldo Emerson arrived and asked him what he was doing inside; the reply, of course, was – Ralph, what are you doing *out there*? Thoreau believed he could make his influence better felt in prison because Truth was stronger than the State's false face, and he could have a better advantage for fighting injustice once he had actually experienced it: 'I saw that, if there was a wall of stone between me and my townsmen, there was a still more difficult one to climb or break through, before they could get to be as free as I was.'

More free than thou! It sent a tremor through the pacifist Left. Thoreau never *sought* the lock-up; he only spent *one* night, in fact, and never went out of his way to do it again. But the new Thoreauvians were soon climbing over each other to be carted off to jail. How logical a home this was for the pride of passive resistance! This was no longer the bitter cage that held the Scottsboro Boys or Sacco-Vanzetti or even Ethel and Julius. It was a holy place now, determined (and transcended) by presence of mind. It was an enclosed stage in which the new leftist hero could act out his morality play. He had the satisfaction of knowing he had not broken any higher law, and probably not a constitutional one either. He acted always with decorum and went limp so that the policeman could carry him off without injury to himself. As he took responsibility for his acts, he had to accept the morality of jail.*

One of the more famous jail-addicts of the sixties was the singer, Joan Baez, clearly in the running for the record of passive incarcerations. She had carried a consistent thread of civil disobedience from the experience of the black movement to the nuclear demonstrations to the more pressing matter of resistance to the draft after the South-East Asian War had flared up. Her

*There would shortly came a time when *not* having been to prison would be a movement stigma. Jerry Rubin and others would declare their mistrust of anyone who hadn't done time. The myth of jail would even outrun the symbolic efficacy of the thing. The sixties were jammed with autobiographies, letters, instructions, declarations and manifestoes of countless revolutionaries in jail. It even became a best-selling racket.

autobiography is dedicated to 'the men who find themselves facing imprisonment for resisting the draft'. She was not content with her own impulse towards jail, but strongly recommended it for others and became a stern sister on this score. When thousands fled to Canada to avoid the draft she slammed them publicly for not staying behind and paying the price (five years) of their anti-war convictions. Her own husband, David Harris, had done several years for leading the fight against induction centres. He claimed that 'one year of organizing on the outside and five in jail does more than six on the outside carrying a draft card . . . It's the only way for my body to be where my words are.'

This had been the crux of every movement's dilemma – keeping the body where the words were. Jail might now weld them together in an impressive moral gesture of defiance which, though politically pointless, could add a few martyrs to the growing leftist list.

*

Joan took her mother to jail with her: 'We did civil disobedience together at the Oakland induction centre. She told me she didn't know if it would do any good, but that it might give other mothers some courage to do the same, or something just as radical.' This was definitely more positive than the 1950s fantasy of informing on the old lady and watching the G-Men drag her away. It was cool: do time with Mom. Where ten years before the political prison-cell had been filled with rumour and dread, she would now find it flaunted, magnified to contain the expansive self inside it. The shame of jail – a paralysis of the parents – was gone (only the parents' shame at incarcerated offspring remained). All of the Red Scare strictures were running to slack. You knew your name was on every list, that you would never hold a government job (who would want to, anyway?), that you had been photographed and finger-printed and processed a million times by cops and by the FBI. You were so aware of it all that rumour couldn't touch you.

A veil had lifted. Credibility no longer ran its tortuous course, for Trust was a new catchword and so was Truth. There would be a lot of chasing after The *(as opposed to: is he telling the) Truth in* days to come, the age of informers serving as bleak reminder of sincerity lost. Language – for a short time, at least – would have to be brought back into the orbit of reason, now that the hysteria and accusation had burned down.

In prison the movement's words at last caught up with the body and it was made whole again, beatified. It was on the landscape of this now relaxing body that the next drama would be played out. All *our prisons – the ones we wrap ourselves in – would be the* guiding theme. *The jail cell could reduce the world down to the* contained space of extremely personal strategies. The process had begun with passive-ism and it implied a profound grace, yes, an aesthetic-politic, if such a thing could then be fathomed, begun at the root of Beauty – Saint ME – an eye of cool, proud defiance on the political world the old folks had lost, running in terror. The children were on the edge of an adventure, that word which housed the maximum of sin in the Communist canon, driving your own engine up that risky road. Somehow, the starting-point was prison, a new medium for self-expression by which you might shine out and where your mother might – with a little coaching – at last be proud of you.

Mind-Expansion as Manifest Destiny

TFL, PhD, in order to save the USA, hoped to turn on JFK with LSD.

This same Dr Timothy Francis Leary – convinced that he himself had been hit by the 'spiritual equivalent of the H-bomb' – would reach the President by first getting top White House aides, including Arthur Schlesinger Jr and Mr (Kennedy)[2], Robert, to swallow the drug; they in turn would flash the message to the Chief. In league with the poet, Allen Ginsberg, Leary had further visions of Messrs (Kennedy)[1] and Khrushchev munching hallucinogenic mushrooms together, in a kind of 'summit' conference, to purge their more dangerous and anti-social games. For here was a pharmacological key to world peace, no longer simply the 'peace' which generations of 'peace' movements had sought between American and Soviet adversaries: no, it was no peace-with-honour peace-in-our-time peace. The new peace required no treaties or United Nations, for it was already compounded with love and diplomatic recognition of mutual godhead – the very peace that passeth understanding.

This was not entirely naïve; after all, LSD was powerful medicine. Then (1960) and in years to come, the various psychedelic chemicals would 'remake' some people completely, awakening sleeping corners of personality. Leary himself had been a stuffy Harvard professor (with short hair!), caught in the higher – (but not 'high' enough) – education rat-race. After several hits of the hallucinogenic 'magic' mushroom he was well on his way to being reborn, a renowned 'dropout' at forty. Of course, the process was not so automatic for everyone; the drama of it wanted at least the complicity of its leading player, someone willing to take a big risk. And who better than Mr President (Kennedy)[1], standard-bearer and seed-bearer, pride of the New England democratic tradition and the American star system, who better than he to champion this latest rendition of the pursuit of happiness?

However, the ideological cornerstone of the JFK programme was education; he could not be expected to sanction a 'dangerous drug' which appeared to subvert the social ambitions of youth, caused many to leave school, and for which this same Dr Leary would soon be fired from Harvard. No, it was Leary's pipe-dream after all – but one inspired by Mr (Kennedy)[1] himself. For JFK had put the romantic melodrama back in vogue, revived the original experiment with subjective freedom. LSD had been synthesized in 1938, but it needed something akin to Kennedy's thousand days to spawn a mass movement (just as the Nixon years would later inspire the unbounded popularity of the substance heroin). It was the most democratic of drugs, bringing a dynamic escalation of the American Dream – every man is God! Further still, it set the unrestful Yankee mind to work again expanding a new continent; as if the vast land mass and overseas imperial clutchings were not enough, as if the new space programme and promised moon were not enough, here was the complex work of old Manifest Destiny, a 'new frontier' in interior dimensions – a most powerful psychic gamble towards self-discovery.

But JFK would eat no LSD. Walter Winchell reported that it made you blind.

1

With the early sit-ins and freedom-rides in the South, and student demonstrations in the early sixties, it was clear the Left was slowly catching fire, and that it had virtually eliminated the Soviet Union from its dreams and/or nightmares. It was called the New Left – although this was stretching the notion of modernity somewhat. There is no doubt that new political values had set in. The witch-hunts had knocked out a whole generation of protest, so there was only a small amount of *direct* influence from the older radicals. But the new groups were as bourgeois and careful as their predecessors had become in the fifties, and clung to the educational and social benefits the elders had fought to provide; nobody was rocking any boats just yet. With the loss of labour, the movement's base of activity shifted from the union to the university confines. But campuses were middle-class fortresses and could certainly accommodate the moderate form of social critique which the Communist casualty ward had passed down to the young students.

The New Left claimed to reject any *a priori* ideology along with authoritarianism. But if the older generation had blindly accepted the Russian model (as the new breed charged), this was hardly from an understanding of theory as much as from a sentimental attachment to the idea of revolution. The heart-felt 'concern' with the plight of the worker and the Negro, the general romanticism of the downtrodden, now passed easily and immediately into the *feelings* of the young movement.

The lingering fear of the Red Menace had an effect on the New Left as well. A sneering anti-Communism was the order of the day, infecting embittered old leftists, clean new protest groups like SANE Nuclear Policy (made up of middle-aged liberals) and sparkling Kennedy-types rising to power. The young movement still held to some socialist principle – if only a vaguer outlook on the anti-humanitarian aspect of capitalism – but it dared not say so. In most European countries the New Left equivalents readily called themselves socialists; but in 1960 America the memory of name-calling still smarted and few groups were actually prepared to admit their Marxist roots.

If the New Left was bound to tradition, it was still attempting to break clear. Its early battles were not fought with the right wing (except in the South) as much as with liberals and ex-radicals who were now entrenching. These were suffering from a corporation mentality which had built up in the New Deal and solidified in the fifties. The sense of industrial expansion was boundless, the central clearing house for personnel was the university (which put the problem directly into the lap of the student New Left). The corporation mind could thrive on a Cold War, peace-time economy or a hot-time in Indo-China; it would accommodate most every change of tune – which the New Left saw as a position of *amorality*. It was a national addict's brain-trust plugged into the perpetual electric fix (more! more!) of the drug GNP (Gross National Product). The movement had a profound distaste for these 'sell-outs' – professors, advertising men, executives who once might have been lured by the Popular Front – because they scampered out of the Red Scare into the safety of half-baked political sentiments and now scavenged off the poor and contributed to an imperialist economy. Not only that, but they also debased the *quality* of life with their boring organizational air-conditioned musak-massaged existence. All these crimes were neatly wrapped in another abstraction – called *The* System – and the New Left declared righteous war on it. After years of peace and quiet, a lull in the desperate hiccoughs which time and again rasped the nation to pieces – a golden opportunity to *streamline* the works, raise the standard of living through an unparalleled industrial efficiency which hadn't been possible during all those Commie strikes – the leftist bastards were at it again, only this time in protest against that very streamlining and efficiency!

The New Left was responding to what *The* System sought to impose on it: the name for it was 'apathy'. Folks had been lulled to sleep and the militants were determined to wake 'em up. Every college newspaper described a panoramic student malaise. Most students seemed to enjoy being coddled by the machine and could not understand what all the fuss was about. Now the attitude of striking at *The* System and the apathetic zombies it excreted would dominate the leftist sixties. The idea that you might be apolitical was repulsive; commitment in itself now became a moral imperative.

The American New Left, however – by dint of being new, Left and American – was not immune to the hereditary paralysis of factionalism. There were, to begin with, natural chips off old blocks, which simply carried on the pretences and the petty squabbles of the elders. The WEB Dubois Clubs kept up the Popular Front attitudes of the CP, looking for pointless coalitions even with the likes of the Democratic Party; the Young Socialist Alliance (YSA) still clung desperately to the myth of the historic mission of the working class; the Young People's Socialist

League (YPSL) continued the belligerent anti-Communist posture of the old socialists – few of these groups, or any of the dozens of other New Left splinters, would be caught dead in the same room with one another.

Both of the primary New Left forces were direct offshoots of older groups. Progressive Labor (PL) had been part of the Communist Party, and SDS (Students for a Democratic Society) a part of the League for Industrial Democracy (LID) – both had to experience serious factional differences before breaking away. SDS hoped to build a non-violent liberal–socialist coalition that would champion 'participatory democracy', the right of every American to determine his own life and political course. The chief enemy was labelled as 'corporate liberalism', and the mechanical universe it constructed was stifling and anti-life. SDS was also profoundly touched by the *The* Bomb morbidity of the moment, fantasizing that it might just be part of 'the last generation in the experiment with living'. The original programme of the group was extraordinarily tame and sentimental, even by Old Left standards. In its founding document, called the Port Huron Statement (1962), there is a complaint that the universities have not fulfilled their age-old function of providing 'moral enlightenment'. The writers of the statement also admitted that 'we are used to moral leadership being exercised and moral dimensions clarified by our elders'. Because of this innocent wonderful eye on the political world, full of hopeful notions that the parents could still steer them on to a right track, SDS could not yet fully admit that much of the old political experience had been corrupt. The important eye-opening here came directly from the parent group. The LID was a socialist organization with an anti-Commie hangover that had little meaning for its student branch. It did not take kindly to the streak of youthful independence which now tended to minimize the significance of a distrust of Communists. When this particular dispute reached boiling point, SDS was locked out of its office (paid for by the old guys) and accused of being Communistic.*

* Although SDS kept its ties to LID until 1965, it moved its headquarters from New York to Chicago after this rift. It was the CP's move from Chicago to New York in 1927 which first indicated a forsaking of grass-

The odyssey of Progressive Labor demonstrates the divisive battle between peaceful and violent strategies already building up in the New Left. In 1961 PL worked itself free of the old Communist Party (rapidly becoming the Venice of the Left, with its history of perpetual erosion, breakaway land mass, its sinking head barely above water). PL believed in arming the masses towards an ultimate confrontation with capitalist power. Their guiding star was the Chinese Revolution, and this was a slap in the face to the still pro-Russian CP. The breakaway group was now expelled for its 'adventurism' which, in CP terms, was rapidly becoming synonymous with Maoism. In 1962 PL branches held a national conference whose aim was the creation of a new Marxist-Leninist political party to carry out new militant strategies (this Progressive Labor Party was eventually formed in 1965). Up until that point a fairly tolerant attitude prevailed among radical students, holding that 'anywhere left of Kennedy' was O.K. Now it was changing, and PL began to telegraph the later crack-up of the pacifist edifice. Now came an old-style elimination of dead-weight and purging of dissidents in the ranks, as well as a further breach with the gentler SDS.* PL also followed the CP tactics of sending members underground, changing names and identities, stirring up crowds in demonstrations and race riots with anonymous acts of violence.

PL's big dramatic moment came with its first visit to the HUAC. In 1963 a group of them travelled to Havana over the dead body of the State Department; Cuba was then a fresh and thrilling model for budding revolutionaries, but the little sugar-cane island seemed to decay the enamel of the JFK smile. The Committee pounced. The PL group was hauled up and charged with travelling without valid passports and disseminating pro-

---

roots traditions. Now the vanguard of the Left was moving west again, and this symbolized a new attempt to gain a mass base and spread over the continent. New York was now destined to lose its status as the centre of the leftist operation, and would become instead the Elephant's Burial Ground of the Old Left.

*The bulk of the New Left, including SDS, considered PL a lunatic fringe at this time. But by 1969 it was SDS's own Weatherman faction that had taken the violent thread much further than the Maoists.

Castro propaganda back in the States. The Committee sought to discover whether this latter act made them agents of the Cuban Government. It was a pointless exercise, since there was very little the HUAC could achieve legislatively. But the idea was to harass PL members whom they knew to be plenty crimson anyway, involved in race riots and anti-war provocations. What the inquisitors did not count on, however, was the amount of crap they would get flung back at them by these latter-day Reds. The intellectual students now buried the witch-hunters under acres of Communist rhetoric. An audience full of screaming groupies came to cheer on the Christians as they drove the lions mad; the hearings were again full of the old tunes – 'Police Brutality', 'Nazi-Fascists' – in tough new lungs. There was also an awful lot of standing on the Constitution, and one man even took the Fifth Amendment sixty-three times in a session that couldn't have lasted more than ten minutes. By now, Committee members had learned a few tricks of their own and barrelled through all responses and lack of response, hoping to catch someone off guard in the confusion. But the kids had the stamina here and mocked the Committee to exhaustion. Those who could recall the good old days, when a leftist knew his place, were baffled at the onslaught.

The new radicals were still trying to flap fossilized Left wings. Whatever 'dignity' and 'integrity' may have been gathered from the ashes of the Old Left, there was just no kick in political activity. The movement was geared thoroughly to student consciousness, and this not only implied an intellectual bias but also the difficulty of true and important contact with the outside world. What happens to the revolution when school's out? Some tiny answer seemed to present itself momentarily during the Free Speech Movement (FSM) at the University of California in 1964, the first and most extravagant theatre piece of the New Left. The timing was perfect. The Kennedy smile had been eradicated and young men were beginning to go all the way to the worm-caskets with LBJ. Worse than these was the threat of bomber Barry Goldwater in the coming presidential election, and the campuses were hyperactive in combating 'the greater evil'. With the Republican Convention coming up in nearby San Francisco, however, the California right wing decided to put the screws on anti-Goldwater activity, concentrating on the notorious 'Red School House' in Berkeley. So what initially appeared to be an internal affair – the campus administration's crack-down on political groups soliciting funds on the main mall – was really a much-needed provocation from the outside world.

The place, too, couldn't be better. Berkeley, California is, for many leftists, the centre of the known universe. The world fans out from this central pivot and all outlying areas are revealed in respect to its primal nerve. It is the core of the radical experience, the State-smasher's very own Hollywood, dream factory of the revolutionary élan. Nostalgic quasi-geriatric leftists are quick to tell how it all started here, as if political life had all been a silent prelude to one blinding moment in October, Year 1 (1964) when several hundred people sat down around – *The* Police Car. It was the capturing of this car (inside was an arrested non-student who had been manning a forbidden table of political activity) which gave the New Left its first dazzling piece of mythology. Off-campus, the police would have simply cracked a few heads and driven right over the leftists, but here (on hallowed turf) the students could pride themselves on the victory of actually hemming in the vehicle. They had not considered the even more dramatic gesture of liberating the man from the car and escorting him to safety. But this would have meant a *physical* tangle with the law, and few were then prepared for violence. Instead, they made speeches – hundreds of them, from atop the police car, all day and overnight into the next day. Most of the more resounding ones spoke of the great de-personalization of *The* System, the IBM punch-out existence of students, the feeling of being factory-fodder, assembly-line products instead of humans. As the man in the police car, Jack Weinberg, put it in later weeks (they had to let him out to pee!): 'You cannot ignore me any longer; and I'm going to put myself in a position where I cannot be ignored, because you're going to have to look at me . . . as you go about your business, and you're going to have to take me into account.' That cry – to be *somebody!* – had been more or less stifled for ten years of Silent Majority-building. The President of the University, Clark Kerr, had written a book some years earlier saying that post-Red Scare college kids were going to behave now and not make any trouble for employers or governments later. Now they had not only revolted, but also captured a fearful symbol of authoritarianism.

Soon the University administration double-crossed the protesters into thinking their demands had been won, and that political activity could resume unhampered on campus. The police car was released, along with its prisoner, and the troops went off that very night to a Joan Baez concert where they were welcomed as heroes. But soon the University backed down on its promises – due to outside political pressures – and, like a computer gone berserk, punched out more and more meaningless and unenforceable rules and regulations over the next weeks. By December it became intolerable. Mario Savio, the student leader, made his famous speech (borrowed from Thoreau) about bringing the machine to a halt when you can't stand it any longer. One thousand students then marched behind Joan Baez (memories of Jeanette MacDonald leading San Francisco – via Hollywood – earthquake victims in 'The Battle Hymn of the Republic'), singing the great hymn of 1960's revolutionary pretenders, 'We Shall Overcome', with its sentimentalist, Uncle-Tom pipe-dream of winning SOMEDAY via moral superiority, whipping up radicals to a pacifist froth and leading them on to Forever-Future-Land. They captured the administration building and brought the machine to a grinding halt – for a few hours – until the gendarmes broke in and bounced them down the stony steps – all gone limp – right into paddy wagons and detention camps serving as prisons.

The FSM had its stars and a few good action moments, but it failed to win any Academy Awards for insurrection. Even its chosen name – 'Free Speech' – which had no relation to the substance of the quarrel, was a safety device, invoking motives no constitutionally minded American could fault. It had the virtue of being a coalition movement and swept in all shades of the leftist rainbow, as one finds in Berkeley. But few were prepared to ask 'What next?' With a few more strikes and the winning of paltry demands, the Free Speech Movement disbanded after one school semester. It radicalized a few hangers-on, some who'd never seen the play of 'Police Brutality' before, but these needed, to be sure, a broader field of exposure with more plentiful thrills.

2

By trying to avoid the false heroics of the past, the New Left failed to provide the crucial hook to identity-chasing. There was great stress on individual participation and choice but these were factors of *conscience* – well-meaningness and well-doingness – divorced from the broader sense of *consciousness* or its American diminutive, *awareness*. 'Character'-building had suffered badly in the crisis of inquisition, and the broad cultural caution which followed was a cold shower for self-expression. The new radicals were keenly aware of this, challenging the mass psychological retreat, but their political analysis hung on vague language and lacked shock value. All feeling for the spectacular had been shunned by the new movement to make room for hard work and hard organizing. At least the Russian model had provided some vicarious thrills and a splash of pageantry.

Then too, the New Left built no bridges to the body. It was a crucial omission, a failure to anticipate that body sensitivity, the essential tactility of the fleshy mechanism, would be one spindle on which latter-day rebellion would turn. The idea of 'participatory democracy' implied the putting of soul and body into the political fight; but it was much too cold a fish, sticking in the mouth even as language.

Where lofty ends such as the 'dignity of the individual' held sway, there was bound to be friction inside New Left groups with regard to less dignified pleasures of the body. There had always been addicts of Puritanism in the Left movements but, in the light of the orgasmic explosions and sensual seminars already beginning in their midst, the reticent quality of some new leftists seems almost reactionary and anti-prophetic. SDS, for instance, was firmly against the smoking of pot, and most members (in the early sixties) rejected sex without the chain-link to love and lasting relationship. The Progressive Labor group had allowed a measure of 'Bohemianism' until an inevitable power coup by prudes (re-living the CP), who crushed out the reefers, ordered couples living in sin to call the preacher and don't forget to cut your hair, comrade! Even during the Free Speech Movement students who had captured a police car, disrupted the machine and challenged the Power were appalled and embarrassed by a lone freak who wrote FUCK on a placard and created his own 'Filthy Speech Movement' on campus. The FSM Steering Committee was quick to steer clear and disown him, after all, *serious* intent of movement, ahem, etc.

So it was that the movement was ripe for a dialogue between expanded consciousness and expanded politics. Without the burden of crusty ideology, a new radicalism could again pursue a wholly American road – which of course meant exploring every nook and corner, the depth of every depth, all possibilities and turns of political tactic. When a CP member took off on a flight of curiosity, he had committed a crime against the Party. Now it was rapidly becoming the order of the day. The overwhelming lure of *experiment* was taking over, and giving vent to the movement's wildest dreams.

Thus the use of psychedelic drugs could become a *political* issue where once (in CP days) it might have been only an aberration or faltering of personality. By the time the movement returned to full activism in the mid-sixties, it was already confronted by drug-stimulated self-awareness syndromes and 'drop-out' privilege. This phenomenon brought confusion to earlier political strides, but also perspective and, in some ways, new strategy and firepower. Hardcore political activity by no means ceased, even at the height of the psychedelic daydream, but ran concurrently and cross-fertilized with it. Also, they had been spawned from a similar cultural need – the regeneration of personality – and both had strong emotional links to the central nerve of pacifism running through the Left.

Before it became associated with the leftist fringe, there had been great social appeal in the drug LSD (d-lysergic acid diethylamide). It was first synthesized in 1938 by a Swiss chemist, Dr Hoffmann, looking for a migraine headache cure; he claimed he was not aware of its hallucinatory properties until he took some 'by accident' in 1943. The substance appears to leave the body soon after ingestion, only stopping long enough to affect the serotonin at the synapses between the neurons of the brain, thereby liberating the perceptual and cognitive areas from their normal 'defences'. Thus it leaves you to do the work yourself, in effect, to be 'yourself' – only many dimensions more than usual. Obviously any such chemical would appeal to American dreaming, to the prying of personality secrets, fixing a wad of awareness in the self all via the express train of accelerated senses; it was only a matter of time before it would be labelled 'instant psychoanalysis'. The justification for this came through dozens of experiments performed prior to the LSD scare. It was discovered that the drug could trigger the process of bringing repressed material up from memory with greater speed than any analyst could, and was especially useful with more obsessional neurotics. The elicited data was much like the stuff of dreams, full of candid revelation. LSD also intensified the affectivity of the subject and allowed him to look with greater clarity on his own defences.

One of the very first experiments with LSD-25 was conducted by the US Army at the end of the Second World War. In its haste to jump the drug warfare bandwagon, the Army asked its scientists to investigate the affect of dropping a couple of *pounds*! of LSD into the water supplies of major American cities; thus began the notorious rumour which has since been ascribed to (and claimed by) hippie agitators. The military was also producing LSD – as well as a more potent psychedelic which later became known in the drug ghettos as 'STP' – to discover ways of 'incapacitating' enemy soldiers.* During the Korean War a joint experiment by the Army and the Air Force attempted to discover whether the Chinese Commies had used the drugs on Yank POWs for evil slant-eye brainwashing businesses. And in 1963 a US Navy commander admitted using LSD for 'application of artificial intelligence to military problems'.

---

*The results of the Army's inquiries remain secret even to this day. But it is known that some soldiers were given mammoth doses under negative conditions and had fearful, long-lasting reactions; a famous 'kooky' pop star is believed to have been one of these guinea-pigs.

In 1959 LSD went like an earth tremor through the Hollywood fault, and some movie stars were paying large sums to get dosed up on the couch. A series of therapeutic experiments was conducted among the glamour élite, the most famous and outspoken of whom was Cary Grant. LSD lifted his masks and performed the ritual psychic defrocking on him. His sessions were filmic, full of coloured lights and mood music, his dosage staggered in size so as to release his defences and memory blocks in short measures. The result was nothing less than a happy ending, a full-orchestra Technicolor 'miracle' for Mr Lucky. His problem with women, the chief stumbling block of his macho-image life, was well on the way to solution (although his wife divorced him years later for taking LSD). 'I have always shied from women who look like my mother,' he noted, before he got the juice in his back-brain. Afterwards he went to visit the old lady whom he hadn't seen for twenty years.

But it was the life and work of Dr Timothy Leary that gave LSD its publicity and, indirectly, its politics. Dropping his load did not come easy for Leary. He was thirty-nine, divorced, with two offspring, an Ivy League psychology professor when some magic mushrooms assaulted him in Mexico in 1959. He brought his discovery back to campus in 1960 and, along with Dr Richard Alpert, began the Harvard Psilocybin Project. These early experiments (1960–63) were conceived in the same pioneering spirit as the new radicalism. Leary insisted that the guide take the psilocybin (a chemical derivative of hallucinogenic mushrooms) along with the subject, that the sessions were to be conducted in sensuous surroundings rather than laboratory conditions and that the nature of the experiments was more religious than scientific. In this, he challenged the very basis of the academic and psychological establishments. Most psychologists believed that expanded consciousness was a kind of temporary psychosis. Leary was willing to concede that the drug state was similar to schizophrenia insofar as it transformed personality and caused hallucinations. But he refused to proceed from a pathological point of view. He was more concerned with turning people on to the amazing new world into which he had stumbled. But being an apolitical creature he underestimated (as he would continue to do with astonishing regularity) the power of the resistance and the resistance of the Power. When he was delivered from his teaching position in 1963 for allegedly giving drugs to undergraduates (denied by Leary), even the student newspaper, the Harvard *Crimson* – making mockery of the Doctor's undying faith in youth – bid good riddance to 'behavior that is spreading infection throughout the academic community'.

Subsequently, Leary founded the Centre for Transpersonative Living at Zihuatanejo in Mexico. Here he dosed up some middle-aged WASP corporation wine-heads and a few psychiatrists in order to research role playing and the elimination of 'hang ups' through use of hallucinogens. But anti-drug publicity crippled the operation and out went the Gringos despite their wholly straight-as-a-gate demeanour.

Leary's early work gives no hint of his later reputation as a corrupter of youth and enemy of the people. It was never 'far out', only renegade institutional stuff. A prisoner rehabilitation scheme he developed in Boston in 1961 was a pioneering venture in criminal psychology. As late as 1966 he clung to middle-class notions like 'curing' homosexuals with LSD. In his autobiography he deliberately avoids talking about his early life – except to hint at an Irish-Catholic background and a defection from West Point – the implication being that life really began (re-began) for him with his first psychedelic hit. Before that, and during the early part of his famous voyage, Leary was quite the good citizen.

But he felt he was bearing a crucial social message, and this turned him evangelical. Leary developed a theory of 'games' for America, out of his LSD experiences as well as Eastern religious teachings: 'Ninety-nine per cent of the activity of ninety-nine per cent of Americans goes into robot performances on the TV-studio stage. Fake. Unnatural. Automatic.' The idea was not to eliminate these, but to recognize them for what they are – the academic game, the marriage game, the President of the United States game or the revolution game – and swing with them, play them lovingly to the full without any illusions as to their importance or your power. When Leary gave psilocybin to a group of prisoners in 1961, many saw themselves as players in the 'cops and robbers' game; to most of them, this was more truthful than being 'cured' of hostile tendencies and sent back into the world of respectable citizens. Leary himself came out of this experience playing the Thoreauvian 'I have absolutely no fear of imprisonment' game: 'I've taken LSD over forty times in a maximum-security prison as part of a convict rehabilitation project . . . so I know that the only real prisons are *internal* . . . I'm the freest man in America today!'

The real wisdom of the psychedelic charge for Leary was in its implications for getting beyond ME-playing, tracing memory in human brain cells far beyond Freud and the toppling of defences – right back to memories of birth, intra-uterine recall, to genetic codes linking twentieth-century man with the first pre-dawn amino acids! But such a divine drama could only be played out on the stage of the mind. Leary found that LSD was only an accelerated equivalent for the 'pure mind' state of Eastern mysticism. The basic religious message was that all bodies and objects are 'one', only gaining separate identities through arbitrary social choices guided by words. But words could never define the divine state, because they had too many set associations. Leary expressed this in a poem about the '   ', that unnamable godhead who produced, in the Doctor, an 'ecstatic gasp':

> He dances out the pattern without ever being recognized.
> As soon as he is caught in the act, he melts in your hand.

All this seemed to render political action and hope for social change pointless. In 1964 Leary and his associates produced a dopester's version of the *Tibetan Book of the Dead* – a sort of *Communist Manifesto* of the interior economy – which stresses a state of *inaction* or passive integration with the world that encounters you. The body is at rest here – though not in a stupor – and yields up spontaneous feelings, similar to 'free association' but with no recourse to words or attempt to interpret the forthcoming material. The silence is all; its aim is 'objective' enlightenment, seeing the world outside the guidelines of personal motivation.* The obvious corollary is that *action* is the property of an *acting* (and, by inference, unhappy) ego. Leary interpreted these lessons to mean that any external action, if not a product of expanded consciousness, was 'robot behavior' and he included in this any protest on behalf of LSD. To him there was no difference between leftists and rightists, between LBJ and Mao, between Ronald Reagan and Ho Chi Minh – all were trapped in the political game.

Some caught in the 'revolutionary game' were baffled. Their first experiences with LSD seemed to confirm Leary's findings. Moreover, many were still locked in the experiment with peaceful personal grace. Non-violence was becoming ingrained, with folks seeking methods for curbing natural anger instincts and self-inflammation. Now a branch of the political movement would carry this urge for tranquillity into an attempt to 'leave' its body, to get beyond its corporeal relation to Power and assume 'pure mind' properties at the most expanded tip of consciousness. It was an odyssey with roots in passive-resistance demonstrations, limbs loose and pointless, the trunk limp and full of gravity for the officer to drag away – a sack of pacifist burden for the rule of law. Now the same arms and legs were smoothing to purpose, turning inward, shanks at rest upon heels, head erect – the lotus position for sensory awareness and passive non-resistance. The leftist body had come to this impasse for a fleeting moment on the path to flagrant pseudo-revolutionary drug-ism.

3

From a private state of divine ego-loss to public nightmares of chromosome-mutant leftists dosing up the water supply with

*This, however, is merely an early phase in a vast process of enlightenment-seeking, leading ultimately to a permanent 'loss' or transcendence of the ego. Leary realized this highest rung of the spiritual ladder was not within the grasp of most people; subsequently he developed the idea of not trying to transcend game reality, merely understanding it for what it is. LSD devotees would almost never reach the permanent summit chemically and would experience 're-entry', a kind of re-birth based on a new awareness – but only a very temporary high.

terror drugs covers a span of some five to six years, an American eternity. Leary's calm religiosity was soon traded in for more dynamic rocking and holy-rolling in keeping with well-known traditions, the Catholic pageant, the funky out-going wisdom-humour of Judaism. Even those who clung to imported discount Eastern mysticism found ways of joining the social parade, be it only through chanting mantras at love-ins to an audience of thousands. It was faith by infection or injection, one of the spurious thousand-and-one last gasps of Christianity in masquerade.

Also, in the broad experiment with changing the *nation's* mind, SDS and FSM seemed to be mere placebos; LSD would have to make its dramatic bid. This was a second phase for the drug culture, hastened in part by the frustrating constrictions of New Left groups. The grey organizational quality of the politicos could not hope to compete with sensationalism and coloured wonder, nor could any movement ever again be 'new' enough. Their capacity for myth-making was slim, somehow it was all still so careful and academic. Even the group names were guided by the stale game of initializing, SDS, PLP, YPSL, FPFC – their post-LSD breakaways would be more like pop groups with names such as the International Werewolf Conspiracy or Yippie or Weatherman.

The old desire for exposure turned the molecular dance at last to a political event. North and South American Indians had been using peyote and other hallucination-inspiring plants for centuries of religious practice, and even European sages like Aldous Huxley had used psychedelic drugs. But the purpose was almost always metaphysical; the fact that the drugs accelerated perception did not mean that the expanding of consciousness was any less than a life's work. Huxley on his death bed injecting LSD-25 probably felt just at the beginning of his climb. It was only when white middle-class Americans popped the pill that the element of *campaign* – with all its implications of hard-sell and speedy obsolescence – was introduced. And it was not only the media that produced it. To a great extent it was the gooey morality of the fringe Left – pushers of 'peace'-dope – that strangled the LSD experiment. The ecstasy of the psychedelic experience is, in itself, completely neutral and non-political; there are no categories to 'pure mind', only the tingle of self in motionless dance. Even Timothy Leary admitted the 'nervous system sees no color, feels no pain, claims no virtue, feels no shame'. The fantasies of 'peace' and 'love', on which the drug culture was weaned and gained its slogans, had nothing whatever to do with expanded consciousness. Such virtue was a hangover from earlier pacifism; at best, this need was *heightened* by the use of drugs.*

In the *Tibetan Book of the Dead* (as 'translated' into a psychedelic manual by Leary and Alpert) there is a vision referred to as the 'Magic Theatre'. Here, depending upon the particular background of the voyager, he experiences a parade of archetypal figures, heroes, daddies, dragon-ladies, Secret Service men, FBI agents, characters out of myth prancing by. There is a warning, however: 'Inability or unwillingness to recognize them as products of one's own mind leads to escape into animalistic pursuits. The person may become involved in the pursuit of power . . .' Leary tried to use this lesson to ease the tensions of role playing, particularly with regard to hallucinations of power. As in the advice of the ancient teachings, the idea was to let the 'magic theatre' pass by without seducing you into games of chance. The final ecstasy would then be one which re-creates the drama – motionlessly, free-floating, full-lotus position – as a perpetually buzzing electric current in the brain. This was the true and final 'dropping-out'.

What Leary's optimism failed to take into account, however, was the element of release, of *projecting* one's personality, essential to most Western (and certainly American) notions of play. To deny the 'magic theatre' and its seductive qualities was to deny the surge towards the power of influence. And now that true political and social power seemed further off than ever, folks were

---

* If concepts like peace and love could be tacked on to a pure mental state and paraded as its inherent properties, surely the opposite could be done as well. The rise of what was later called 'psychedelic fascism' – the brutal shamanistic power trip of demon acid devotees – had no causal relationship with the swallowing of LSD. It was rather a direct offspring of leftist/hippie purism. Where there is sanctity there will always be sin in a punishment-addicted Christian culture.

seeking just such substitutes in the realm of sensation. They would not be denied, and ancient Nirvana would have to be re-interpreted as psychic discharge.

Thus the atomic tingle in the nervous system could not be confined to the space of a man's internal works. The acid rush in the brain, after all, produced a great spectacle; the affairs of the head, now flashing on an indoor screen, were astonishing – *demonstrably so*. It is the normal temptation of an acid-tripper to want to express his magic vision as if it were the world's first and best (although it is difficult to imagine a Navajo Indian at a peyote ritual turning to a fellow brave and saying 'let me tell you about my trip, man'). Some had now taken the literal meaning of 'psychedelic' – *mind-manifesting* – and stretched it to US borders where it gained the amendment: *upon whom*? The LSD high became unsatisfactory until it could be staged.

Dr Leary often spoke of LSD in terms of television imagery, electronic brain impulses on an inner screen, receptacle of imprints and exposer of set rituals. But now that it had become a *cause*, this was too constricting. Whatever acts of 'revolution' followed the LSD syndrome took on the proportions of the drug itself; nothing less than cinemascope would hold it.

The landscape for it was a curiously revived Americana. The inherent democracy of LSD – rendering everything as 'one' – as well as its sense of spectacle brought back the old romance of the Republic. 'Inner space' had no sooner been demonstrated as a dimension of consciousness than it was being explored and exploited to the full. It was an expansion of the personality continent, a Manifest Destiny of the brain cells. In a 1966 speech at a Boston church, the poet Allen Ginsberg advocated that every American over the age of fourteen and in good health take LSD at least once. To give historic weight to his argument, he invoked the name of Thoreau as one who believed in the dominion of 'individual soul development' over the 'illusions of the political state'. He then carried this further, promoting the use of psychedelic drugs as tools in the old business of re-dreaming America: 'I am speaking from this pulpit conscious of . . . my transcendental predecessors in this city, with all the awesome prophecies about these States pronounced by Thoreau and Emerson . . . and the more naked Whitman . . .' We must 'set forth within the New Wilderness of machine America to explore open spaces of consciousness in Self and fellow Selves. If there be necessary revolution in America it will come that way.'

In spite of his persistence in keeping life apolitical, it was finally Timothy Leary who took up the thread of myth-making and gave LSD its major shove towards a public platform. The most dangerous sort of socio-political animal is the Johnny-come-lately, one whose personal past has no strong social bias and who – once he's heard the message – beats a frantic path without caution or sense of background. Leary was just such a changeling, shot through and through with missionary zeal. LSD had packed a powerful wallop in his soul, far too powerful to be contained; it would be his gift to American culture. He spoke now of expanded consciousness as the 'Fifth Freedom', proclaiming every man an artist when he communicated My Trip and, further, every man was God. On this level, he proposed that everyone should found his own religion and start his own country.

In the early days of his experiments, Leary – like many others – was fired with the New Frontier and the Kennedy myth. He believed the Kennedy brothers would be responsive to his work because they themselves were in a similar process of altering the nation's consciousness. But it was especially their youth that attracted the Doctor, and his particular fantasy was that America could be remade through the ecstatic stream of Executive sperm: 'The crucial variable in today's political equation is age. The basic areas which now divide men are hormonal . . . The issue which determines who will be elected, who will be listened to is: How much time did you spend making love last week? . . . The Kennedy strategy board understands this secret.'

In 1960 Leary was already concerned with getting his message out to those he considered 'influentials'. He and Allen Ginsberg wanted to give psilocybin to famous writers, artists and politicians, to get them on 'our team'. This was precisely the Win-a-Date-with-a-Star strategy of the old Communist Party, as if one's work might be blessed by the proximity of such notables (not to mention the publicity). The 'big-name bit was intriguing', said the Doctor.*

Leary later organized his International Federation for Internal Freedom (IFIF) and ultimately created a tight-knit psychedelic community at Millbrook, New York. Here it was all very reasonable and adult, thoroughly bourgeois, with a vegetable garden planted in the shape of a sacred mandala. There were professional guides, medical degrees, all quite legit. But in 1966 the harmless Millbrook (which had been operating unharassed for several years) was busted on trumped-up marijuana charges. Symbolically – and practically – this was a downhill turning-point for the drug movement. But it was not the baptism of the older folks which brought on the repression of the Doctor. Leary was now being made to pay for his supposed influence on the children of America, who were not only 'tuning in' and 'turning on', as he had suggested, but worse – 'dropping out' of bourgeois, ambition-oriented culture and running away from home. Inevitably there were casualties, middle-class strays from stifling booze-homes who got broken by the highly dangerous LSD. The more lucid, however, used their new awareness to make further war on the conventionality of the old folks, like, daddy, your whole life is colourless and grey, stuffed with personality blocks and poison gin, you pollute the landscape with your Ballantine Beer cans and, moreover, your head is shorn like a de-sexed chicken. Oh brother, the humiliation of it! Somebody must be responsible for bringing them to this conclusion! After an early mushroom meal, Leary had declared he would dedicate his efforts to the 'disenchanted young, the sons arising'. He did not, however, advocate generational warfare, only an honest drugged interchange on the nature of game reality: 'I can't imagine parents being turned on without wanting to turn on their children. I know no child over the age of seven who hasn't been given drugs and I know many of them.' But it was for playing the Pied Piper

* One of those Leary succeeded in turning on was the ex-Communist Arthur Koestler, whom, for some obscure reason, Leary called his 'beloved Whittaker Chambers'. Koestler, however, did not get along with the mushrooms; on a previous trip he even had horrific visions of inquisition and Stalinist confession terror.

game that he would finally be paid off with indictments and prison.

Because LSD was legal in nearly every State until 1966, the authorities had to rely on the stand-by catch-all for political dissenters – the marijuana laws – to stop Leary's children's crusade. (So desperate were they to pin the rap on him, however, that they would have waited until his tissues were 'aflame' with LSD electricity and then busted him for infringing fire laws.) In December 1965 he was railroaded for possessing some shreds of weed into a five- to thirty-year, $30,000 sentence in Texas. This was eventually squashed (1968) by the Supreme Court because Leary had been charged with non-payment of the absurd Marijuana Tax which is self-incriminating and clearly unconstitutional. None of this mattered to the Federal Government which continued to slap charges on him like wallpaper for the next three years. It kept him a prisoner to the courts and to the pressures of legal fees.

All this brought graduated stardom upon the High Priest (as he calls himself in his autobiography). He tried to use this to effect in 1966, by calling upon youth to initiate a unilateral 'cease-fire' on the expanded consciousness battlefront; this would, he believed, allow for cooling of passions and the re-uniting of the generations. This strategy – beneficial to Leary's legal defence – naturally went unheeded. It is unlikely the mass of young dopers had ever really paid him more than passing respect. Nice old guy.

It was probably the stress of finance as well as the crunch of fame that led Leary to perform a My Trip-style theatre piece in New York in 1967. He alternated nightly 'The Incarnation of Christ' and 'Illumination of the Buddha'. With guru Leary all in white, full lotus downstage centre, a combined lecture-light show-ballet occurred, taking the spectators through a dramatization of sex and murder fantasies, Hindu gospel and the death of the mind. Once Tim had finished his hushed holy riff there was audience participation. He called upon everyone, politely including the narcotics agents in the crowd, to re-enact Jesus' trip with him, assuming all the sins of deathly Western culture so as to exorcise, once and for all, the good-evil dichotomy which was hanging everybody up. This was all augmented with elaborate stroboscopic effects and mandala spectacles, blazes of white purist costume and Eastern gear. After some friendly words of advice Dr Leary hastily abandoned his acting career.

In December 1968 he was again busted for marijuana in Laguna Beach, California, where he had founded the Brotherhood of Eternal Love two years before. (This was the last in a chain of religious groups he founded, including the League for Spiritual Discovery, designed to give him an air of legitimacy; all were suppressed.) For possession of two joints he was given a sentence of six months to ten years. At the same time he was going to be re-tried on his Texas arrest, despite having been acquitted by the Supreme Court. Then there were conspiracy charges pending against his Millbrook colony, on and on in the unfolding autobiography of the 'freest man in America'.

One of the most outspoken opponents of the drug culture was Ronald Reagan, the actor who once worried about Reds splashing sulphuric acid on his good looks; now he panicked that their children would lace his drinking water with the lysergic variety. LSD horror stories helped to get him elected Governor of California, along with his general promise to stamp out student dissenters and weirdos. One of Reagan's pet hates was Leary himself, recently become a resident of the sunny State; so when the Doctor decided to challenge him for office in 1969, the Governor was not amused. Not that the good burghers of California would dream of electing the High Priest to high office, but his very presence in the election made mockery of the thing. Yet, Leary was dead serious about running. He proposed to make the police the highest-paid citizens in order to keep them happy and unaggressive: 'My politics will be based on a system of rewards, not punishments.' He planned to conduct a series of love-ins up and down the sunny coast, with the playful erotic campaign slogan 'Come Together', in order to pull in votes. But Reagan saw to it that he got no further than the Orange County Jail. Leary was denied bail under the new Bail Reform Act of 1966, and was put away for an indefinite period pending the appeal on the old marijuana charges. There are two reasons, under this act, that a judge may withhold bail. The one which nailed the Doctor indicated that his freedom presented a definite and overwhelming danger to the community. No one paid much attention to the

other clause, seemingly irrelevant in Leary's case, which denies
bail if a man is likely to attempt an escape.

Once the psychedelic experience was raised to the level of public
platform, with many left-ish people reaching curious new peaks of
self-promotion, the authorities fell over themselves in their determination to cut it down to size; this rendered it even more of a
political issue. As long as there was a possibility of practical
application and social benefit, the Power had turned a more or
less blind eye on LSD use, or at least provided loopholes for
legitimate experimentation. But now the drug culture had carried
it into an unadulterated pursuit of happiness. And pleasure that
had its roots in sensation or, worse, in the cosmic ecstasies of
gooky religions, was frowned upon in an America founded on
Calvinist ethics, material happiness and the denial of joy even
in the privacy of one's home. The equation of hedonism with sin
was aimed at keeping children underfoot, a social motivation
which had been passed down through the ages. The increased
sexual licence that accompanied the mass use of LSD put the
finishing touches on the authoritarian fear. All of this added up
to a *natural* official aversion to the psychedelic campaign. One
sure proof of this lies in the fact that barbiturates and heroin – far
more dangerous and physically debilitating substances, but with
no associations of pleasure – were never suppressed with half the
conviction or media-scare as were the hallucinogens (including
the safe marijuana).

In 1965 Senator Thomas Dodd proposed the Drug Abuse
Control Amendments aimed at 'the pseudo-intellectuals who
advocate the use of drugs in the search for some imaginary freedoms of the mind and in the search for higher psychic experiences'.
In 1966 three separate States, including California – the 'highest'
of all – enacted anti-acid legislation. And by 1968 LBJ mentioned
only LSD in his war on dangerous drugs in the State of the Union
message. 'The time has come,' said the President, 'to stop the sale
of slavery to the young.' On top of this, the drug-influenced
'subculture' was experiencing a classical sabotage of the Left – via
narcotics agents and informers – a memory of days long past
when you had to think twice about trusting yourself. Psychedelic

chemists, some of whom had become millionaires overnight, were forced underground – like Reds on the run – to brew their alchemical wonders, creating secret codes and paranoia-languages.

On the date of the California law prohibiting LSD (October 1966), some of the more religious drug devotees from San Francisco issued a 'Prophecy of a Declaration of Independence': 'We hold these experiences to be self-evident, that all is equal, that the creation endows us with certain inalienable rights, that among these are: freedom of body, the pursuit of joy, and the expansion of consciousness . . .' This was followed by the usual expression of 'love' for all the genocidal hate-addicted people of power and plenty, another daffodil handed to grizzly bears. But the implications of the declaration were wrong, not only in pretending the Power would protect the Bill of Rights on behalf of left-ish freaks, but also in presuming that there was a legal mandate for expansion of consciousness. In fact, there is no constitutional guarantee whatever for thought or experience. At best there are the freedoms of speech and religion of the First Amendment; Leary tried constantly to get his organizations recognized as religions in order to claim protection for the swallowing of his sacrament. One argument was that peyote is legal when used by Indian tribes in ceremonial fashion – so why not the technological Brand X taken by palefaces? It could be countered (and was) that peyote is confined to the reservation and to a small number of takers, while LSD presented 'a clear and present danger to a substantial interest of the State'. Freedom of conscience can be interpreted as a guarantee; but expanding consciousness in this instance involves the ingestion of a substance – this constitutes an *act*. It is the act that is finally illegal, not its effect. Certainly a case could be made for anti-marijuana and -LSD laws contravening the Eighth Amendment which forbids cruel and unusual punishment; but this would require proving that these substances were not dangerous and did not merit stiff sentences. At a pinch, LSD could be labelled a 'poison' since it is a derivative of ergot, a black fungus which usually develops in rye seeds; in the Middle Ages ergot caused a disease called St Anthony's Fire, in which limbs became blue and gangrenous and fell to pieces. The case was closed.

It wasn't only the Power that weakened the drug movement, but its own internal logic as well. The situation of an LSD trip is highly precarious; the taker is in an extreme state of susceptibility throughout, wide open to an infinite variety of pressures. This was now reflected on a mass scale. The drug culture wasn't two minutes old before it was up for grabs. The psychedelic market was overrun, bought, sold, raped, plundered, cheapened. Naturally, there were the dream-spinners and dollar-shuckers and needle-dopers and rip-off leeches that haunt any American free enterprise, and these did not hang back from staking instant claims. But there were more benevolent dopesters whose motives were Utopian: 'I think it is a moral exercise that every one of the thirty million who are using psychedelic drugs should take a turn at dealing,' said Dr Leary. It was the notion of personal initiative all over again, every man a pusher: The New Deal. This counter-cultural 'Robin Hood' – as described by Leary – would be a mythic replacement for cops and robbers, a righteous agent who worked with fellow pushers in 'brotherhoods'. (Ironically, a 1966 Senate subcommittee said the same thing, from a totally opposite point of view, charging that the LSD market had become a *Cosa Nostra* operation.)

Others simply wanted to turn on everyone everywhere. Taking dope was quickly replacing going to jail as the new cocktail-party Left moral imperative ('here, try this'). This tended to obscure further the non-social nature of LSD. The notion of drug 'oneness' suggested perhaps a relation of man to nature, never a mass movement. But self-advertisement – the projection of My Trip – was once more at full throttle after the fearful first treads of the pacifist movement. A band of LSD gypsies called the Merry Pranksters, led by novelist Ken Kesey, drove a huge Technicolor bus to every American border, their catchphrase 'further' written across the front. Their game was being totally 'up-front' with one another, creating a breakthrough in defence-less self-expression. Towards this end, each prankster was considered to be in the process of acting out his 'own movie'. Even the more institutional trippers broke ranks and jumped into the new movement. *The Psychedelic Review*, edited by Leary's Harvard gang (and often Leary himself) since 1963, had always had the cut of a typical university medical journal, the square intellectual squeeze of square binding. By 1969 a full-colour trippy dream-package, it announced its move from the 'tradition-bound East to the liberating West'. It was all happening now in San Francisco; Leary himself had made the California move, trading his guru pallor for a Berkeley suntan.

Naïvety had always been a property of movements that challenged American order, but here it crept in with a vengeance. The 'peace and love' terror was partly to blame for disarming the more susceptible young and confusing them with gestures of conciliation to the forces of law and order. But there was also the effect of the drug itself, the haze that blurs the corners of the inner screen, a magic that insinuates itself 'cosmically', establishing spectrum upon confusing spectrum in the broadening of personal horizons. It could cloud up your telescope on the known world and bring on a delirium of vague 'universal' thinking. It was this quality that made the experience honey in the fists of religious wizards skilled at creating substance from vapour. Language, too, suffered in this last outpost of pacifist abstraction. The great 'oneness', the dreamy 'all is equal' mentality – in the mouths of the untrained – now expressed almost every action as doing 'our thing' (*la cosa nostra* in the Sicilian). So too all the world's extraordinary *Angst*, all the dilemmas of self, the stretches of human misery and waste might now be flattened to 'hang-ups' – with its image of the organization man caught by a hook at the back of his three-piece suit, dangling helplessly in his 'uptight' – yet another – life. It was a language of the '   ', of pseudo-religion, but even more a product of the great whirlpool of spectacle – an event of body and brain for which words were not enough, or too restrictive, not yet evocative enough to catch the speeding back-brain phantasms – expressed while drowning.

So that when the question of 'revolution' was once again raised, the lack of specific thinking and precise language posed acute problems for getting anything *done*. Even if it could now be only a 'cultural revolution' (an historic admission), it would still need some clarity to it. The first broad hint of the dilemma came at the 1967 San Francisco Be-In. With the blissful logic of '   ', some 30,000 humans gathered to demonstrate for no purpose whatever, a pure carnival of zero presided over by multiple gurus, acid flowing like lemonade. Throughout the afternoon the the South-East Asian War spectre was hauled in by conscience-creeps to whom pleasure without political guilt was an obscenity. The budding hippie, but still devoted leftist, Jerry Rubin, addressed the throng on the escalating dangers of the Indo-China conflict and the worse danger of everyone simply doing his thing and doing nothing to *stop that War!* To most folks his words were lovely crimson soap bubbles, they could *see* his conscience shrieking Red in the breeze. There was, to be sure, a certain hope and ecstasy for a revolutionary future here but it did not revolve around any notion of *act*, had, in fact, little more than faith from the bounce forward that Mind had taken. Dr Richard Alpert, a prime mover of the event, saw the Be-In as a promise of a Glad State shining up ahead:

In about seven or eight years the psychedelic population of the United States will be able to vote anybody into office they want to. Allen Ginsberg? Sure . . . Imagine what it would be like to have anybody in high political office within our understanding of the universe. I mean, let's just imagine that Bobby Kennedy had a fully expanded consciousness. Just imagine him in his position, what he would be able to do.

He meant 1973.

4

The Glad State was not to be. Soon the anti-face to the love delirium would express itself in random murder fantasies and more bitter chemicals whose goal was contraction of body capacity and simulated suicide. But LSD only accelerated the changes in social mood of the sixties, and cannot be blamed for creating what was already in the works. The leftist heritage of shifting ground and perpetually overhauling political strategy was now ingrained. This was not merely a change in life-styles and tactics, but endless inter-breedings and troop defections which precluded an effective mass movement. It was not enough to change your mind; you had to *discard*, to renounce your recent past as you sped up another blind alley. The experiment with experiment had won the day. Forty years after anarchism had ceased playing a role in the American Left, phased out as it was by a more orderly Communism, it was back in style – only nowhere near as ideological or purposeful as before. The late sixties were charged with rebellions within revolutions, condemnations and exclusions, all electrified by the idea that no eruption was shattering enough in the cause of liberating the person, that any project might be abandoned in pursuit of its contradiction, that memory and assimilation of past political experience did not serve the purpose of self-promotion, that phases of revolution might come to feel as obsolete as last year's Buick.

So it was that Moonshot Hallucination exploded on firing of second-stage rockets. But the volume of its psychedelic debris was immense and far-reaching. Every edge of the Left caught fire of it if only by contamination, the rage to disown it or persecution by one of the new 'acid gangs'. It knocked off balance the old-style political action and its residue in the New Left. It bred the later American movements of neo-Buddhism, environmental sanctity and cocaine. And it gave the movement its first-ever dose of real fun. Not giggle-fun, but exposure-fun, terrorist-fun, foaming-at-the-mouth-fun, gun-fun. The renewal of counter-violence to the State was only a further stage in the puff of pleasure blown up by the hallucinogens, a visceral reaction to the cold porridge of pacifism. So the immediate enemy (because yesterday's pal) was the naïve bubble of psychedelic transcendentalism. A flyposter disseminated on New York's Lower East Side in 1968 by a post-'peace and love' gang called Up Against the Wall, Motherfucker (The Motherfuckers) condemned Timothy Leary for dragging organized religion into the subculture and 'not for expanding the mind but for limiting the revolution'.

These Motherfuckers had broken with their SDS-traditional New Left roots to develop a fresh outlook on urban militancy. They carried forward the Communist thug tradition of busting up meetings of rival groups – in this case liberals, socialists and SDS-types. Theirs was a reaction to peaceful negotiation and blind hatred for the failures of past movements. Their new alternative was laced with LSD: 'Only when we simultaneously see our magic drugs as an ecstatic revolutionary implement, and feel our bodies as the cellular macrocosm and galactic microcosm will our spiral/life energy destroy everything dead as it races over the planet leaving us alive spinning at the pineal eye.' *The Last Trumpet*, nothing less. Everything 'dead' is swept away, leaving behind the rush of the acid pure state. It was the stuff of messiahs, cutting away the fatty excess of the body politic, sub-machine-gunning the money changers out of the temple. No dim hope for revolution expressed as transference of power; instead, gestures of extermination. Of course, most such white barks were far worse than their bites; the Motherfuckers achieved next to nothing in the way of lasting strategy. But they show how quickly some of the 'love culture' could grasp for the pleasure of spiritual murder. Naturally their fiercest growls were directed at the old folks, fat burghers ripe for enforced euthanasia by the 'sons arising'. Here the Motherfuckers changed their name to the International Werewolf Conspiracy, carrying Leary's gentle Pied Piper game to B-Movie ends: 'Gentlemen in pajamas rush to their windows . . . Women in curlers clutch the blankets close around themselves as the shadowy, howling shapes move through the streets . . . When morning comes . . . their stomachs sag with the weight of a satisfying feast, and their fangs drip with the fresh blood of their victims. THE CHILDREN OF THE TOWN RUN BESIDE THEM.'

The parents and the police are the intended victims in the killing pageant. But the liberal Left was the only group they ever persecuted. The Motherfuckers were three fourths muscle-flexing and one fourth myth-making. Their need for gestural warfare and simulated street violence would find a niche in the world of explosive devices yet to come. Their momentary rage was a strange wedding of Freud and Stalin, with a taste for leftist purification in vampire-fangs.

There was a more palatable psychedelic cry – Utopia Now – an attempt to demystify the religious blur along with leftist pretence to dream futures. It was the guiding theme of the San Francisco Diggers who haunted that city's famous 'Summer of Love' lasting from 1966–8.

Their name was well taken. In 1649 Gerrard Winstanley formed a community of 'Diggers' to cultivate some common land in Surrey, England, in the belief that the earth was a 'Common Treasury'. The land had been laid waste by economic wars and the Diggers refused to find a place *within* the system that created such devastation and poverty. They simply *took* what they needed, in the spirit of 'mutual aid', ignoring the godless claim to owner-ship of property. Winstanley planned to store all harvested crops in warehouses so they might be distributed free. Naturally, he never got that far, blocked at every turn by Puritan oppression.

It was not merely Winstanley's primitive communism that appealed to the originators of the San Francisco group, but also the gutsyness of his procedure. The English Diggers had already applied their spades to the Common and were carted off to prison several times before they issued their manifestoes. Even then, Winstanley made no *demands* of the Power: 'But I do not entreat thee, for thou art not to be intreated . . . I Command thee.' There was no protest. The San Francisco Diggers also made certain they would never demonstrate for or against anything. A social effect was either in the works already or not worth speaking about; no conferences, no caucuses, no programme. They assumed, like Winstanley, that the world of buying and selling was created by thieves, and all people needed to do was take back what was al-ready theirs.

The SF Diggers despised leaders (as did the New Left which nonetheless relied on them), but they had gone even further into a highly un-typical posture of anonymity. Their street handouts, poems, papers and leaflets were never signed (at least not with real names), they indulged in almost no media play and, with few exceptions (one has finally written a 500-page autobiography), their identities remain obscure even now. Still, by the time they disappeared from the San Francisco scene in 1968, they had either started, or were in the process of starting, a switchboard information centre to coordinate all services and provide com-munity assistance, newsletters, etc.; a free food storage and dis-tribution outlet, plus the provision of free food daily to anyone with a bowl in the public park; a distribution service which gave out free food on a door-to-door basis; a free garage with semi-professional mechanics (who also taught you how to mend your own car); free legal assistance; free housing for the transient population, especially crucial when the runaways descended on the city; free medical aid from clinic doctors who dispensed no guilt and didn't even wince when picking off the crablice.

They were debunked as a 'hip Salvation Army', devoid of syntax and political awareness. But there was no saving of souls or conversion therapy as there was in fervently religious Marxist groups. Nor was the Digger mystique confined to boring social service. On a broader plane, they inherited from Winstanley (perhaps without knowing it) the idea of 'levelling', destroying economic consciousness. They pretended to be scornful of money (up to a point), burning ten-dollar bills at random – but they were even more wary of being outguessed in their tactics. So they drove their Free City Distribution truck around wealthy neighbourhoods as well as poor ones, handing out free food to mink-lined matrons.

Some hardcore left-wingers argued that the limited vistas of the Diggers were demeaning the prospect of revolution in America. But whatever small success they may have had came precisely from their refusal to be swept into the romance of smashing the State, concentrating instead on one small 'Free City' community in San Francisco's Haight-Ashbury district. Their zeal was there directed not against broad and chiefly invisible power, but at the vultures who circled over the ego-death of easy-prey LSD-takers. These included the trippy psychedelic shops with overpriced artifacts based on false prurient fantasies about the 'subculture'; merchant groups who hired starving runaways for crap-work at wages below the minimum; the dope dealers who bled and cheated the community. Also included here were the neo-Buddhists and Learyites with their oracular newspapers, seeking Nirvana-corners in a hostile urban set-up. As such, the Diggers were conducting a religious war, scourging the usurers, crusading against the dishonest pretence to a new anti-materialist ethic. This was in proportion to the social crisis. Thousands of love-children arrived to play at poverty (their trust funds and bank accounts safe for their twenty-first birthdays back in Iowa), brought there by overblown marketing and image-making, falling unwrapped into Frisco (which has one of the coldest summers in the US). Hepatitis and VD epidemics from unsterilized needles and casual copulation abounded. When the LSD supplies ran out for a few days, there were always amphetamines and heroin (or anything, anything) which the blacks of the nearby ghetto were quick to dispense. The Diggers did what they could to prevent locals from making a profit off the situation. This meant providing free services where possible, but they also tried to make life miserable for the merchants. They stole what they could and gave it away. They instituted a scheme (which never worked, surprise, surprise) whereby all proprietors, rock musicians, dealers, etc. would donate one per cent of their earnings to a Free Bank, from which anyone at all might draw funds. Also, they used their physical prowess and fierce grimaces (several were professional actors) to harass and cajole. One noted Digger, in his autobiography, claims the merchants approached him 'as if he were . . . John Garfield . . . That is to say, they showed him a condescendingly fearful respect.'

The difference was that the new John Garfield incarnations had been re-routed round the hallucinogens. As much as they despised the soap-bubble aspect of the drug charge, many of the Diggers had been unhinged by LSD. Yet they emerged wholly corporeal, insisting on a concept of man as 'meat' to counter the Learyesque thin-air disappearing act. LSD also gave them a more visionary cut, one which might have seemed like pure acid weirdness if they hadn't already been putting some of their ideas to work. If the community was microcosm, the planet became macrocosm, and the Diggers were among the first counter-cultural champions of the ecology. Where their language carried them out of the idea of the city it became futuristic: 'Reverse a colored city map to see Planetedge. Here the parks are blonde and black but the tenements are full of trees, BOTANICAL APARTMENTS . . . Live oak walls, branched eaves . . . Swaying bedrooms . . . Old timers remember planting their houses.'

It was something just short of hallucinogenic communism. Curiously, Winstanley had conceived his communism in a trance, during which a 'voice' called out to him: 'Work together, Eate Bread together, Declare this all abroad.' Winstanley expected his revelations to produce sweeping changes in human nature, a world of FREE, no one holding power over anyone else. The SF Diggers were also filled with righteous fervour, seeking to level *with* – if not simply level – the lying greed culture around them. One Digger Messiah believed that 'so much that should have been done in the Book of Revelations wasn't done and now had to be done, so there would finally be something new under the sun'. It would all come now via the familiar American method of rooting out the phoneys. The Diggers broke up left-wing conferences and community meetings whenever they had been invited to state their case. But they pushed neither violence nor peace, stressing that the only way to deal with the Power was to outfox it, not to cry on its shoulder for your rights or waste human energy trying to smash the State for the television audience.

The Diggers began from the notion that there was no success like failure, and despised especially the syndrome of revolution as achievement. They hated the pattern of desiring something and then proceeding to build structures (verbal and conceptual) between yourself and it. For them, the future could never be won; the only goal in life was tactical competence in the here and now. If you want it – it's yours; but you have to take it, not ask for it. The Left wouldn't touch it. There was a world to win. You could not build a revolution on the prospect of nothing to gain, nothing to applaud or sing for.

The Diggers felt that leftist protest was a thoroughly humiliating exercise by tear-jerking grovellers. By dramatizing the will to failure, they felt they were pointing up the preposterousness of the revolutionary spectacle. This was not nihilism, but rather the belief that personality could only expand at a level where it could not be tricked, where it had no illusions and where it could predict its own limits. Accordingly, they simply disappeared when the local conditions that bred them could no longer accommodate them.

One of their few culture-heroes was George Metesky, the gentle 'Mad Bomber' who placed thirty bombs in New York public buildings between 1940 and 1957 to express his grievances against the set-up. He claimed to have contracted TB while working for the Consolidated Edison Co. in 1931, when a gush of gas from a backfiring boiler hit him full face and filled his lungs. The company failed to compensate him, put his claim in their 'dead' files, and he spent the rest of his freedom in jobless seclusion with his two spinster sisters. In all his bomb notes he signed the initials 'FP' which, he explained to arresting policemen, stood for 'Fair Play'. He was caught after seventeen years and finally declared insane because he smiled all the time and freely admitted to all the details of his acts. In one of the letters he wrote to a New York newspaper before his capture, he said: '. . . my one consolation is – that I can strike back – even from the grave – for the dastardly acts against me.' The Diggers had fun with the Metesky image, even signing some of their leaflets with his name. They felt he had carried his protest to absurdity, playing it out for keeps. His one-man revolt was anonymous, effective for seventeen years and without presumption. In this spirit, the Diggers conceived of huge demonstrations that had no meaning at all. For the 1968 Presidential election they held a mock convention whose theme was 'Vote for Me' or 'A Vote for Me is a Vote for You', in challenge to the leftist call to get their troops out to Chicago to persecute the Democrats. If they had been locked out of the Great Society, they equally shunned its pretentious undoing.

Yet they could not anticipate the George Metesky syndrome that would shortly develop out of political frustration, where their failure game would be interpreted as luxury. Social impotence would drive the Left further into random acts of rage and discharge, working backwards – the fire-bomb arm swung back to fill the wide screen – from the striking point of grudge.

*

Mr (Kennedy)^2, Robert, convened his 1966 Senate subcommittee – looking into drug abuse – by slamming Dr T. Leary for not having warned America's youth soon enough against the hazards of LSD. It was an unfair crack seeing as how the Doctor always spoke highly of the 'erotic' promise of RFK's presidency. But the Senator from New York was determined to prevent 'future LSDs' from getting out of experimental laboratories and invading the sanctity of our campuses and ghettos.

RFK's remark was in reference to Leary's testimony one week earlier before yet another Senate subcommittee, this time Senator Dodd checking out the causes of juvenile delinquency. Tim – by now up to his Third Eye in court cases – felt compelled to declare that the use of psychedelic drugs was out of control. He suggested that there be college lab courses in LSD which might put an end to indiscriminate use. But there was a surprise guest sitting in on the televised (natch!) hearings who didn't appreciate the idea. 'What's going to happen to the boy who doesn't get to college? Are you going to offer high-school courses as well?' scowled Senator Edward Kennedy. The Doctor answered that that would have to be left to further research, and finally the peeved Mr (Kennedy)[3] broke in with: 'Mr Leary, I don't understand what you're talking about!'

Leary was shocked at the youngest Kennedy's hostility, for even the old reactionaries of the subcommittee had been polite. But EFK or TFK or whatever FK he was waxed indignant; he was surprised that health officials weren't more concerned about stamping out the Colourless Menace called LSD. It gave the lie to the Doctor's theory that there was hope in those politicians who were as yet pre-menopausal. If the sap of life still flowed in the vas deferens, he believed, then the juice of the ecstatic brain would not be long a-coming.

But the only sap was Leary himself. Aside from his cocksure grin which (Kennedy)[3] couldn't stand, he had gone and told the hearing that alcohol was more dangerous than LSD, one sure gauntlet thrown at the feet of the son of a millionaire whisky merchant, a Senator who is known to prefer his drop.

It was a lovely dream – cortical messages crackling between generations, hallucinatory power shared between governors and governed, the State in a state of grace, a psychedelic convention of these States – while it lasted. But the Pied Piper might now be led by his own flock who had outrun him and were moving to a stage he himself would reach four years later. They took the original adventure well beyond his Hindu dispositions, crawled out of his divine tunnel into tunnels of their own devising, of every shape and strategy, now lust, now terror, now the terror of lust and lust for the terrible, the Four Horsemen of the Apocalypse pushing cocaine, not to mention the arousal potential of distant yellow wars. And for every one of these aberrations there lurked a corresponding official suppression of it, tailor-made to cut off experience at the pass. The shudder in the synapse was now a war of nerves.

The American Wet Dream

Into the political prisoners' club at Lewisburg Federal Prison, Pennsylvania – here were Red Roundup captives like Alger Hiss, Harry Gold and David Greenglass (from the Rosenberg trial), Harvey Matusow and others – came an outsider. Most of the leftists had been in for several years already (it was 1957) and knew little of the controversy which chased him into their midst. One of the ordinary criminals – alerted by scandal sheets – wised up the others: 'It's the sex-box man!' Who? 'The sex-box man. He's got this box, see; it's an aphrodisiac. They go in there and fuck like rabbits!'

It was the public image of Wilhelm Reich and his Orgone Energy Accumulator. Reich claimed to have discovered the 'life energy' or 'orgone' which, when harnessed, could aid potency, stimulate sick tissue, provide healing for numerous aberrations of the human organism. The accumulators, large enough to hold an adult human being, were built so that orgone from the atmosphere would filter in through their walls and collect inside. The subject was usually naked so that the skin would more readily absorb the vital energy. This gave rise to rumours that Reich's science of orgonomy took its root in 'orgy', word and deed. The US Food and Drug Administration concluded the boxes were medical fraud and by 1954 had obtained an injunction against their use and distribution.

Arriving in the Promised America in 1939, Reich had hoped to continue his pioneering work in eliminating 'armouring' in human character and muscles, perpetuating the idea that sickness and unhappiness are caused by an inability to experience guiltless, loving, full-bodied orgasm. This carried its own political message: it was the purpose of nearly all political systems – in the maintenance of power – to encourage sexual fear and misery. Reich felt his discoveries would help to expose the cruel suppression of sexual instinct by the elders against children, adolescents and against their own natural desires. He promoted a 'sexual revolution' of the body against the body politic, one which required no violent over-throwings, but which would nonetheless render all aggressive authority null and void. He had once hoped that socialism could bring about this liberation but, he had finally grown disillusioned. Only the US, he believed, would prove to be progressive 'sex-politically', and he clung to the Old World image of American passion for scientific experiment. Such beliefs earned him the burning of his books and a season in the slams.

1

In the old people's home of protest you could already look back on that first date with psychedelic drugs as youthful folly. Even that fire had proved insufficient – in itself – to light the way in the personality pageant. At the same time, mounting American intervention in Indo-China made it difficult to reconcile *conscience* with continuation of the drop-out experiment. For a while the idea was promoted that acting *against* the war was the same as acting *in* it and accepting the premise of its grim reality. Initial anger had been directed at the 'immorality' of the conflict – a safe posture towards a distant holocaust. Now there was a massive call-up of men to reckon with. They were coming to take away the corporeal-You attached to the drugged-You, there on the eth-ereal plateau. Only with this implication of flesh – American flesh – did the South-East Asian War provoke an appropriate leftist response.

Matters of self continued to deflect the precision of a political analysis, confusing choice of tactic with questions of sensation and emotion. But there were some who argued that these were not distractions or side-issues; war or no war, there could be no peace *within the movement* as long as authoritarians, Puritans and male supremacists ruled the roost. The problem was compounded by the fact that the growing peace movement was not the domain of any one group, but gathered under its roof all the remnants in the leftist rag-bag as well as the flashy experimenters – all tooting their own horns. This was not merely an echo of old Stalinist–Trotskyite quarrels; life-styles were coming into opposition more than platforms. It was even possible to interpret the war, on one level, as a reaction against the growing emancipations of mind and body. Stubborn military escalation demonstrated machismo, sexual frustration gone lunatic and an insistence on public zombie-compliance – all targets of the 'cultural' revolution.

In the opening stages of this intra-movement battle, pacifism unquestionably held the upper hand. The non-violent Left had operated even in the midst of the drug movement, moving slowly out of civil rights into an involvement with the war. Its early demonstrations, around late 1964–early 1965, were of a calculatedly symbolic nature, still reflective of an inbred caution from the Red Scare. Actions at this point consisted of 'teach-ins' on numerous campuses to debate the issues and get them out of government-made closets; non-payment of that portion of income tax which went to finance the war (a gesture out of Thoreau), sporadic arrests and minor civil disobedience; theatrical displays linked to awareness of *The* Bomb. Since older liberals managed to promote an anti-Communist line, there was no support for the National Liberation Front of South Vietnam. The idea was to de-escalate and get America out, not to condemn its actions or give comfort to the 'enemy'. The younger groups were equally wary of provocative actions and positions. SDS continued to tread a careful path until well into 1967, even though it adopted the famous clenched fist salute (thinking tough) after its 1963 convention. The group's main concern throughout its early years was with 'consciousness-raising', working at a grass-roots level. It developed the Economic Research and Action Project (ERAP) which sent students into poor neighbourhoods to push for immediate reforms. That such social action was pointless as long as public funds were pumped into the war was not quickly apparent. The Free Speech Movement and its more militant offspring, the Vietnam Day Committee (VDC) in Berkeley, gave some fresh example for action; from 1965 SDS began to abandon its accent on domestic issues to concentrate on the war. But when the group's leaders called for mass resistance to the draft, in the middle of that year, the rank and file voted them down because such action would be 'illegal'.

The huge Vietnam Teach-In on the Berkeley campus in April 1965 proved to be a watershed. All colour of opinion assembled here to express solidarity, the first major gesture in building towards a new mass movement. But the speeches tended to demonstrate, instead, some sharp divisions. The famous baby doctor, Benjamin Spock, ignored the more immediate political reference and worked hard to remind folks of the probable incineration of us all via nuclear holocaust. We were teaching our kids (couldn't keep him off the subject) delusions about distant enemies and, in the course of it, 'losing our sense of reality'. The old socialist stand-by, Norman Thomas, jumped back even further out of date than Spock, baiting those ever-not-to-be-trusted Communists – with specific reference to the Viet Cong – while condescendingly mumbling about the 'so-called "new left"'. Others had a bash at fifties liberalism, some advocated non-violence and a return to the principles of Thoreau, a song-fest of oldies. There were very few calls to militant action of any kind and none to violence against the State. There was almost no anticipation of things to come in the next years except perhaps by Paul Potter, ex-President of SDS, who expressed the fear that the movement could be easily accommodated by the Power.

Yet despite the clear voice of yesterday booming over the throng, there was the germ of a feeling that such endless analysis-without-action was on the way out. After all, the event was staged in the not-yet-cooled-off precinct of the FSM demonstrations, and a distrust of compromise was in the air; there was a definite connection to be made. The universities played a major role in the war effort, developing sophisticated methods of mass murder in government-sponsored projects. Recruiters for officer material were an institution on campus, and napalm-pushers like Dow Chemical sought personnel openly within university confines. Moreover, explained FSM's Mario Savio at the Teach-In, students were a kind of home-grown Viet Cong – no one recognized their existence as a legitimate pressure group, nor would any of the big wheels negotiate with them. The same deaf and dumb State-machine doled out repression via military officers in Indo-China and university officials on campus. The smooth operation of that machine had to be thwarted at *all* levels, urged a statement issued by the VDC, for the war was no further away than FSM or Watts.

After this point the movement divided into distinguishing postures of 'peace' and 'anti-war', the one expressing concern, the other motion. All were agreed upon the new moral imperative of relating to the war and keeping the public aware of its atrocities. But it was still so distant, and verbal antidotes carried the experience even further off into abstraction.

On the New Left it was again Progressive Labor that set the tone for the future. Although incapable of any significant mobility, they dared to be pro-Viet Cong – outspokenly so – as early as 1964, advocating victory over the US aggressors. This was in line with their pro-Maoist/Albanian stand, and they proceeded to donate blood and solicit funds for the NLF throughout 1965. Naturally this earned them a second Command Performance before the Committee in its 1966 hearings on aid to the enemy in time of undeclared war. This was the HUAC's first foray into the Vietnam racket – proposing a bill which would make it an offence to give aid and comfort to the yellow peril – and they got a reaction worthy of the protest moment. The leftists were, of course, the usual smart-asses who gave Nazi salutes on being sworn in, scoring the Committee's 'racism', 'fascism', 'imperialism', you name it. Two brash witnesses almost begged to be asked the famous question, 'Are you now or have you ever been a member . . .' and blasted out their you-bet-your-sweet-ass-I-am replies before the inquisitors could finish the interrogative. A PL member, Steven Cherkoss, electrified with bravado, was one of the most ornery critters ever to face the witch-hunters. He leaped all over questions with a stream of rhetoric, read a long boring preamble to the PL Constitution (without interruption), told the Committee their days were numbered, that the American working class would rise up and take over, cutting imperialism off at the pass. The Chairman's set response (they *were* learning) was always something like: 'So, I take it you admit to being a member of the Comm—' and wham! – off Cherkoss would go again, a shower of revolutionary vomit bouncing off the air-conditioning, the Committeemen too mesmerized (or fast asleep) to pull out his plug. He certainly had the best HUAC exit line for ages, while being escorted out of stenographic hearing by US marshals: 'In the words of John Quincy Adams . . .'

But the Committee was keen to get a piece of the peace movement action, and was not about to be cowed into submission. Accordingly, it began to hit below the belt as it had done so brilliantly in the 1952-3 Hollywood investigations. It subpoenaed membership lists of anti-war groups from the top Red schoolhouse at Berkeley and the University of Michigan; both administrations obliged, although there was no strong compulsion to do so. But the real coup was the buying off of an ex-rebel named Phillip Abbott Luce (cheap at a measly thousand bucks!), an organizer of PL's Cuban trip. At the 1963 hearings on Cuba, Luce had shouted at the Committee: ' . . I believe along with Thoreau, Emerson and other people throughout American history that certain rules and regulations must be broken.' Now he was witnessing for the bad buys, giving names, talking against PL and revealing stories of arms caches and increased underground activity. Luce had been one of the most outspoken militant leaders of the movement, and was the first major New Left renegade in the Stalinist tradition.

SDS, too, was becoming more aggressive on the war, if not yet ready to flaunt the NLF flag as it later would. In April 1965 it organized a march on Washington against the wishes of its parent organization, the League for Industrial Democracy (LID), which still kept a fatherly eye on it and dropped a few pennies in the poor-box now and again. 30,000 people showed up, about three times the SDS expectation. This was a great boost for the group, and its ranks swelled in the next years, with hungry outsiders like PL and even the CP looking to make 'alliances'; LID flipped its lid at the prospect and waved a final good-bye. But even the new vanguard status of SDS failed to have much impact. Marches came and went by the dozens, and futile feet were getting restless. Joan Baez – still going steady with the struggle – announced, at the Washington Monument after a big march: 'I don't think the President gives a damn.' It wasn't until 1967 that

SDS reversed itself and voted to move out of protest into *resistance*. This meant shaking up military-industrial death vultures on campus, primarily Dow Chemical. But it was also the beginning of an effort to aid deserters and provoke mass action against the draft.

Still, the question remained of how to kick the verbal habit. Committees, resolutions, leaflets, petitions, talk-ins all seemed to pale against the implications of napalm. People were being raised to a pitch where only concrete action could release pent-up angers. One of the new strategies of Berkeley's Vietnam Day Committee was to attempt to stop troop trains on their way from the nearby Oakland Army Base to Vietnam-bound ships. The idea was to put your body on the line (literally). Protesters, among them Jerry Rubin, would stand or (more impressive) lie down on the rails, as in the old cliffhanger serials. On one occasion a phalanx of coppers walked in front of the train, bashing peace creeps out of the way as they went. After that, they saved time and manpower by instructing the engineer to keep going no matter what. The engine bore down at ten m.p.h., scattering folks like flies although, on one dramatic demonstration, two people jumped only at the very last second while the locomotive ripped their home-made banner in two. Attorney-General Ramsey Clark pointed out that since the demonstrators knew the trains would not stop, they must surely be in it for the publicity. But finally, on another occasion, a protester managed to get on the train and pulled the airbrake, stopping its forward motion. Jerry Rubin puffed: 'We were victorious warriors. We were ecstatic . . . We stopped the War Machine dead in its tracks.'

Symbolism was still the order of the day, on or off the rails. The Berrigan priests poured napalm on the records of a local draft board, and Barry Bondhus of Minnesota outclassed them by doing a similar number with two buckets of grade-A shit. But LBJ could always do it better – and un-symbolically – heaping up charcoal-broiled gooks like steerburgers. Eventually, American flesh responded. In March 1965 a University of Kansas student cut his wrists to stop the war. Others, more practical, cut their wrists at draft examinations to avoid Uncle Sam's greetings. Then, in November, a Quaker named Norman Morrison sprinkled himself with kerosene and lit up right in front of the Pentagon. Morrison showed no signs of mental disturbance in his lifetime, only a deep 'concern' over the immorality of the war. In the prayer service for him a fellow Quaker pointed out that pricking a finger on a pin is more painful than the *idea* of Buddhists burning in Saigon. Only the body could grasp it. Morrison, naturally, achieved nothing in his act outside his own brief experience of it – except perhaps to show that the Indo-China genocide was chiefly a war against the human body, symptomatic of the building of a Silent Majority at home, cold and wholly out of touch.

2

All the opening shots against the war ricocheted, producing anxiety and further feelings of impotence within the peace movement. This tension, as usual, was now directed back into the Left where radicals could proceed to take their frustrations out on one another. But this time the rift was dynamic, a far cry from the normal petty squabbling. In the main, the war was conceived – and to some extent directed – by Ivy League professors, corporate executives and Kissinger brain-types, all devoted to a better, more *manageable* America – as was the liberal Left. All these – and to a large extent, the New Left – were united by similar codes of morality and social demeanour. Only by distinguishing themselves from the spirit of decency and reform – which nonetheless tolerated racism and genocide – could radicals ever bring the Left to a climactic divide. The drug experience had already brought matters close to a following of instincts, but it was becoming clear that this was the *meaning* as well as the method of the new revolt. The shunning of 'reason' and 'good taste' signified another step in the long American search for natural impulse.

This was a revolutionary dialogue anticipated some thirty years earlier by Wilhelm Reich. Little had changed in the nature of leftist organizations since Reich's Communist activity in Germany in the early thirties. Uptight comrades tended to get more entrenched and authoritarian because they could not see the key role played by personal liberation in the political struggle. Reich ultimately came at revolution from a complex biological viewpoint, and his *direct* influence on later movements is accordingly small. But his works form the most powerful frame for the 'sexual revolution' that occurred in the late sixties in America, although his original ideas were changed drastically to suit the American temperament.

Reich – a star pupil of Freud's – began with the idea that a neurotic symptom showed a misdirected anxiety, the root memory of which had to be traced, usually in psychoanalysis. But instead of concentrating on the symptom, Reich observed the entire character structure that housed it. He believed that compulsive habits and social postures always express a sexual energy which has not been properly released in orgasm. Character itself is a substitution for the natural flow of bodily feeling, and Reich considered it as an illness. The body forms defensive blocks – called 'character armour' – to protect against psychic pain inflicted by the outside world, but also against its own inmost desires (as society demands). Later, he insisted that this armouring was not so much a function of character as of the muscles. The body is a sensitive retainer of psychic impressions – usually learned in childhood – and expresses these in the form of muscular rigidity.

Breaking through the armour is a stepping-stone to liberation, to 'orgastic potency', a total, involuntary convulsion of all the muscles, releasing defensive tension. Just before orgasm, energy concentrates in the genitals; the greater the concentration, the higher the pleasure. On discharge, the excitement flows back from the genital 'centre' to the 'periphery' (the rest of the body), ending in relaxation and renewed vitality. A true Reichian orgasm (not merely ejaculation) has to be free of anxiety, otherwise energy is directed 'back into the self' instead of outward, in effect, *at* the world.

Unarmoured beings are called 'genital characters', open to all sensations of joy and pain. But few are so naturally endowed. Getting there means proper use of the body's energy resources, breathing and muscular apparatus. Reich provided therapeutic answers which changed along with the major phases of his thought: strict 'character analysis' (roughly 1923–34); the relief of muscular rigidity (vegeto-therapy, 1934); the discovery of the orgone (1934–9). One through-line in all these phases (and in the techniques of Reich's latter-day disciples) is a dynamic theatricality. This therapy is still practised in the US and provides a real alternative to psychoanalysis. The latter is wholly dependent on words, on the patient sputtering forth his traumatic autobiography to a *detached* analyst; it has all the attributes of cunning seduction. Reich was a bold rapist. If illness was bound up in the total character, nothing less than an assault on bodily gestures and defensive postures would suffice. The Reichian doctor is a full actor in the drama and is as aggressive as the physical response he wants to elicit. He ruthlessly attacks the armoured areas, calling attention to defences time and time again, tearing down any phoney sense of self-control or insincerity he may see. Reich believed that a patient who seems calm and untroubled is often hiding something, and that his imperturbability is itself a signal of trouble inside.

Reich's early character-analytic method did not cure so much as give the person an objective view of his own armour, experiencing it as a foreign body in need of purging. Later Reichians concentrated on the body, manipulating key centres of tension, e.g. neck muscles, all the while encouraging full breathing, leading the patient through stages of sensation. The experience can be excruciating, and the victim is taught to give vent to his pain by screaming, crying or letting any other natural reaction come out. Once the chink in the armour appears, the patient's naked rage is often turned at the nearest receiver – the Doc. Some early Reichians resorted to using dummies to prevent violence against themselves: 'Today the patient threw the dummy on the floor, stomped on its belly and then put it back on the examining table and choked it. Loud screaming accompanied all of these actions. The second time he . . . began kicking its shins and pushing its head upwards . . . The third time . . . he looked at me while pounding the dummy. It appeared that this was to indicate to me that it was *me* he was pounding on.'

Towards the end of the therapy (possibly years), when attention is usually directed towards loosening the uptight pelvis, the drama reaches climax. Here the therapist asks for constant shimmying of groin and buttocks, accompanied by full breathing, attempting to bring about what Reich called the 'orgasm reflex'. A spasm of the full muscular structure – with the pudenda as centre of gravity – is simulated on the doctor's cot. The patient supposedly has brought his body to the point where it can break out in uninhibited convulsions and *act out* sexual intercourse – sans partner – in therapy.

Health is the revolution. An unarmoured person has the power of 'self-regulation', which means he follows his natural impulses rather than social morality. Reich believed that failed sexual potency leads to a lack of self-confidence and submissiveness, allowing aggressive types to take power because they supposedly have superior knowledge and moral awareness. But this is an unnatural process propagated by authority itself to keep its control; if people were more self-regulating, the State would be in trouble. This was a world-view rooted in the natural goodness and innocence of human beings, the idea that primary instincts are joyful, while destructive ones have to be learned. Here Reich's road diverged unalterably from Freud's, and the distinction is the key to each man's impact on the American Left. Freud held that moral codes, shame, guilt were inherent factors in personality, and against his own 'pleasure principle' he pitted the 'reality principle', designed to let the external world have the final say over the course of individual desire. In 1929 he adopted the view that civilization *needed* the suppression of certain impulses if it was to flourish, that excess sexual energy should be diverted towards more ennobling goals in the service of society: 'The liberty of the individual is not a benefit to culture.' Reich, on the other hand, felt that Freud simply accepted an authoritarian *status quo*, failing to see that 'the ruling class has a reality principle which serves the perpetuation of its power'. He also claimed that guilt, sadism, sin, as well as Freud's later idea of a 'death instinct' in man were 'secondary drives', perversions by authority of natural feelings.

Fear of being free, that is, inflexibility of the body, can be expressed as aggression and sadism as well as submissive introversion. People who take out their sexual aggressions on others, whether viciously or in the name of social welfare (i.e. anti-pornography committees), have been stricken with something Reich calls the 'emotional plague'. This sickness is manifested everywhere, and is the major prop of authoritarianism. Fascism is the 'basic emotional attitude of the suppressed man of our authoritarian machine civilization and its mechanical-mystical conception of life'. The State maintains power by advocating the 'atrophy of the sexual apparatus' through compulsive morality. This social 'anchoring' takes place in the first four or five years of life, where the 'pleasure principle' is massaged into conformity by the pressures of authority (Don't touch!). Morality calls this *self-control* and gives it reference to 'honour', 'duty' and other frozen postures. When these compulsions are assimilated by the child (in Communist as well as capitalist countries) the result is character-prison, the turning off of the orgastic tap and – top of the list – paralysis of the will to rebel.

'Mysticism' is a central weapon in the continuing war on free sexuality (into adolescence and adulthood). Religion not only insists on abstinence for perpetuation of its power, but religious fervour itself is a sexual substitute. False excitations are also brought about through sport (football is a breeding-ground for reactionaries), rallies, heroes, leaders, marches, as well as the *sentimentality* to be found in the 'behavior of the audience at a third-rate musical'. In this last business, the wool is pulled over the spectators' eyes as their brains are addled and eros stimulated to ungratified frustration, gushing an orgasm of programmed tears, inducing hypnosis while social institutions (marriage, family, chastity, etc.) are reinforced: e.g. *The Sound of Music* as a fascist epic.

The primary reinforcer is the family. The State propagandizes marriage and family, and the family in turn recapitulates the authoritarian function in the home. This follows the usual means: suppression of genital sexuality in the child, who then becomes compliant to all bosses from daddy on up. Reich felt the Oedipus Complex played a major role here, for certainly the very first DON'T TOUCH required by society is the taboo on relations with the mother. In adolescence the child is prepared for bourgeois marriage through propaganda about monogamy. This of course requires the further clampdown on natural sexual urges so that the structural cycle can begin again. The young marrieds are then fed the myth that sexuality is a by-product of procreation (Reich believed the opposite to be true) so they can get on with the 'marital obligations racket'.

Reich felt there was no hope for revolution as long as the bourgeois family persisted. Simple rebellions of sons against fathers were meaningless unless 'that human structure which craves a Führer' could be eliminated. He saw no chance of the elders bringing this about. They were already armoured and pre-conditioned, obsessed with stability of economy, social order and their own 'self-respect' as leaders of the family unit. In all his work Reich never seems to have addressed the sexual needs of the old or middle-aged, merely scoring their 'fear of youth's sexuality' or denouncing the anxiety-sex they practised. All his hopes rested with the 'child of the future', to whom he dedicated his last books and whom he endowed with a mystical grace: 'Its eyes sparkle with a gentle glow and look into the world with a quiet, deep gaze. It is soft in its touch of hands. It can stroke so that the stroked one begins to radiate his own life energy.' From his earliest Marxist days he championed children's rights, and the scope of his vision is still decades ahead; any revolutionary movement would be at pains to catch and match it. Genitality in young children must be utterly respected, i.e. no restrictions on mastur-bation or healthy sex-play with other children. Adolescents, upon reaching puberty, must have free rein (not to mention encourage-ment) for their desires. He saw little hope of this coming about naturally, nor was his programme of sex education – designed to limit the authority of the parent – quite enough. Such protection had to be legally binding and, to this end, he lobbied the US Congress in 1942 and 1952. The second time he sent a proposal 'On Laws Needed for the Protection of Life in Newborns and of Truth', which would provide protection for kids against 'emo-tionally sick mothers and other sick individuals'. This revolution-ary notion also contained a bit of later obsessional Reich, wanting to *prosecute* what he called the 'biopathic individual' for not telling the 'truth' to children.

Reich's theories of sexuality, especially as they relate to the biological freedom of children, brought him persecution from psychoanalytic communities and public administrations, but also gained him the malice of the Left. A dedicated Communist and Party worker, he was sent packing from the German CP (and the Danish CP – while in exile there – which he claimed he never joined) the minute his sexual politics became too hot for the commissars. This hurt Reich deeply and his later work is filled with bitter diatribe against the 'Red Fascists'.

Reich was a threat to the Party because he exposed the vapidity of social theory which paid little heed to personal needs. The fascists gained the love of the masses because they knew how to manipulate the more perverse compulsions for strong daddies and erotic substitutions; only when the Left could learn to appeal to people's healthy sexuality would it gain a mass base. To the argument that sex was a private matter and did not concern the organization, Reich countered that anything which preoccupied a comrade, such as sexual frustration, interfered with good political work. Furthermore, most comrades really joined the Party in search of a partner, and many dropped out because of its Puritanism and the rigours of discipline. The kind of problems he worked at in his 'sex-political' clinics, and which he hoped the Party would also tackle, included: the abolition of homosexual laws; free abortion with no 'social' reasoning necessary; the dissolution of compulsive marriage; the availability of contraceptives, again with no excuses of a social nature; nurseries in factories; sex education courses; finding a compromise between Communist asceticism and bourgeois glamour, for the sake of women; most important, the establishing of housing conditions conducive to happy intercourse (as opposed, say, to the back seat of a car).

Upheavals in economy were not enough. He was sceptical of '. . . the suppression of liberties unlivable in a trap, and the Unions for Civil Liberties within the trap . . . so-called "progressives" who fought and suffered and died at the gallows for advocating more freedom within the trap.' Nothing short of sweeping social and personal liberation could produce the Glad State. Yesterday's tactics also had to go. Reich was especially wary of political 'shouting', a simulated discharge of protest at the emotive vocal level. He fantasized that in the great revolutions where Russian peasants or American pioneers gained their own freedom, a purified silence accompanied their acts. Slogans had no value unless they were calm and concrete. *All* sex-energy substitutes would have to be eliminated for the revolution to succeed. Music and marching and political rallies were damaging because they misused vital bodily resources, and also served to fortify ideas of discipline and leader-following: '. . . children and adolescents will march just as happily to fascist music tomorrow as they march to liberal music today'.

Above all, Reich bashed at the stifling morality of the Left which – through 'good' motives – strengthened repression and preserved the social order. He saw a classic leftist tale in the changeover from Leninism to Stalinism, from passion to bureaucracy. Unless *health* became a guideline, old forms of patriarchy, male chauvinism and symbolic child murder would be carried over after the revolution. A new society would pass the burden of regulation on to the individual who would learn to live without leaders and authority-codes; only anti-social destructive acts would be governed from outside the person. Reich called this harmony of nature and culture 'life-affirmative'; he believed it could work if there were no recourse to *conscience* or fears of ethical chaos. There was no chance of this Utopian vision being applied by the 'vulgar Marxists' who, by the late thirties, were no better than reactionaries for him; nor could the liberals, those most character-armoured of ladies and gents, carry forwards the revolution in their horse-drawn cart of reform. Naturally, he placed his naïve future in the hands of the kids. 1946: '. . . in the course of thirty years the human race will have been biologically renewed; it will come into the world without any trace of fascist distortion.'

In the American late forties Reich was too wrapped in his cosmic engineering to notice the subtle cultural shift taking place in the midst of the Red Scare. Where he had argued for getting out of the 'trap', the newer social 'reform' was designed for the better management of impulses, to make life more comfortable and efficient. Reich had once believed that psychoanalysis would undermine middle-class ideology by exposing its most repressed secrets. But now it had adapted itself to re-integrating the individual with the social set-up and seeing that he did not rock the boat. This view – studded with principle and conscience – was a cornerstone of American bourgeois liberalism.

The protest movement of the thirties had been spawned, for the most part, in households lorded over by crack-the-whip European daddies and 'don't make trouble' mammas; in the streets, the air stank of chastity propaganda aimed at keeping children in fear. Now these gave way to a new spirit of 'enlightenment' in child-rearing. It was understood that overt threats to child welfare and clampdown on desire could induce submission, but also a powder-keg situation. The new social engineering needed both the stick of authoritarian fear and the carrot of liberalized culture.

Enter Dr Spock. From his earliest government-published pamphlets in the mid-forties, the famous baby doctor gained his reputation for creating the 'permissive' attitude towards bringing up children. But nowhere along the line is he out of step with the process of turning out 'good citizens'. Many of his pearls of wisdom are descended from Freud, but these never appear to be part of an overview of childhood. Spock's concern is that Mom knows how to deal with each crisis as it comes, what not to say in reproach when Junior wee-wees the bed, and so forth. 'It is better to say nothing to the child about masturbation', or '. . . some remark such as "People don't think it is very polite."' You curb the little rebel with love and understanding, not with harsh discipline.

Speaking to children two years or so before puberty he warns of '. . . nature . . . saying "Whoa! Before you can be trusted with a powerful body and full-grown instincts, you must first learn . . . to control your wishes and instincts for the sake of others . . . understand the laws of conduct in the world outside your family . . ."' Mom is not likely to question the Doc when he attributes to a child's 'nature' what is nothing more than his own middle-aged puritanical bias.

After the Spock child has learned in school 'how to get along in the world', he is ready for his teenage, a time when he must begin to discover his place. As for sex–Spock's ideal adolescence, as of *1970*, was: no 'dating' until sixteen or seventeen; no 'petting' until you are 'going steady' for at least a year and confident of each other's love; nothing beyond kissing and embracing until there is a firm commitment to marriage (after yet another year); then, after two full years – and only after eighteen years of age – you better watch out, kids: 'The touching of breasts and genitals even through the clothes is much more exciting and is likely to carry you beyond the point where you can use judgement.' Now you are ready for the penultimate experience in the Spockean universe – a workable marriage and its inevitable offspringing. And, as the cycle begins over again, the Grand Comforter churns out his 'don't-worry' wisdom: a young boy will form a dependence on you, Mom – let it be; a child will gain all its notions of the Ideal from its glorification of the parent – let it be; from this he intuits the pattern of necessary authority and benevolent social leadership – encourage it. 'This web of idealizations sustains the whole community . . .' Daddy, Boss, Sergeant, President.

Spock's massive influence, especially in the forties and fifties (more paperbacks sold than Jesus), puts him up as kingpin to popular child-rearing and invests him – *ipso facto* – with *political* power. Of course, there is no questioning his political intentions. He makes it perfectly clear he believes in regaining the 'higher values' America lost, along with its belief in the dignity of man. He hopes to make whole individuals out of shipwrecks and build a society of peace and 'brotherly love'. Towards this mini-Utopia, he never says 'you mustn't' without providing further explanation, and never *demands* self-control and abstinence; he merely helps you understand why these are good for you.

Spock demonstrates the liberal tactic by which the promise of a sexual revolution could be distracted. Spock-babies were already pushing puberty at the time of the Red Roundup, and were not especially viewed as a threat to the red, white and blue-tinged future. The Doctor's books would not be burned.

Reich's were. His discovery of the 'orgone', the basis on which he lost his scientific standing and eventually came to trial ('mad scientist' v. sane State) was a logical outcome of his early work. If the entire muscular structure was convulsed on orgasm impact, followed by relaxation and renewed excitation of the body, surely this must be the function of something more than semenal fluid. The energy which gathered in orgasm and then re-filled the body with health he called 'orgone energy'. It was in the air like all-pervasive 'ether' and could be seen through scientific devices and sometimes with the naked eye (spots in front of eyes, etc.), always manifested blue. All factors of living conformed to this universal.

His renegade Marxism and renegade Freudianism had never provided Reich's detractors with a convincing rebuttal to his crusade for full genitality. Now they had it: he was simply a 'madman' and the sexual revolution only a pre-orgone lunatic fancy.

In February 1954 the Food and Drug Administration slammed an injunction on Reich and his fellow-therapists who had established a research centre called Organon near the town of Rangeley, Maine. Reich ignored the injunction and in March it came into effect. It stipulated that all Orgone Energy Accumulators were to be destroyed, along with all written matter pertaining to them or mentioning the *existence* of orgone energy. In April 1956 Reich was summoned on a charge of contempt of court for ignoring the injunction. He refused to appear, arrogantly stating that scientific truth was not a matter to be debated in courtrooms. Three days later he was arrested and brought to trial in Portland, Maine. His defence was typically self-aggrandizing (and fraught with the atmosphere of the American B-movies he loved so well): he said he resisted FDA agents by shooting at them as they tried to gain access to his land; he had instructed all the men at Organon to tote 45s, and even asked one to dig a grave for him since he was prepared to die resisting. He was given a two-year jail sentence, fined $10,000 and told that the conditions of the injunction would now be carried out. By 1957, the higher courts had turned down his appeal.

Although Reich's trial seemed a straightforward contempt proceeding, there were many questions it left unanswered. The FDA first investigated the accumulator in 1947, and yet took seven years before it built a clear-cut case on interstate commerce statutes. At the time of the trial there were only about 150 accumulators in existence, and these were yielding Reich almost no profit. They were used in treating cancer patients, in the hope that orgone could revive sick tissue; but Reich made it clear that this was purely experimental and that he could claim no definite cure. At most, the accumulators were a 'fraud' on the public, but certainly caused no harm – not nearly as much as electro-shock therapy – nor was any scientific evidence presented against them. Why seven years and several million dollars in man-hours and procedural expenses to bust a supposedly empty box? Finally, no explanation can whitewash the burning of Reich's books and pamphlets. Originally, only those which referred to the accumulator were to be destroyed; but FDA officials seized copies of earlier works, *Character Analysis*, *The Sexual Revolution*, *The Function of the Orgasm*, *The Mass Psychology of Fascism* – which make no mention of the orgone box – and incinerated these along with the others in two shifts in 1956 and 1960.

The future may show that the harassment of Reich was nothing more than the prancing of some power-starved bureaucrat. But the date of the event cannot be overlooked; Reich was surely a victim – if only indirectly – of the national mood of the Nixon-McCarthy era. There is no evidence of any government plot to silence him (after all, his work was scarcely known in the US at the time), and yet, in an age when the Conspiracy Theory became an American way of life, when the nastiest, most *unimaginable* plots were plotted, who can be sure that the promised 'children of the future' did not strike a note of apprehension in the corridors of public authority? It is almost unthinkable that such a a trial and a *book-burning* could have occurred at any other time. Reich was naturally branded a Communist, but the Red Scare fear of weirdos and men with extraordinary ideas stretched well beyond political bounds. There were rumours of patients being masturbated in the accumulators, and that Organon and orgone and orgastic potency were really Soviet-inspired codes.

Reich was also a victim of the Red myth through his own fantasies. He felt the 'conspiracy' against him was directed by Moscow, whose agents in the Food and Drug Administration were out to steal his secrets and so deprive the US of the benefits of orgone. He repeatedly reduced his trial proceedings to paranoia, referring to the arresting agents as 'Beria-type hoodlums' and pointing out – in unconscious imitation of McCarthy's 'numbers-racket' – that 200 'traitors' had recently been cleaned out of the Department of Health and Welfare which was linked bureaucratically to the FDA (as if this fact could prove conspiracy). His late writings spoke of 'Chinese Red Devils' and he even stooped to the clandestine-Commie syndrome by exhorting the CP 'snipers' (i.e. FDA men) to come out of the 'BUSHES'. His disciples were often worse in this respect, not at all above the fashionable character assassination of the historical moment. When a woman journalist denounced Reich and the accumulator in a noted leftish periodical, one orgonomist retorted that she '... wrote the article primarily on behalf of a certain political party whose basic tactics is slander and defamation; she published it in the *New Republic*, then under the editorship of Henry Wallace, about whose loyalties the American public no longer has any doubts whatsoever.'

Reich's American-dreaming and flag-waving now linked him with the reactionaries he hated, and he even believed his work was being secretly patronized by Eisenhower and the US Air Force. He proposed to change the name of the HUAC to the 'Congressional Committee to Safeguard the Process Toward Self-Government'. Here '. . . only the people who are *right* . . . will fight the CP, and not the wrongminded people, who are clearly *against* self-rule *themselves*. We shall no longer feel embarrassed to sympathize with the exposure of spies and destroyers of human freedom as we do at present.' Above all, he felt that America was 'life-affirmative' and that Nixon-McCarthyism was only a temporary blight – inspired by Stalin – on the Statue of Liberty.

Reich's relation to the era is further characterized by the silence/ complicity of the liberal-intellectual community at his demise. Only the American Civil Liberties Union and a few scattered writers protested at the burning of his books, and there was virtually no public outrage at his jail sentence. True, 1956 was hardly the time to come to the defence of an enemy of the State. Also, the importance of his early work – which might have brought him more respect – was not nearly so well known as the orgone publicity (which was Reich's own fault). No doubt his own voluminous arrogance and paranoid obsessions got him few fans outside his own worshipping devotees. Yet, it may be that those Left-leaning people who damned him and then clammed up at the outrage against him were distressed at the very real possibility of the sexual revolution breaking out in their very schools and living-rooms. Some of these *had* read Reich and saw him as a threat; they knew the children's revolt could never topple the Power, but it could wobble Daddy's authority and also divide the Left down the middle. It may have then been too early to fear orgy-freaks breaking up civil-rights symposiums and fornicating in the aisles. But they did fear that life was on the verge of becoming unmanageable.

Ironically – in his own peculiar way – Reich expressed similar apprehension: 'Like an arrow released from the restraining, tightly tensed spring, the search for quick, easy and deleterious genital pleasure will devastate the human community.' He always insisted that the orgastic life must be free of rape, child-molesting, motherfucking, exhibitionism, perversion, obscenity, pornography (or any fantasy attendant on these). So worried was he about being taken for an advocate of ordinary 'free love' that he re-named the sexual experience the 'genital embrace', a reaching-out past the partner towards the world, space, everything. He created a holy war of – in his own terminology – 'love' against 'fucking', in which he himself assumed the role of Christ who 'abhorred the dirty fuck out of nowhere into nothingness'. At his death, Reich feared that anarchy might be pulled by mistake from his magic hat, and despaired the sexual nightmare he sensed approaching as 'the fucker chaos'.

He got it.

3

The American version of the 'sexual revolution' – dependent as it was on the social peculiarities of the late sixties – was bound to outrun a complex strategy like Reich's. Some leftists tended to believe – in keeping with WR's thinking – that the Indo-China War was a demonstration of repressed eroticism gone sadistic. But with its unthinkable skin atrocities, it seemed even more expressive of *anti*-sexual trends in American life – urbanization, mechanization, religious revival, the push into body-warping drugs. On the home front, the middle class was building its war counterpart in the form of a pornographic epidemic, a rash of pudenda magazines and massage masturbation parlours, frustrated sex-radio dialogues between fantasy merchants and aching housewives. All this was a totalitarian purgatory known as the 'permissive society' in which the State was kind enough to *permit* you to follow through on your own desires, only to lumber you with guilt and anxiety afterwards.

On the 'healthy' side of the coin, the sixties heightened the tendency for getting 'in touch' with other beings. This took the form of sensitivity-training and body seminars, demonstrating a slight trend away from psychoanalysis, cutting through the fat of words to the 'real' of the flesh. Also, alongside the growing political movement (and often in intercourse with it) sprang Sexual Freedom Leagues, more or less orchestrated orgies, the new moral imperative of removing your clothes in public (requiring the *act* of removal – not merely nudity in itself), gonorrhoea gone-awry and a general openness of mind and aperture.

The political 'awakening' of the sixties was fraught with all the pain of tough body therapy. It was full of rage and Reich's hated 'shouting', employing sexuality as a weapon rather than using it to understand the proper distribution of body energy. It was primarily sexual *rebellion*, convulsive and exhibitionistic, full of rampant scatology and pubic publicity. In 1970 the President's Task Force on Pornography and Obscenity claimed that the new wave of filth 'strongly parallels the rise of certain extremist groups of nihilists in America', mentioning only SDS in this context. But the State was not the prime receiver of all the new shit-slinging. It was for war inside the stodgy household of the Left, meant to be rubbed on Daddy's liberal grey-flannel suit. What the spirit of reform represented politically it expressed through repressions of the body; the new political in-fighting was first and foremost a swift kick to the older movement's groin. It was by no means the rational orgastic revolt Reich dreamed; it was *orgiastic*, obscene with a malice, deliberately offensive and teasing, full of the thrill of watching the old guys squirm. Jerry Rubin: 'We were dirty, smelly, grimy, foul, loud, dope-crazed ... a public display of filth and shabbiness, living in-the-flesh rejects of middle-class standards ... We pissed and shit and fucked in public...'

This threw the anti-war movement into further schism. The New Left had provoked ideological crises but had basically kept to the optimism, morality and cleanliness of the liberals. Together with the older well behaveds these carried the banner of conscience as far as they could in the midst of the rising sexual rave-up. In 1968 Dr Spock and several clergymen, writers and young teachers deposited hundreds of draft cards – collected at numerous rallies – with the Justice Department. Spock had joined the peace movement in the early days of S A N E, fearing that *The* Bomb would deprive all those Spock-babies of their idyllic adolescence. Now, to the astonishment of the Moms of America, he was busted and brought to trial for conspiracy to aid the draft resistance. In the courtroom, middle America expressed its delusion that Spock was responsible for their over-permitted kids turning weird and rebelling. The prosecution's closing argument: 'As there may come a time in the government of individual families where permissiveness goes beyond the bounds of reason, so, also, there comes a time in the government of nations when duly constituted authority must assert itself and face up to unwarranted challenges.' Spock argued for the right of 'symbolic speech' provided for by the First Amendment, which he hoped to stretch so as to include counselling young men against taking up arms. His challenge was against the 'immorality' of the war, he pleaded, and his sorrow was for the loss of American prestige in the world. But the Government had taken care to see that there were only fathers on the jury. Their conviction was later overturned in the higher courts.

It was not conscience's last stand, but purist protest was being momentarily pushed into the background. Many old-timers would have nothing to do with the movement now that the 'crazies' were getting into the act, and simply beat a retreat, dragging their shopworn strategies with them. Body politics and pleasure were winning the protest day. For the first time since the pacifist takeover of the Left in the early sixties, revolution-making lost the millstone of personal sacrifice.

The newer political therapy was based on *gesture*, the *look* of the action. In previous leftist strategy, the meaning of any single manoeuvre was at least bound up with (or gave lip service to) a broader theoretical or moral purpose. Now the emphasis was wholly on the expression itself, and its only wider 'reason' was self-satisfaction; you might now demonstrate for just a thrill. A line-up of arrogant Black Panthers in leather jackets, bandoleros, Magnum rifles, black berets on blossoming Afros and dark dark frowns said more and gained more young Panthers than their excellent Party programme ever could.

This Politics of Gesture, relying on individual exhibitionism, gave a massive boost to the leftist star system. Among its most exposed celebrities and manipulators of the new spontaneity was Jerry Rubin. Rubin had been through the Free Speech Movement, awakening there out of short-hair consciousness and a liberal heritage. He had been moving slowly out of traditional Left postures, seeing his real breakaway come at the 1967 march on the Pentagon: 'I was furious at the censorship within the Peace Movement. All over forty, they were planning a demonstration in which young kids, fifteen to twenty-five, would shed their own blood and go to jail, another one of those scenes where the old motherfuckers are on the platform and the kids in the stands.' One of the factors which divided the gestural freaks from the older and more rooted leftists at this event was the idea some of the former had of levitating the Pentagon by mystic incantation, then exorcizing its demons while it was air-bound. The old-timers didn't wait around for it to happen. After their speeches, most of them rushed back to their chartered buses and sped home, leaving the young militants to take on the police.

Rubin and others, like Abbie Hoffman, fancied they saw political potential in the swarms of LSD-takers, but realized these would have to be engaged theatrically, on the already generated level of costume, hair and exhibition. They formulated the Youth International Party (Yippies), consciously exploiting media vicariousness and public thrill-seeking. They held a mass Festival of Spring in the 'main ballroom' of New York's Grand Central Station, complete with jelly beans and popcorn, removing the hands from the station clocks and painting peace symbols instead. They also rained down dollar bills from the balcony of the Wall Street Stock Exchange while marketeers panicked and stampeded below.

The 1968 Democratic Convention in Chicago was the major proving-grounds for the Politics of Gesture. A 'Festival of Life' was announced for the streets to oppose the 'death' politics inside the convention hall. The Yippies nominated a pig (called Pigasus) for President, parading him through the streets and vowing to eat him after he won the nomination. They distributed leaflets promising that 'several hundred Yippie friends with press passes will gorge themselves on 800 pounds of cocktail onions and puke in unison at the nomination of Hubert H. Pastry.'

To everyone's amazement, these inventions touched an exposed nerve somewhere and were taken seriously. The famous Blood-In staged by the Chicago police – thoroughly out of proportion to the threat posed by the demonstrators – cannot be attributed simply to the brutality of that notorious gendarmerie. Chicago was filled with old-timers, peace-creeps, liberal Democrats, most of whom were thoroughly disillusioned with the party, many of whom had thrown their support behind Eugene McCarthy's candidacy. The Democrats, led by H. H. Humphrey, needed desperately to solidify their strengths and win back their splinter groups. But the circus in the streets brought them to a peak of humiliation, spoiling any shred of hope for a mass leftist reconciliation. Moreover, the gestural freaks were holding up a teasing mirror to the fading of both their ideals and their sexuality. It was one thing to be shouted down politically and have your meetings busted up by idiot-children, wholly another to be publicly mocked for personal frustrations. If the rage of the police was not directly brought on by the liberals and high-ranking Democrats, it was certainly sanctioned by approving silence or feeble protestations.

Rubin was one of eight men of differing leftist temperament and persuasion to be indicted for conspiracy in the Chicago affair.

His response was characteristic: 'I realize the competition was fierce, and I congratulate the thousands who came to Chicago. I hope that I am worthy of this great indictment, the Academy Award of Protest.' He was also summoned for a Committee encore. In the 1966 hearings on aid to the Viet Cong, Rubin had appeared in a uniform from the American Revolution, carrying parchment copies of the Declaration of Independence (he never got a chance to testify). But this seemed too *clear* a protest against the denial of founding principles. In October 1968 he appeared before the HUAC wearing Viet Cong pyjamas, bells, a toy M-16 rifle, his bare chest exhibiting nipples painted with psychedelic designs. He was motivated this time by sheer orneryness, as was cohort Abbie Hoffman, dressed in an American flag shirt, swinging a yo-yo.

Also brought before the Committee in these hearings were movement leaders Tom Hayden, Rennie Davis and Dave Dellinger. Dellinger, an elder pacifist-militant, demonstrated his generational bias by invoking the name of Hitler and likening the HUAC to a Nazi tribunal. Symbolically, his testimony was interrupted by the Chairman announcing that Mr Rubin was outside, dressed as Santa Claus, asking to be admitted to the hearing room (he was not). Hayden and Davis came out of structured New Left positions, the former having drafted the Port Huron Statement as an ex-president of SDS. Theirs were still strategies of theory and language, although both had travelled extensively in North Vietnam and had coordinated the militant Chicago demonstrations. They had only neck-length hair and flashed no beads but it was obvious their politics had been touched by the personality upheavals, and they tried to give voice to what the inarticulate Rubin implied with his looks. Davis threatened the Committee with the certainty that their own kids would defect from the Great Society and overthrow them. Hayden pointed out that no one picketed the HUAC any longer, signalling the end of their reign. The Committee would vanish for having been demystified. Equally, events like Chicago had taken the sting out of LBJ and Nixon and all politicians, doomed to lose their authority now that young folks had learned to laugh them away.

Such arrogant proclamations of the victory of the young and

loving were particularly 1967–8 delusions and would not even live out the decade. Yet these were the conceits which resounded through the movement – the feeling that every street battle was a blow against the Empire, that every demonstration was a further brush-stroke in the glory-canvas called *The* Revolution. Here was the old leftist logic of dramatic 'moments' climaxing in a struggle deemed 'revolution' by virtue of nothing more than its own energy dynamic. The kids had free bodies because they *acted* as if they had; the State was on the defensive because our guys *said* (and wrote!) that they had it backed against the wall.

But the maraschino cherry atop this revolutionary cream-pie was the war-cry, 'The future belongs to us!' Jerry Rubin: 'We have infiltrated the ruling class at its most intimate level – womb of the mother and sperm of the father.' Furthermore: 'We, the first generation to revolt, will not have an antagonistic split with our kids.' Of course, the years just after such sentiments do not indicate any mass break-out of youth, and surely the *wish* for it had leap-frogged its own enthusiasm into 'fact'. But so it was with the whole of *The* Revolution. It was as easy as . . . Do It! – from the Rubin autobiography of the same name. The mechanism was sexual discharge: 'Riots, campus struggles, demonstrations – the longer, the better – are social, community orgies . . . The mind is lost in a spiritual orgasm, adventure . . .' Movement myths have to be fabricated, says Rubin, to replace John Wayne and Tarzan with new blood (guess who?): 'Didn't we have a responsibility to the millions of young people out there who accepted us as models?' Even the 'out there' seems to conjure up televisionland, viewers, a catapulting to fame through a mass audience. Old Reich can help us out here: 'Self-aggrandizement is, as it were, a biopsychic erection, a fantastic expansion of the psychic apparatus . . .' Puff, puff, it gives us Jerry Rubin splashing his own reflection everywhere in a rage of random semenality: 'America destroyed language, and we are trying to revive language.' His logic is that what he feels so powerfully as revolutionary motive must surely be the same experience for the bulk of American youth. 'We are everywhere' – the title of his second autobiography – the hairy and disaffiliated, the goons and gooks, the smokers and the jokers.

Some could not, however, be accommodated in *The* Revolution. Even now the leftist experience could not be complete without a sense of Us and Them. In the Rubin pageant: beware of anybody who doesn't light up a joint or hasn't done time in the slams. The uptight, too, get a kick up the tight rear: 'Puritanism leads us to Vietnam. Sexual insecurity results in a supermasculinity trip called imperialism . . . Amerika has a frustrated penis, trying to drive itself into Vietnam's tiny slit to prove it is The Man.' And cut off swiftly and irrevocably are the old folks. At the Chicago Conspiracy Trial: 'We looked at the jury as a jury of our mothers. We felt Mother might forgive, while Father would punish.' Rubin's autobiographies are haunted by the parent, and nowhere does he aim so wrathful a dart as when urging their demise. There can be no revolutionary satisfaction until the spirit of the elders has been dispersed.* Rubin's brash self-exposure gains him a turn as a social irritant, but even this dubious place in the sun requires pressing the blame elsewhere for years wasted, mind adrift and body suppressed, the violation of the middle-aged – so much that these can become *The* Revolution itself, phantasms shook off momentarily by his sperm-shot in the dark, dropping his radical temperature to exhaustion.

In the massive discharge known as *The* Revolution one loud man could shout out his ecstatic delirium and have an instant following on the strength of it. Some of these radical powerhouses managed to create entire fictive civilizations out of their own visions and desires. One of the more celebrated of these was John Sinclair, leader of the Michigan White Panther Party. It was one of his intentions to organize in the high schools and turn youth away from the elders, allowing the old culture to atrophy and

*There is a strong resemblance in tone between Philip Roth's novel *Portnoy's Complaint* (1969) and Rubin's 'factual' account of his own misdeeds. Both culture-heroes develop out of the liberal Jewish tradition, and both seek deliverance from its leeching and guilt-making properties, Portnoy looks for it in acts of sexual aggression against his own person (in the main), Rubin through exhibitionism and pseudo-terror against the State. Portnoy has accommodated himself to public order, but hungers for a channel to house his masturbatory fantasies. Rubin does not keep his to himself, but nonetheless disguises them in acts called 'revolution'.

putrefy. For such sentiments he was awarded, in 1969, an astro-
nomical ten years in prison on a rap of handing two *free* marijuana
joints to an undercover narcotics agent (Sinclair was released in
1972). From his cell he wrote numerous manifestoes and open
letters to the 'underground' (the most *exhibited* in leftist history)
press, most of which assumed that American youth had completely defected from the bourgeois set-up and joined the 'street
people'. This new community had swelled to a 'family', and,
ultimately – bursting at the seams – 'We are a people. We are a
nation.' The nation had its own life-style, an inbred unity, no
leaders and was totally anti-consumer (this despite its addiction to
overpriced clothes, LPs and stereo equipment, colour television,
not to mention that most urgent of commodities – dope).
Moreover, the people of this nation were 'colonized' by the
fascist pigs of the 'Mother Country' (*her* again) who tried to
suppress their uninhibitedness and inevitable takeover: 'The
white honkie culture that has been handed us on a plastic platter is
meaningless to us! We don't want it! Fuck God in the ass. Fuck
your woman until she can't stand up. Fuck everybody you can
get your hands on. Our program of rock and roll, dope, and fucking in the streets is a program of total freedom for everyone.'

Sinclair's visions were also symptomatic of the new movement's
fawning over black revolutionary experience. This reflected a
driving need to create a pantheon of brave heroes (yet another sin
of the leftist fathers visited upon the sons) – and who braver than
non-whites? Accordingly, Sinclair imagined his circle of comrades to include the Black Panthers and Mao-Tse-tung, all the
while ignoring the central thread of discipline and anti-pleasure
running through their ideologies and programmes.

The White Panthers demonstrated another paradox of the
Politics of Gesture, claiming to be free while *demanding* freedom
from the Power. To his credit, John Sinclair could point out the
absurdity of being 'free' while the pigs came and broke your
head. He recognized the need to organize a community of *purpose* as well as looks. This required first of all 'kicking out the
jams', no holds barred, buster, check your character armour at the
door of the love-in. The 'total assault' on personality and culture
meant you must never get bored and fall back on bourgeois

Amerikan 'honkoid' life. To do this, you had to be immersed in
perpetual sensation: '. . . when you become inundated with high-
energy culture, you simply become *incapable* of operating in a
low-energy context.' But this presupposed a nation of revolutionary Supermen jacked up to drug-buzz capacity at every turn. It
carried no idea of revolutionary *rest*, and could only herald the
massive movement exhaustion of the next years.

4

The public spectacle of *The* Revolution created a logic that
cracked it wide open. Even as it gathered in intensity mini-
revolutions were springing up faster than any Bolshevik could
count. Nothing could be more obvious than that *everyone* would
deserve and expect a hunk of that liberation pie. Before several
years were out every pressure group from Polacks to baseball
pitchers could be seen throwing out a clenched fist or V-sign of
I WANT. For the first time since it lost the working class, the
American Left had actually provoked the democratic thrill.

The most inevitable of these schisms was the women's movement. The longest and largest of oppressed groups, it was only
surprising the break hadn't come sooner. This attested to the
deep-seated masochism of the female Left, and now it was quick
to invoke the bitter memory of frightened silent sisters at movement meetings. But nothing could better demonstrate their demeaning position than the announcement, by movement men,
that sexual liberation had arrived.

Women in the Old Left had not spoken on their own behalf
because of the influence of Communist conditioning.* Even when
they did rise to power – as some did in the American CP – the
issue of women's liberation was hardly raised. This heritage
passed down even to the post-Red Scare liberal Left whose codes

---

*The example of the Soviet Union is in evidence here, with its accent on
motherhood and the morality of the Communist family unit. Reich pointed
out that all the advances made in sexual emancipation (of both men and
women) after the 1917 Revolution were squashed a decade later by bourgeois Stalinism.

sanctioned, at best, tea-and-pickets groups like Women's Strike for Peace. The women's movement laid much of the conceptual blame for this at the feet of Freud, whose strong opinions on feminine neuroses were coloured by his own misogyny and problems in relating to women. Decades of psychoanalysis and Freudian cultural thinking tended to exploit the myth of female hysteria and turn out ladies 'cured' enough to return to male supremacist households. The specific application of Freudian doctrine to American life was made by a number of pseudo-psychologists, both in and out of radical circles; one of these was that Johnny-come-lately leftist, Dr Spock. His main concern was to see that boys will be boys and that girls remain girls. To this end, Daddy must approve daughter's pretty dresses and her yummy-yummy home-made cookies. When she approaches puberty, it is Mom's job to wise her up and tell her just how far she can't go. The entrenchment of roles is naturally geared towards making comfortable marriages where each partner respects the other and does not rock the sexual boat. Spock distinguishes the sexes by pointing out that men are used to dealing in abstractions and analysing problems, which is why they become philosophers and explorers. Women are not meant to tread this road because they *change their minds* more than men. Women's virtues are all bound up in the idea of non-aggression, and those who tend to become feminists are, more often than not, simply envious of men.

Spock not only popularized trends in psychoanalysis, but kept up to date the core of the liberal Left that had raised their daughters by such wisdom. In this respect, many of the young people who entered the fray as new leftists were Spock-marked from birth to puberty, ladies *expecting* to sit quietly listening to the profound abstractions of the world-changing boys.

The New Left came under fire in the early days of the women's movement (1967–8), with special emphasis on the role of the 'vanguard' SDS. The women had always been 'content' to advance themselves to positions of minor power in the organization. Any glimmer of revolt was greeted with penis envy/castration catcalls and let's get on with the 'greater struggle', girls. The guilt implicit in the idea of diverting attention from the 'broader' issues stopped many feminists cold. The anti-war movement was already in big trouble, what with LSD-crazies and personal salvation syndromes. But more militant feminists began to point out that you don't get radicalized fighting for someone else's liberation while you yourself are underfoot. One writer summed up her relation to the war in no uncertain terms: 'Shall I work to bring the boys home from Vietnam . . . so that they can turn their violence against us instead of the poor women of Mylai? . . . I shudder at the thought of having to deal with these whore-mongers and ear-collectors when they return.'

On the home-front, their very own slogan was amended and flung back in the faces of SDS males, that 'participatory democracy begins at home', which means your turn to scrub those dishes tonight, Ho Chi Minh. Also, no more hierarchical structures of domination within the movement; 'cock power' – out, the collective – in. Some feminists went so far as to demand all male leadership out of the Left since it was so corrupt. All this shook SDS profoundly, although it insisted on accepting women's demands only within the 'greater struggle'. When the militant Weatherman faction broke from SDS in 1969 some of its prime movers were radical women. Others left the group altogether and formed or joined the numerous all-women parties which began to evolve. Too long under the shadow of leftist polemics – and many of them unmarried or childless – radical females realized they had been out of touch with the dilemmas of women outside the movement. Many groups like the Redstockings and the Feminists devoted themselves solely to questions like wages for women cleaners, child-care, abortion and subjects the movement as a whole had considered beneath its dignity. The staunch day-to-day feminism which Reich had practised in 1930 – without any reference to 'women's rights' – had found its American niche. But the matter of full political struggle remained a sore factional point. In the early days of their 'consciousness-raising' meetings – a round-robin confession syndrome – women were torn between working with men against war and racism or simply recognizing men as the chief villains of the piece. What was the point of working for socialism when socialist countries treated women as badly as capitalism did?

The new open culture of freewheeling sex, orgasm-scandal mags with more-free-than-thou mottoes, tight-panting pop stars, offered little comfort where women were still treated as sex kittens. Some of the worst offenders were the new militants who had learned to provoke political reactions with their bodies. Their political performance was, in essence, a flashing of sexuality, in much the same way as the sex 'act' had often required good *performance*. Most prominent in this respect were the black radicals with their shade-eyes and super-cool machismo, consciously exorcizing all trace of 'feminine' softness along with faggot-honkie-jive culture. But the pale clowns also postured and pranced, often in rank imitation. Disassociating from the 'pansy-assed' Old and New Leftists needed a flourish of manhood, a tough new John Garfield with shoulder-length hair. This had the effect of speeding up movement women's sense of their own sexual dread. Many who had played safe – concentrating on political questions – now went straight to the groin of the matter. One of their challenges was an argument over the dynamics of the female orgasm. Freud designated a woman as frigid if she could not achieve orgasm with a male partner. Even Reich believed that problems began with an 'inhibition of vaginal feeling'. But now feminists were pointing out brashly that orgasm occurs, in fact, in the clitoris, and that women have not been frigid but that men have simply missed the point. The greater implication was that a feather or a finger could do the trick as well as (if not better than) John Garfield's appendage. Biologically, this denied variations among different women as to their specific centre of gravity. Nonetheless, the very expression of the sentiment said that many women were now prepared to go (and come) their own way.

This psychological breakthrough against the male ego led to increased militancy; in many cases, women were opening up whole new territories of revolutionary thought while the men scampered to catch up or merely continued to Marx time. Movement women – by showing up the false pretences of the new radical enlightenment – actually helped put the 'greater struggle' back on to an activist track. They burst the bubble of imminent victory over the uptight established war-creeps, as well as the deception, in the teeth of increasing police repression, that the cultural revolution would 'pull down the State with its dope and music and its so-called liberated sex'.

A certain gestural theatricality rubbed off even here, as the women necessarily moved down an *American* road. Demonstrations were manifested against bridal fairs, the Miss America pageant and against *Playboy* magazine every time it sent a speaker to a college campus. A New York group called the Emma Goldman Brigade paid homage to their anarchist namesake by chanting the slogan, 'Emma said it in 1910, Now we're going to say it again', at Goldman-style street-theatre demonstrations. The group known as WITCH promoted the idea that the expression of female-hood was an act of ritual, containing aspects of masque, magic and spectacle. Even the Yippies had a branch of craziettes: 'The Women's Liberation Caucus within the Youth International Party, being through a rigorous analysis of the thought of Mao, Susan B. Anthony, Che, Lenin, and Groucho, considers itself bound by the historic necessity of becoming the vanguard party of the progressive women's revolution because we fly higher.'

There were some who understood the dangers implied in the Politics of Gesture. Unlike most leftist movements, choosing sides was not a *goal* for the women. The idea was to expand the awareness of *all* women, right up to Pat Nixon herself. Instead of resorting to male violation tactics and 'shouting', women had to softly widen their net. Sloganizing and picketing and guerrilla theatre had had the effect, for example, of humiliating the contestants in the Miss America parade, potential sisters frightened off.

Yet physical gesture could be used as a warning to the men, and the tougher sisters followed hallowed tradition by busting up meetings, seizing public microphones and taking over leftist newspapers. In 1970 a collective representing numerous groups grabbed the offices and works of the New York 'underground' paper, *RAT*, which had been stewing in its own liberated juices for some time. This proved to be one of the strongest media voices to come out of the women's movement, identifying itself with militant struggles in the Third World and in US ghettos – to the embarrassment of other 'cultural revolution' papers – as well as printing info, girls, on how to change a flat tyre.

As if all this weren't enough for 'serious' political types, the faggots had to go and rub it in! All those years the Left had spent countering McCarthyite accusations of homosexuality in the ranks, and now! – the queers were leaping out of their closets, poof-ing up our *The* Revolution!

Gay Liberation was directly inspired by the women's movement, but even some women's groups at first rebelled against it. The idea that a lesbian might be doubly oppressed did not come easy for ladies whose consciousness was still adrift in the rice-paddies of Indo-China or the sweaty kitchens of home. To think that traditional psychology might be wrong again here was too much to swallow in the same revolutionary breath. But eventually the sisters softened, and it even became fashionable to 'come out' and admit your own homosexual experiences and fantasies. Even Joan Baez publicly confessed that one of the grooviest loves of her life had been a girl.

Male gays found it more difficult breaking into the movement as full-blown 'come out' queers. Up against the New Left they met strong resistance, even though the women had broken much ground in advance. Uptight comrades would cringe when boys got up to dance together at leftist functions. The Gay Liberation Front provided new colour to the usual drab Vietnam capers, but caused embarrassment for straight politicos who couldn't relate to ideas like 'bring the beautiful boys home' or 'suck cock and beat the draft'. The gays hoped that the new hip culture with its concern for sensitivity and encounter, body politics and the trance of costume and long hair would instigate awareness of a 'feminine principle' even in heterosexual leftists. But radicals, for the most part, had trouble distinguishing a new openness of community touch from its implications for the maintenance of their heterosexuality. To point up the dilemma the GLF disseminated a pamphlet cutting Jerry Rubin to the macho quick. In *Do It!* he poked fun at men like Edgar Hoover and Mayor Daley of Chicago by implying they had fucked each other. The gay brothers pointed out that, aside from there being nothing wrong with that (if only they were human enough for it to be true!), the Yippie only deflected the real political argument against such pigs through defamatory sexism and character assassination. Every time a movement spokesman called Pat Nixon 'Tiny Tits' he was slurring his flat-chested radical sisters.

Despite the difficult birth-pangs of the 'come out' movements, they soon performed a measure of surgery on the ailing body of the Left. A new attitude towards homosexuality grew out of the GLF's numerous confrontations with movement meetings and psychiatric conventions. The various experiments in communal living, diet and physical health, as well as the new concern for the environment all owe much to the 'softening' effect of the sexual liberation movements. There was also some fresh example for strategy. The voluminous Women's Liberation writings were, for the most part, precise, pragmatic, un-Utopian (except by implication) and unburdened by 'stars'; those few supersisters who did emerge were mostly media-bred and not generally looked up to by most movement women.

Also, the men had to learn to make coffee. Many were shaken to response, questioning their male chauvinism and their hasty declarations of mass liberation. Men's Liberation groups started up, trying to cope with male supremacy as well as 'getting in touch with our own gayness'. A West Coast newspaper, *Brother*, described itself as a 'forum for men against sexism', hitting out everywhere at 'phallic imperialism'.

Inevitably, too, came the Stalinoid confessions. It was, of course, not enough for movement wiseacres simply to mend their ways – they had to publish their transformations abroad. Suddenly the 'underground' press was teeming with 'I Was a Male Chauvinist' revelations. Abbie Hoffman re-wrote the introduction to the paperback of his autobiography, *Revolution for the Hell of It*, denouncing the book for its male ego-tripping. John Sinclair wrote from jail saying he was humbled by people calling attention to his sexism ('Fuck your woman until she can't stand up'), telling how he had described all things in the masculine; he was hard at work now, he assured his readers, cutting all the evidence out of the proofs to his forthcoming autobiography. Also from Sinclair:

'Some of the worst examples of the filth that still exists in our culture are a lot of the rock and roll songs we've held up as exemplary . . .' But the new 'rainbow culture' would purify all this by taking a fresh look at bad habits learned from 'the honkoid culture we grew out of'. Jerry Rubin also did it! But, like Sinclair, he argued that he really didn't know what he was doing when he was doing it: '*Do It!* poured out of my Amerikan unconscious, shaped by a male chauvinist point of view: The yippie as Superman.' Even Huey P. Newton of the Black Panther Party wrote an open letter to his black soul brothers, claiming that homosexuals and militant women had to be related to as revolutionary comrades. The implied message was: the same system that oppresses blacks oppresses women and gays. Most important, black brothers were only manifesting their own insecurity by persecuting these groups, insisting unnecessarily on false notions of black 'manhood'. This letter was signed by Newton, as usual, designating his position in the Party: 'Supreme Commander'.

*

Reich, in prison, waited for the flying saucers.

The prisoners would tease him mercilessly as he sat aloof, waiting to check out their books (he was prison librarian), inventing little dialogues for him to overhear: 'Hey, you see the little guy who came to my cell last night? He's gonna get us outta here in a couple of weeks!' This was a reference to Reich's belief that his father was from another world and had mated with his earthly mother, and that men from other worlds would eventually come and rescue him. Something or someone called the 'Silent Observer' (SO) seemed to be keeping watch over him. One of his favourite films was The Day the Earth Stood Still, *in which just such an observer comes down to Earth in a spaceship and gives, in W R's critical estimation, '. . . the full truth about both the plague abroad and at home, ruthlessly, relentlessly revealed for all to know . . .'*

This was merely a final plateau for a consciousness whose expansion knew no limits. It had progressed from the genitals to the muscles to the air and now reached into infinity. What had been a war between the life energy OR (Orgone Radiation) and EP (Emotional Plague) now extended itself (in conjunction with the persecution of Reich). The challenge was now against 'Life' (read: Reich) and could not be the work of mere armoured beings; the real adversary was now DOR (Deadly Orgone Radiation), developed by destructive leaders and scientists who hoped to take over (or destroy) the world. OR alone could not defeat it, and this task was therefore being carried out by CORE men (Cosmic Orgone Engineers) who hailed from other planets. WR was doing all he could from his Earth-bound vantage, using his own 'cloudbuster' to make rain (successfully in Maine and Arizona), just as he used the accumulator to create health in armoured man, living as he did in an 'emotional desert': 'The desolation of emotion, the dehydration of tissues . . . alcoholism which serves the stimulation of what is left over from an original sense of life, crime and psychosis . . . last convulsions of a thwarted, frustrated, badly maltreated life . . .' Reich saw that DOR was sustained by the recent atomic blasts, and also spoke of 'the sparkle of life that went out of the landscape'. Certainly he was not 'mad', in this sense, only providing an early parable for the fight against nuclear fallout and deathly pollution in the atmosphere. Supremely arrogant, however, he insisted that everything he said was based on scientific fact. In the same way, he re-wrote all his early classics – confusing his most brilliant work – when they no longer conformed to the 'facts'. He evolved his own language where more common words and phrases would have made his ideas more accessible, built his own science and cosmic categories. He played out his mysticism to the tune of: I am the facts. *All the deadly traps of authority and power he avoided, only to arrange his own private cosmos in the end, himself reflected everywhere.*

In such a voluminous state he was forced to share his last days (he died a prisoner in 1957) with the victims of the Nixon-McCarthy era (his despised Reds). Like these men, he had upset the political balance in some small way; one purpose of the Red Scare was to redress that balance by making examples to see it didn't happen again, to frighten the future speechless. Ironically, the protest impotence which resulted was not overcome until a 'sexual revolution' of sorts had occurred.

But just as Reich could not gauge the reaction to his call for liberation, so the new movement could not understand that it would suffer the consequences of telling 'impotent' men that they are impotent and that their offspring are defecting. No 'liberated' man needs to flaunt his erotic priority. Of course, there was no 'fucking in the streets' as promised, only the bombast which spoke it. But squirting even imaginary freedom-sperm in the eyes of the State only served to bring out the more deadly tear-gas and riot squads.

Reich's 'orgastic potency' required no enemies; 'Power to the People' did. The movement's body was not satisfied to linger at its moment of pleasure, and bolted again for the higher stakes of personal power. It was the same crossroads at which Reich had forsaken his own 'sexual revolution'; it could not be otherwise in 'life-affirmative' USA. Sex-energy substitutes were on the rampage. The new power for the 'people' could only mean Woman Power, Black Power, Chicano Power, Flower Power, ME-Power, Not-You Power – all in contention for Microphone Power at the demonstration, Spotlight Power on the political stage, a cacophony of 'come outs' pressing each other – and The *Revolution – to incoherence.*

VI: Anti-climax and Grand Finale

Desperadoes in Wargasm

Model prisoner Leary pinned his last hopes on Supreme Court Justice William O. Douglas.

In his several months at various California jails, the LSD-doctor managed to convince everyone from prison officials ('he seemed unlikely to be violent or try to escape') to his arch-enemy Ronald Reagan that he was worthy of transfer to 'minimum security' incarceration at San Luis Obispo. He gave no press conferences, made no public statements, and even the jail memoirs he was preparing for publication could not be construed as inflammatory. On one occasion, when he helped prevent a violent fight between a guard and an inmate, Leary was balled out by an SDS militant in his cell; by stopping inevitable confrontations between the 'people' and the pig power structure he was only prolonging revolution. The Doctor countered that a revolution had already occurred – in consciousness – and he was distressed that his very own acid-spawn were now 'using violent tactics which were light-years removed from the accelerating and rapidly evolving realities of our space and time'.

But even minimum security proved trying, and the prospect of further court cases in three States made it imperative that he be free to deal with his future. The lower appeal courts had upheld the denial of bail, still maintaining Leary was a public menace. He looked, with characteristic optimism, to Douglas. The ageing liberal Judge had recently scored himself an eighteen-year-old bride (he ought to be responsive to politics of the pudenda) and had written a book called Points of Rebellion *about the coming revolution and its relation to American founding doctrine. Leary was certain of getting bail from him, and even expected to win the later court case. But Douglas's decision came up razzberries for Tim.*

There was nothing left for him but to perfect his yoga. In September 1970 two Federal agents came to take him to New York to stand trial there. They gave him the option of driving cross-country with them there and then or waiting out the weekend to fly back on Monday. The high flyer chose the latter, and spent the weekend composing a public statement. Seven months in prison and the further dampening of his pacifist hopes led him to write: 'Arm yourself and shoot to live . . . To shoot a genocidal robot policeman in the defense of life is a sacred act.' The full text was carried somewhere on his person as he crept out at night under floodlights where the guards paced. He was half-way up the ten-foot-high chain-link fence (or twelve feet, depending on who tells the story; stay tuned for the film), topped with barbed wire, when he noticed his hands were cut. At this suspense-filled moment he doubted he could make it. He hung there on the fence, not knowing if he'd been spotted, and thought (so legend has it) that if they shot him, he must manage to fall over the fence so people would know he was a-tryin' to be free. But as a 'brother' now in the heroic People's Liberation Struggle against 'The Man', he was not about to let himself be cut down before he had his chance to 'off the pig'. With a final burst of acid-will he was up and over the barrier, where a car-load of armed shadow-figures lurked to carry him to safety.

1

Before *The* Revolution became just another disposable commodity in the American dustbin, it was milked for every ounce of fresh experience it might yield. Political tactics were stale after one or two years, but even some of the more sweeping 'cultural' changes were quickly discarded, revised or, in some cases, turned inside out. One certain cause was the radical breathlessness of the late sixties, which could only end in breath-catching confusion. In early 1969 Jerry Rubin circulated an open letter round the 'underground' press, saying the movement was 'suffering the greatest depression in our history'. He pointed to all the local revolutionary heroes already dead, jailed, exiled or just pooped out. Even Dr Spock had been convicted and, if the Government could get away with that, there was no stopping the tide of repression. This letter showed little more than one weak-pulsed over-30 winding down from a self-made summit, projecting, at the last, even his personal ennui on to the greater frame of the movement. There was, in fact, a lull before a new storm, but it was no more than the instant disenchantment which troubled great periods of the sixties. The 'cultural revolution' and all its delicacies failed to feed the hunger of an era whose motto was 'What Next?'

Some people had gone so far into themselves that there was no place to go but backwards. The many personal frustrations of rapid change even led to a new (though brief-lived) romance with the *organization*, the collective, the commune, the party. It is true that the old political styles continued to drone out their ritual chants throughout the upheavals around them. Some of these got caught in the gravitational pull of the Politics of Gesture and were altered, or else they lost membership to other political phenomena. But a slow process of returning to the 'theoretical' fold had also begun, even in the midst of rampant self-concern.

When SDS opened its doors to all comers in 1965, Progressive Labor went to work inside the more influential group. Because SDS had no strong centrality and allowed its local branches complete independence, it was easy for the Maoists to gain a foothold and proceed with a takeover plan. This was made possible by the fact that PL was a disciplined group (never having lost its CP training) whose members voted in a block, did what they were told and accepted a vision of revolution so rigid as to paralyse the very idea of dissent. Theirs was the hereditary certainty that only the working class could make the revolution – and there was no veering from that line. That it could still be retained by young Americans in the late sixties was miracle enough; PL also managed to attract political drifters to the idea and make it seem an exciting possibility. In March 1969 a non-PL newspaper put out by Ohio SDS boldly announced: 'The New Left has been agnostic and "anti-theoretical" for many years, and the importance of theory . . . has only become clear in the last six months or so.' PL now established a Worker–Student Alliance in which students helped organize labourers on or off campus. Leaders also urged them to go out and get jobs – in the summer, of course – so they might understand what it actually feels like to *work*. Leafletting and 'rapping' – airing labour grievances – became useful political tactics again. 'Solidarity Forever' (an old union hit-parade favourite) hung in more throats than 'I Can't Get No Satisfaction'. Moreover, old style labour jargon was back in vogue; university authorities were now the 'bosses', the cops were their 'goons' and anyone who bucked a student strike was a 'scab'. At the Columbia University strike in early 1968 Mark Rudd (later to become a Weatherman) talked publicly of the need for redistribution of wealth, freedom from imperialism, and gave an astonishing new revolutionary name to it all: 'In the movement we are beginning to call this vision socialism . . .'

The PL Maoists proved to be stern opponents for those who'd gone round the psychedelic bend and now come full circle. They were down on dope and free sex, and their movement was based on self-control and, of all things, patience. When a branch of SDS became the Motherfuckers (before breaking away), PL tried to have their drugs and shaggy heads voted 'out of order' at a national council meeting. PL also considered the Black Panthers counter-revolutionary because their issue was race, not class; women's movements were also divisive in the workers' struggle. Even North Vietnam was condemned for negotiating with the Americans and especially for using *Soviet* weapons! The Maoists also fought bitterly against the rising influence of the sage, Herbert Marcuse, on the New Left. Marcuse believed, in contrast to the old industrial divinity, that social workers, students, teachers and professionals constituted a sort of new middle-class– working-class which would make the revolution.

At the same time, 1968 brought militant student rebellions around the world and at home (Columbia, San Francisco State), black riots throughout American cities, the great Tet offensive of the Viet Cong and the Chicago offensive of the home brigades. The May riots in Paris had a strong effect in the US because they combined a thoroughgoing Marxist analysis with real-live *action*, and because they appeared – to some near-sighted observers – to prove that a Western power could still be overthrown. (This overlooked the fact that the French Government was by no means toppled, that a doubly oppressive police state followed the revolt and that workers had been fighting in the streets alongside students – which wasn't about to happen in the US.)

These stunning examples of a new student/youth *power* set US campuses aflame (often literally). Students began to see themselves as an oppressed class, as the 'new nigger', and this implied that middle-class kids were 'gettin' ready' to join up with blacks and browns and yellows in mortal combat with the forces of piggery. There was, naturally, not *that* much of a hurry in this and, before actually confronting the outside world, they would practise on Mother College. In May 1969 the Permanent Subcommittee on Investigations (Joe McCarthy's old committee) issued a study of recent campus 'disorders'. Over a two-year period they found 471 disturbances at 211 (out of 2374) colleges, 25 bombings, 46 arsons, 598 injuries, 6158 arrests and 207 buildings occupied. A modest beginning, about a C+/B− for Elementary Insurrection, and not much for a limb of Congress to fret over. Their real concern was $2·2 million in *property* damage between 1968 and 1969. This was even worse when the kids graduated with a big A between January and June of 1969, causing $4·5 million worth of university damage. By the time of the subcommittee probe there were already nineteen bills in the House of Reps and two in the Senate for clamping down on student unrest.

For some reason campus insurrection took the Power by surprise. It was not considered a spontaneous phenomenon (which it mostly was), so the prominent SDS was singled out to take the rap for *conspiring* to make trouble. And who better to root out this plague of bonfires and broken windows than the Committee itself. This withering ancient had only recently been saved from euthanasia, oiled and lubricated, polished, given a name change from the old HUAC to the shiny new Internal Security Committee (ISC) and, to a large degree, given a new image. Gone were the subpoenas for hostile witnesses; the HUAC never got anything but stick out of those creeps, and the new group wouldn't even try. Instead, they would rely solely on info provided by informers (paid and unpaid), concerned citizens and assorted 'experts'. Of course, anyone named in testimony would finally be given the chance to come and respond to charges (if anyone still cared, which was doubtful) but only 'on condition that the witness conduct himself with propriety and decorum and that he will be available for cross-examination'. And if this wasn't enough to cool things off, Chairman Ichord moved the whole shebang into a smaller hearing-room where he could more easily maintain order. It was a bright new Committee worthy of its mentor in the new-look, low-temperature White House. By cutting out all the fun, the publicity-mongering, the dramatic episodes which had thrilled the multitudes for twenty years, the group might even function effectively at last and take on a meaningful investigative role, almost like a shadow of the FBI. If its days of scaring the Left were over, the new Committee would nonetheless outlive even its youthful critics as a social force.

It opened for business in 1969, and SDS was one of its first customers (June–August) – although no members of the group were asked to appear. The bulk of these hearings was taken up with boring damage reports and itemizations, as well as the boring opinions of university presidents and 'model' students. But this was all right for the new Committeemen, appearing more like corporation executives than witch-hunters, oh so reasonable and patient. And not unbright: '. . . every radical movement has made a contribution in the field of literature', one member pointed out, '. . . Jack London, Jack Reed, Max Eastman . . . But here, for the first time . . . we have a movement which has made no contribution . . . and which is remarkably inarticulate.'

But there were some hangovers from times gone by. Aside from its own spies, the Internal Security Committee encouraged the awful spectacle of college administrators and professors informing on their own students; many did so gladly, even providing the Committee with ID cards, leaflets, SDS pamphlets and photographs of the protesters at revolutionary play. All these pillars of academia plugged the same theme: we have urged reform of US institutions, de-escalation of the war and have made the campus a more liberal place; its just a handful of rowdies who upset the majority of the academic community. They described in vivid detail demonstrations against police and CIA recruiters on campus, government-sponsored anti-guerrilla projects, Indo-China holocaust research, and especially against the ROTC (Reserve Officers Training Corps), a strong source of officer material for the war. They also gave names of disrupters (some of which the Committee didn't already have) and spoke freely about them as individuals. Many academics turned stool-pigeon out of a mounting sense of despair and the feeling that the universities were becoming, as one Committeeman had it, 'scalps on SDS's belt'. One administrator claimed 'there are hundreds of deanships and presidencies going begging because nobody wants to get up there and stand in the center of a shooting gallery and have his head shot off'.

Another gesture to yesterday was the Committee's concern with – of all things – the Communist Party's influence on the kids. They recognized that SDS was formulating its own brand of communism, 'with a small *c*'. That was OK and they were not going to persecute the heretics or the dissenters who were merely expressing their democratic privilege. But a theme which pervaded the 1969 hearings was the possibility of SDS being taken over by some more sinister band. Members still asked their stooges if a given radical 'advocated violent overthrow of the US Government'. They were also concerned to discover whether financial support for SDS was coming from a foreign power.

Curiously enough, the Communist Party did begin to have a very marginal influence round about 1968. The growing interest in Marxism made the Party a likely source of theoretical education. But some CP members were actually recruited into SDS in order to provide some discipline-addicts to help organize against PL. Still, this was hardly the power struggle to seize SDS which J. Edgar Hoover reported was taking place between PL and the CP. The Party sensed it had arrived too late and, in typical 'what went wrong?' fashion, flagellated itself: 'Why was the Party slow to see the new situation which developed around 1966 which made it impossible to unite most of the left movement among youth under our banner while still guaranteeing the emergence of a Marxist trend?'

2

The Great Liberation had opened up the floodgates. Women, Red Indians, blacks, Puerto Ricans, Chicanos were speeding ahead with *urgent* political battles and chided the counter-culture for being self-indulgent and counter-revolutionary. The white male Left, hereditarily given to self-doubt and guilt, would now have to work overtime to catch up. The only way this seemed possible was to clutch the coat-tails of the darker brothers, following up their accent on personal bravery. Gun fantasies were adopted, rendering whites fierce by association. Words like 'honkie' and 'the pig' (who must get 'offed') were accepted without translation into whitey's rhetoric (a throwback to 1920's jazz-vicarious white culture). But black militants, at this time, were firmly on their own road and keen to obliterate the liberal notion that whites could do their liberating for them or even provide significant aid and comfort. It was a similar blow to labour leaving the fold some twenty years before. But if leftists could no longer work white fist in black fist (as in the old CP posters), they would simply try, for a while, to run alongside. The idea was to make so much internal trouble for 'The Man' that he would be forced to take some of the pressure off the blacks. It took some time before folks figured out what this would mean in *practice*: that only a serious *military* solidarity could prove that one was not just jiving and playing pansy-assed honkie games.

At the same time, the white Left attempted to use its influence on the new political awareness growing up in the high schools. The teens were supposedly 'getting it together', mimicking much of the counter-culture and its thrills. Hundreds of 'underground' papers started up in answer to the familiar official high-school organ which was usually geared to printing sensitive poetry and news of the senior prom. Now there was info on how to act in a dope bust, the making of Molotov cocktails and the re-capturing of youth culture that had been 'co-opted' by the capitalists. Kids were openly demanding an end to suspensions and expulsions; open admissions to colleges; free speech and press; black and Puerto Rican studies programmes and the ousting of cops and narcotics agents from school premises. It was an extremely volatile situation, for high school had always been the central reinforcer of accepted values or the turf on which you made your rebellious stand before settling down at last to 'reality'. But even where a certain percentage traditionally ran out of control, they never before sounded like this: 'We're going to claim our birthright – dig that Manifest Destiny – we're going to be Americans and what's more American than REVOLUTION?'

Hundreds of SDS chapters now opened in the high schools. Yet the youngsters snidely wrote off the main group as liking 'to think of themselves as fathers to the high school underground . . .' and insisted on an independent status. SDS believed the teens would love them for the new exemplary heroism they were practising: 'These high-school kids eat it up when they learn that we're beating up Harvard professors.' But when two SDSers attacked a Columbia prof with a club, one high-school paper said they were no better than the Chicago pigs with their pointless violence. In effect, SDS failed to have any real impact, owing chiefly to something the little snot-noses called the 'generation gap'! These over-the-hill over-20s didn't know anything about making a revolution: '. . . they're really hung up trying to organize the working class.'

The cross-breeding of generations and interest groups and issues gave an impression of mass fervour which smelled like it might just be revolution. But instead, it served to diffuse and weaken the movement. Every rally now, no matter what its ostensible purpose, had to have its token women's liberationist, Chicano, teenager and drag queen – all shouting counter demands and vying for the power of the amplification system. This once-welcomed turn of events led to a need for re-examining personal strategies so that one might fly higher in the revolutionary cluster and be *recognized*. More than this, there was now an unspoken challenge in the competition for vanguard status: how far dare you go, comrade? The only winning answer was to go for broke.

This is not meant to minimize the turn towards 'revolutionary violence'. For the leftist hero it was the serious culmination of years of fretful inertia, the recognition that *The* System was not programmed to be any more than 'reasonable', if even that. The age-old American *ambition* to scratch your name on the Republic, to be *somebody*, was still at work. Despite the few short years of unlearning it, of drugged 'ego-loss' and freedom from the desire to be a good citizen, the need to bear impact came quickly back with a vengeance. Stark violence would be its new *modus operandi*.

It had to be learned. Self-defence was only a beginning; *provoking* confrontation was another matter altogether. One of the first groups to anticipate the pseudo-military cut of the white Left was Up Against the Wall, Motherfucker. As an SDS chapter from New York, the Motherfuckers gave voice to what many other members only dreamed in 1968 – a ferocious antidote to 'issue' politics even in the midst of the new theoretical surge.* It was a flashback to one of the primal rivalries – anarchists v. organized leftists – complete with sabotaging of meetings and provocateur actions. The Motherfuckers saw the student as a privileged character (after he'd officially sanctioned himself as 'oppressed'): 'Students in France, in Japan and especially in Mexico, are struggling and dying in the streets in the real fight . . . and revealing the poverty of our movement and the terrible artificiality of our "struggles." '

Unlike the later Weathermen – who were their descendants – the Motherfuckers paid little lip-service to the capitalist power structure or to oppressed peoples. They struck a blow (if they were lucky enough) for the blow's sake; any political theory would have to *follow* that. They introduced 'motion tactics' to SDS early on, the idea of running wild and taking out a few windows (and, if you were really brave, a pig) on your way, but keep moving, brother, don't stop long enough to get caught or let down the momentum. Improvisation was essential; they tried to turn orderly leftist demonstrations into street riots – hitting and running – hoping that others (for whom the demo had an original meaning) might pick up the thread and carry it through on their own polit-

---

*The creative imagination of the Motherfuckers came from the fact that many of them began as painters, coming at revolution by way of demonstrations against museums and art galleries. Their earliest culture-heroes were the madcap Dadaists and Futurists from the early part of the century; in a sense, their 'revolutionary' street actions were only a further stage in a long search for viable artistic expression.

ical terms. At the same time, they hoped to turn fence-sitting dissidents on to the extremist *fun* of it.

Their first big move came – appropriately – during the New York garbage strike of 1968. They set fire to great piles of rubbish and then dropped bricks from rooftops on firemen who came to fight the blaze. One of their favourite numbers was wading into police with karate chops (so goes the folklore), then running away to lure lone cops down back alleys where hidden Motherfuckers would be waiting to jump them. They were able to move in this manner by dividing themselves into 'affinity groups', street-gangs of up to twenty-five, but *with an analysis!* not just free-form hoodlums. Again, the point was to act as catalyst: 'The active minority is able, because it is theoretically more conscious and better prepared tactically, to light the first fuse and make the first breakthrough . . . encouraging action without claiming to lead.'

One of their final gestures (before disbanding) of provoking 'reality'-terror in the Left came at an SDS regional council meeting in March 1969. Here they circulated a leaflet giving the recipe for a Molotov Cocktail, followed by: 'A "White Radical" is three parts bullshit and one part hesitation. It is not revolutionary and should not be stockpiled at this time.'

From 1968 a series of pitched campus battles with law and order forces marked the turn towards dynamic confrontation. None of these proved to be a catalyst to mass rebellion, but they yielded up a bevy of white martyrs and fresh heroes. These Great Scenes from *The* Revolution spanned a period of two to three years, increasing both in firepower and publicity. They were self-defensive for the most part and, although the only serious victims and casualties were leftists, all these battles – like the off-campus fight in Chicago '68 – came down through movement folklore as *victories*. The basis for this claim was that the power structure had been provoked to acts of unspeakable brutality which would – so it was believed – serve to politicize hangers-on and draw the sympathy of the Silent Majority.

In that merry rebellious month of May 1968 the first police riot of major proportions on a white campus took place at

Columbia University in New York. The specific 'issue' was the university's building of a new gymnasium on a park site in adjoining Harlem, one of the few open spaces for black children to play in. However, by the time the situation heated up, other demands crept into the picture, among these the removal of the Institute of Defense Analysis – which organized the development of weapons systems for the war – from Columbia. There were other 'firsts' here, what with outsiders (blacks) pouring on to the campus, turning the matter into a community affair (which it was anyway); it was not simply a call for better conditions within the sanctuary. Whites made 'alliances' with black militants on the spot, until they discovered the dark brothers were toting six-shooters, rendering this no ordinary academic insurrection. The frightened pales were left to capture their own buildings which they did with style, taking over the President's office and breaking out his imported sherry and best cigars (Havanas?). There was even a wedding in one of the seized buildings between some 'children of the new age' who spent their wedding night with bleeding skulls and their honeymoon in the slams. But it was still too early for the Left to fight back and, when the Tactical Police Force pushed past the barricades, they found the same old non-violent lambs waiting for the slaughter. As one of these lambs described it: ' ''We Shall Overcome'' were the words that were being sung when the Gestapo came in. Circling us, our song got louder. The captain in charge . . . sicked his animals on us. They began beating, kicking, using crowbars and the debris from the barricades in their sadistic game.' Somewhere in the midst of the action, the school's electrical system was rendered inoperative: it was the Motherfuckers.

Berkeley had come a long way in the battle-scar sweepstakes since the days of the Free Speech Movement. In those early days, police merely revved up their motorcycles to put the fear into students jammed around the famous police car. But they did not come wading in indiscriminately, truncheons ablaze – this would have been unthinkable on a white campus in 1964. Even when demonstrators were pulled down the steps of the administration building, few were seriously injured. Although 'Police Brutality' had been a movement theme since the early sixties (no one had time to shout it when it really happened), the protesters hadn't seen nothin' yet. In June 1968 some young socialists attempted to hold a street rally to show solidarity with students rioting in Paris. They had not got permission, and the constabulary proceeded to clear the streets. The university's long-range policy, since the FSM, was to deny radicals a base of operations on the periphery of the campus. Now students were made aware that standing on the corner or just 'hanging out' in the street could become acts of revolutionary dimension. The police certainly thought so in their determination to clear the streets, and they provided the first-ever *large-scale* tear-gassing of white students. But it was kid stuff compared to the following year.

In May 1969 a group of Berkeleyites took over a vacant university-owned patch of land and built People's Park on it. Technically, this land was designated for campus rebuilding, but had stood empty for years. Nonetheless, after a month in which the growing Park became a new symbol of 'community', the university threw up a fence around it and demolished everything that had been built or planted inside. They also surrounded it with cops, begging confrontation. The police ran an American flag (insult of insults) up what had been a children's Maypole and gave the Park the radio code name: Fort Defiance. It was the war come home, and radicals warmed quickly to the idea. They became the local Viet Cong, their 'turf' overrun by the imperialist aggressors. As soon as word of the occupation spread, a mass meeting was called on the edge of the campus, just a short way from the Park. The usual leftist speeches were made *ad nauseam* until someone in the crowd shouted 'Let's take the Park!' The spontaneity of it startled the old-time politicos who were left literally with open mouths as the people's militia strode forward to *take the Park!* There were no demands for better conditions or fair play; the Park was tangible and folks could at last feel they had experienced the object of their struggle. This did not satisfy the socialists who saw the movement eluding them again. Progressive Labor said: 'Workers can't relate to parks. Workers can only relate to racism and imperialism.' But most people saw it as the climax to a process of repression begun in 1964, the containment of youth and radical culture in Berkeley.

It was also, in miniature, an allegory of American destruction of the environment. It was Vietnamization and defoliation, therefore answerable to the people's wrath.

Halfway to the battleground – after smashing a Bank of America window – the Cong got the willies. Up ahead were the notorious 'Blue Meanies', blue-clad coppers specially trained for turning such situations un-pretty, named after the suppressors of love-culture in a Beatles film. The instant Left commando operation wiggled down to the old caution again. Someone then turned a fire hydrant on the Meanies – just what they were waiting for. They picked off their targets with great accuracy. Sixty demonstrators were hospitalized with gun wounds on the first day alone, called 'Bloody Thursday'. Two thousand National Guardsmen were on the scene in no time at all, a thousand arrests were made. To compound the Indo-Chinese parallel, helicopters appeared overhead and rained down poisons even black rioters hadn't yet sniffed. CS gas and 'pepper-fog' were used indiscriminately so that children in nurseries miles away were overcome. Astonishingly, Berkeley was being used as a testing-ground for new sophisticated weaponry – the armed forces could not have made a better symbolic choice. The only consolation for demonstrators was in learning the trick of wearing gloves (from now on) so as to throw tear-gas cannisters back at the pigs.

The real escalation of the Berkeley People's War came with its first white martyr, an onlooker named James Rector who'd had his belly blasted open by a shotgun. The police claimed that only birdshot was in use, but it was later discovered that Rector had stopped some 00 buckshot, normally used for bagging deer. This gave the movement an opportunity to use soap-opera one-liners like, 'We have to struggle harder so that James Rector will not have died in vain.'

The rage at the killing and maimings (another onlooker was blinded with buckshot) seemed hopelessly spent. As a man on the spot put it: 'Street people had run out of rocks. The next step was guns and nobody was ready, plus the State Power was too huge . . . they had tanks and armoured cars waiting for us.' By the end of the week the guerrillas threatened to enlist the aid of the 'people', calling for 50,000 to descend on Berkeley, from all points, to *tear down that fence!* Only 35,000 showed up and these were forced back into symbolism. When they saw it was impossible to get at the Park for the swelled numbers of cops, they put down their sacks full of soil and trees – wherever they happened to be on the street – planting 'instant parks' everywhere. But it was not an ending with a cheerful lesson: the Power was now prepared to aim its ugliest guns at *white* youth. Said one protester: 'Our paranoia has come true.'

Still, that was Berkeley, and you could expect it in that hotbed of radicalism. But when the National Guard gunned down four sons and daughters of the Silent Majority at Ohio's Kent State University it seemed, to some, altogether another story. Kent State was a mid-western fortress before 1968, seemingly untouched by *The* Revolution. Jerry Rubin had visited the place and was laughed back to New York when he urged students to get out and kill their parents. But it was a measure of the Great Liberation that such a campus, by 1969, could find itself the subject of an Internal Security Committee investigation into radical activities. For this set of hearings, the Committee's choices were strategic. They were not interested in any of the Big League Red Schoolhouses like Columbia or Michigan or Berkeley. Instead, they concentrated on SDS activity at relatively 'quiet' campuses like Georgetown, Kent State and American University. Naturally, they could count on more cooperative stool-pigeons from these places. But the selections were also calculated to show that the enemy could infiltrate even into corners of Middle America, creating little trouble-pockets where activism would have been unthinkable two years before.

At Kent State the Committee uncovered evidence about SDS activities beginning in 1968 with a demonstration against the Oakland, California Police Department (notorious Black Panther chasers) who were recruiting on campus. The trouble-makers later concentrated their attention on the Liquid Crystals Institute, supposedly looking into cancer research on a *Defense Department* grant. Liquid crystals were also used in a heat-sensing device ('the sniffer') which, radicals claimed, was used for tracking down Che Guevara (who was eventually caught and executed) in the jungles of Bolivia. It was a fantasy worthy of American truth, and students attempted to inflict property damage in protest. In April 1969 SDS-Queen, Bernadine Dohrn, spoke prophetically at Kent State. According to a Committee spy, she 'stated that to date no whites had been killed on campus, but this would eventually come, and then it would be necessary for . . . SDS to carry guns . . .' To combat the growing influence of SDS, Kent State officials obtained injunctions and restraining orders, preventing certain agitators from entering university grounds.

Nixon's invasion of Cambodia in 1970 came as a 'shock' even to SDS, for whom the war had de-escalated as an issue. But it surprised only those already propagandized by the false and sinister expression, 'Vietnam War' – as if the situation hadn't included Laos, Korea, Thailand and Cambodia all along. American radicals were equally to blame for this, and their outrage bore all the trappings of their dim sense of history. Nonetheless, the feeling of 'deception' helped to kindle new movement flames. One of these caught in the ROTC building at Kent State from the impact of some liberated woman's liberated tampax soaked in kerosene and packed in a Molotov. It brought out the National Guard as well as the fury of Ohio politicians bent on saving Kent State from radical infection. On one sweltering day soon after, some irritated, rifle-bearing guardsmen felt they'd had enough of being pelted with rocks, and consciously conspired to deal a little fireworks in return. When the shooting began, some folks shouted 'It's only blanks', but four extras never got up off the film set.

Yet it had a strong reality to it, provided by the element of 'surprise', the sheer 'momentary murder' of it. It did not seem like any long-range plot to silence radicals (as in Berkeley). Yet, in many ways, this is precisely what it was. For the same reason the Committee had singled out Kent State a year earlier, the repressive finger of history might fall there in a bout of murder. Radicals no longer scared easily; as in the previous Nixon era, it was Middle America that needed a warning. If it chose to protect agitators – even on the basis of academic freedom – it would have to pay the (if only 'accidental') price. Many leftists now felt the killings would radicalize the great middle. And certainly some moderate students joined the ranks after their bitter taste of gun-fire. But this lasted the length of a single outrage, and leftist pro-phets were wrong again on one of their primal fictions. Nixon's bullets closed up the middle, just as they were 'intended' to.

Still, the immediate scoreboard showed some 400-plus cam-puses closed as a result of the 'Kent State Martyrdom'. Many fires were started and windows smashed. A huge Kent/Cambodia march descended on Washington, but slowed quickly to a groan. Dr Spock was arrested again and, by August 1970, the *New York Times* reported him wearing – at a Black Panther trial – a badge showing a hand clutching a rifle.

3

Radical masochists could bear only so much escalation of police force before knuckling under or turning to – revenge. As soon as it took power in 1969 the Nixon administration piled on the abuse, not just through isolated displays of firepower, but under the counter, unceasingly tying up activists in the courts, throwing up new legal loopholes and smiling repressions faster than even paranoia could handle. It was enough to send many scampering back to passive resistance or community projects; others simply 'disappeared'. The Cambodia demonstrations, far from being another great renewal of movement spirit as predicted, proved to be a signal of retreat. By the end of May 1970, the Kent killings hardly one month cold, it seemed like it was all over including the shouting. Then, on 9 June a bomb ripped through a New York City police building, causing extensive damage (and em-barrassment), injuring several cops. Soon after, the Weatherman saboteurs made it clear that this was retaliation for Kent State.

It was evident from this that, although the movement was in collapse, there were some bravos willing to play out a final hand. These did not begin as dyed-in-the-wool vigilantes, however, and their road to personal apocalypse paralleled the upward course of the State's trigger-happiness. But their impulse took root not only in struggles against the Power, but in power struggles out of leftist tradition.

Flashing back: In an attempt to solidify against the takeover bid of Progressive Labor, more open-minded SDSers tried to build up their own coherent politics. They felt American labour had become a privileged class; before any purely 'socialist' revolution, it was necessary to make the workers conscious of US aggression against the Third World, and their own inadvertent role in this aggression. Each side in the growing ideological dispute dropped turgid tracts like gauntlets, mouthing pseudo- and crypto-Marxist dogma at each other. It was as if the freshest item in the chase after a new thrill was *boredom*; the excitement of all the cultural changes of the just-gone past might only be excelled now by a thorough drop in temperature, the great snore of Left rhetoric. Meetings began to divide down the middle in the old socialist manner. One group would establish a caucus, meet in secret chambers, fight amongst themselves, bring their differences to a vote; whichever position got the most votes *was* the group's position. Soon there were slanging matches where the two major factions – now both more or less Chinese-oriented – waved Red books at each other, the PL-Maoists chanting for Mao Tse-tung, while the SDS-almost-Maoists one-upped them with cries of 'Ho Ho Ho Chi Minh'.

It came to a head over the issue of the Black Panther Party, considered by all but PL to be the vanguard of revolution. The emulation of groups advocating armed resistance led to a point where anti-PLers longed to be part of that heroic band which ran riot in the streets of Paris and which held the pigs at bay in Oakland. They had to go through a process of initiation to get there, starting small by calling themselves the 'Jesse James Gang' or the 'action faction', picking up Motherfucker rhetoric and getting into threatening slogans like 'Less Talk, More Action'. All this led to a showdown at the SDS convention in June 1969 where anti-PLers displayed full solidarity with the Panthers present. They also came armed with a weighty new work of literary radicalism called 'You Don't Need a Weatherman to Know Which Way the Wind Blows'. The gist of this endless document was that students were not really oppressed after all; on the contrary, they were an élitist class hiding behind something known as 'white-skin privilege'. It was now necessary for armchair radicals to MOVE, to get out and seek a base among white lower-class youth, the disaffected and the downs-in-the-mouth. Black brothers had to find their own identity and were taking care of business well enough. The way to help them was – as Che Guevara had it – create 'two, three, many Vietnams', make life so difficult for the US Government that it would not be able to protect itself against constant insurgency both abroad and at home.

A dramatic rupture occurred at this convention. PL had gained in strength and numbers and was ready to take over SDS with ease. But the militants jumped the gun, first walking out *en masse*, then re-emerging to announce that PL was 'expelled' (a final act of accidental homage to the Communist Party). Then they moved out quick enough to get to downtown Chicago where they liberated the SDS office of membership lists, files, bank accounts and printing press before PL even knew what was happening. (It was 1919 all over again.) Both groups now claimed to be the 'real SDS', although the action freaks also called themselves the Revolutionary Youth Movement (RYM). At New York University, in July 1969, PL tried to enter an RYM meeting and had fire extinguishers turned on them. The groups stalked one another on campuses, stomping on lone members of the opposition, but PL finally won the vendetta through sheer strength of numbers; most of the organization had lined up behind PL after the June split. RYM itself soon had a fracture; the breakaway group calling itself RYM II (called 'running dogs' by RYM I). In the next months RYM II underwent three mitoses (presumably calling themselves little RYMs III, IV and V). There were also 'third forces' to both the original factions in SDS, these called the Radical Student Union, December 4th Movement and Mad Dogs. Not to mention the Molotov Cocktail Party of Berkeley who described themselves as 'anarcho-Communists inspired by Hell Riders, a cycle club; Herbert Marcuse; the Motherfuckers of New York; and the peculiar state of war in which they now find themselves.'

The Revolutionary Youth Movement was soon re-named Weatherman and, in one sweep of the seasons, its politics and strategy proved changeable as the weather. The powerful influence which Progressive Labor and the return to Marxist theory had on SDS slowed the new militants down at first. Early Weather reports were full of half-baked dogma, in search of the 'correct' ideological position. They later toyed with half-way creations like 'armed love' – popular amongst White Panthers and Motherfuckers – a glance over the shoulder to LSD mellowness and up ahead to the ·45 (revolver, that is, not phonograph record). This had a lot of advantages – you could pretend to be fierce, shoulder-holster a-bulge and, at the same time, you might avoid serious implications by claiming you only shoot when attacked. Eventually, this was dismissed as self-indulgent; revolutionaries don't wait around for 'The Man' to come and get them.

Although the Left had graduated from its calculated passive resistance, it remained on the receiving end of the physical punishment. In response to brutal beatings, sophisticated weaponry and now State murder, the most it was geared to achieve was to 'smash the glass of the ruling class'. Here was a Reichian nightmare in the bud. The impotent struggles over the years, the dammed-up angers and hunger for power-packed self-expression – all this worked now towards eliminating those who *didn't dare*, leaving behind those who might – with a bit of nudging – just take a chance. There came a point where calling a busted skull a 'victory' for the movement just wouldn't suffice. The white American leftist hero set out to learn the hardest lesson he possibly could – how to *inflict* pain, to take the initiative to cause suffering, mutilation and even (perhaps) death for 'The Man' and his 'running dogs' who'd caused all the misery up to now.

It was a tall order. This was hardly a natural instinct, and building towards it required a cruel and masochistic therapy. Their more or less liberal upbringings had armoured most Weatherfolks with non-violent characters, with a penchant for tenderness and sentimentality, all of which they slung together now as 'bourgeois hang-ups'. These had to be swept away and there wasn't much time. As they increased their determination to lead *The* Revolution, the old idea of Marxist *selflessness* crept back into their experimental actions. The cultural revolution's message – that even revolutionaries could be gentle – was ignored as

Weatherman collectives moved towards a bitter version of the classical Communist purification rites. They toyed with a kind of Puritanism which didn't entirely work out, although it tended to deflate the hedonism of the past years. They held community LSD sessions to try and eliminate the sense of the individual. The family had to be erased because it was a major link to the past. Many of their fathers were moderately to extremely well off, captains of industry and commandants of Pig Amerika – the fact that these villains sired you had to become irrelevant. Weather-Jews had a special way of shirking original identity and giving substance to the old parental refrain 'You're killing us!' To have a coherent ideology in support of Third World anti-imperialist forces, you naturally had to be pro-Fedayeen. For some radical Jews this proved a critical problem;* many were lost to the movement over this issue, made even more poignant by the Panthers' fierce support for the Arabs and their rampaging anti-Semitism. But for others who needed a tool to sever the cord, backing the Palestinian cause was just what my son the doctor ordered.

The women's movement was essential in shaping Weatherman, and even eventually forced a change of name to Weather People. For these, the prospect of picking up a gun and offing the pig was the road to women's liberation. But the building of a pan-sexual army precluded, first and foremost, the practice of monogamy; the collective had to take precedence over the individual partner, and sentimental attachments were now counter-revolutionary. At the height of Weatherman's preparation, marriages were broken up and children sometimes given up for adoption. After one weekend council meeting, a large women's caucus decided to cancel instantly several hundred relationships. A Weatherwoman: 'At first, there were all kinds of crises around it. People made it on the sly, and then didn't make it at all for fear of being male chauvinists. That was clearly a bummer and . . . we did a kind of flip-flop from celibacy to a near orgy state. Fucking became pretty impersonal – if someone was a revolutionary, that was a good enough reason to make it . . . That didn't work either . . .'

* Even at Columbia University – a kosher hotbed – Jewish S D Sers clashed with the militant Jewish Defense League over such questions as allowing Israeli officials to speak on campus.

Obviously, there was a need to take stock of the new situations coming fast and furiously, and here Stalinism provided an exemplary answer. An early Weatherslogan was 'Criticism – Self-Criticism – Transformation'. This meant a gruelling, often sadistic group 'rap' in which the collective demanded massive changes in personality, and then followed this up with a critique that too much emphasis was being put on personality. Fear of actually being able to carry through some of their political and physical threats proved a major obstacle; this problem was 'handled in groups with people encouraged to bring it out and keep talking . . .' This allowed for new power struggles and mind manipulation within the collective, and stronger wills were able to lead these sessions towards a kind of therapeutic terrorism. The overriding theme: how far are you willing to go?

It all came down to factors of bravery. Despite the women – perhaps, in part, because of them – Weatherman became an exercise, yet again, in the promotion of virility. Confrontations with the police were provoked in the presence of white working-class kids, bikers and greasers, ostensibly to win them for converts by showing how tough we are, we ain't no faggot radicals like you've seen in the past (conjuring 1965-ish memories of Hell's Angels stomping on peace creeps 'cause they was too chicken to go in the army and fight like a man). During an action in Detroit, the Weather brigade bragged of 'defending' an NLF flag which the pigs tried to take away from them (and what macho patriot could quarrel with *defending your flag*?). From Detroit: 'We've become fighters this summer. Our study of karate makes us strong, and our practice makes us real to young people.'

Needless to say this new new gutsyness would first be rehearsed against the liberal Left (starting as modestly as possible). Weatherman conceived of itself as a 'moral force' – righteous brothers and sisters – and the growing political lethargy of the movement at large was intolerable in the light of their own zealous energy. The jive-ass honkie Left needed some shaking up, and who better to do the job than these new breed Stalinists. In November 1969 several Weathermen attempted to put the screws on the Vietnam Moritorium Committee, a liberal/pacifist group which was planning yet another peaceful march on Washington. Weatherman is reported to have asked a $20,000 payoff in exchange for behaving itself at the demo. Although the liberals did not want any violence on the march, and were already in the process of publicly disassociating themselves from the lunatic fringe, they told the blackmailers to piss off. The Weathermen decided not to 'off' them right there and then because the meeting was presided over by a Moritorium official who just happened to be an ex-member of the Washington Redskins football team.

The leftist movement itself became the last bourgeois cloud to be blown away. It had not been 'real' enough and could not provide a heavy turn-on. This was in part a reaction against Weatherman's own earlier flirtation with 'socialism'. Now – one year later – it seemed to them a washed-out ideology, so rooted in its historical premises that it was incapable of MOVING. Also, Marxists tended to denounce them for being just what they were – 'adventurists', personal courage mongers. In place of their recent Marxist-Leninist-Maoist-Marcusan-Pacifism came a whole new eclectic Weathermythology based primarily on images of brutality and revenge, one which had to be built up afresh to provide stimulation for the new 'Red Army'. They were not content at this stage – as were the Motherfuckers – with random violence for its own sake; it had to have some meaning. The influence of the crazies (and of LSD) was still strong, and helped turn Weatherman off of debilitating theory and on to the Politics of Gesture. But their religious fervour required tried and true icons. They believed they could wage the 'people's war' as conceived by Lin Piao, never questioning the preposterousness of the Chinese model in a US context. They idolized the Japanese students who hijacked a jet using Samurai swords (but probably would have taken less notice if this had been performed with guns). They adopted the existing movement syndrome of promoting trial victims via the new numbers racket – the Panther 21, the Chicago 8 (or 7), the Seattle 7, a group of Weatherwomen called the Motor City 9 or MC9 (not to be confused with the MC5, a revolutionary pop group) – thereby establishing a whole new order of Stars in Court.

And there was Che. No longer could they respect Martin Luther King types who just stood and took abuse, nor even the old leftist hero who could punch back. John Garfield was now traded in for a new Errol Flynn-type champion, one who could hang by his teeth over a thousand-foot precipice, wondering where in the world he might find some 'real' danger. Handsome, swashbuckling Che Guevara was just the thing, and he was Number Onederful throughout *The* Revolution (although, leave it to the broads to point out that even he insisted the *muchachas* do all the cooking in the guerrilla camp!). His image as a warrior (not as a strategist) was built up and projected everywhere. One theatrical piece made him fucker-extraordinaire, orgy-master and king-stud of the sexual revolution (which he probably would have denounced). Committee Chairman Ichord even conjured him up at Kent State: 'I don't know who they are trying to imitate, Che Guevara or someone else, but just looking at them and the television pictures leads one to believe they are potential troublemakers.' But Che was hardly more than Castro's sidekick until he became a notch in some Green Beret's gunbelt. *This* was his fascination for Weatherman, just as it had applied the same heroism to daredevil Viet Cong: the greatest amongst the new god-men were those who professed or demonstrated a *willingness to die*.

The 'death trip' initially took a purely vicarious form, dreams of murder sharing popularity with the act of dying. They replaced the two-fingered 'peace' symbol with a three-fingered 'fork' symbol to commemorate Charles Manson and his collective who offed some bourgeois pigs (Sharon Tate, etc.) and then plunged a fork into their fat. (Later, Manson was dropped from the roster of culture-heroes when it was discovered he was a male chauvinist!) Their new cartoon Superman-replacements (in leaflets and in the 'underground' press) shouted Weatherjargon like 'Eat leaden death!' or 'Taste the sweetness of destiny, racist pig!' as they finished off their middle-aged capitalist victims. One Weatherman waxed ecstatic over a pop group called The Up, sixteen-year-olds who played with bayonets attached to their guitars.

Weatherman beefed up its new black and Third World folklore by adopting a lingo with counter-cultural roots. Their new tracts and communiqués increasingly gave up their Marxist mouthings in favour of 'outtasight', 'fucking us over' and that delightful new curio, 'getting our shit together' (oh toilet-trainer Spock, where are you now?). But none of these isolated effects or heroes made sense without a reason for being and struggling: the making of revolution on behalf of – *The* People. It was a glance back to leftist fawning over the worker in the thirties, but never so grovelling and self-effacing now, nor so limited a thing. The implications of giving All Power to *The* People, Serving *The* People whose Spirit was Stronger than The Man's Technology, was an act of righteousness, not merely a symbol to organize around.

It had almost everything going for it now, celebrity, motive, ferocity, Cause. 'Cadres' (this old leftist word caught on like wildfire now, the icing on the military cake) were ready and conditioned for action. They practised karate and weaponry, and steeled themselves for inevitable beatings. Group analysis rooted out those who weren't willing to give *everything* for the struggle. Now it only wanted a theatre of operations.

Weatherman entered its second major phase when it planned the Days of Rage for October 1969 in Chicago to coincide with the famous Conspiracy 8 trial in progress there. Its theoretical basis was shelved in favour of total physical militancy; Chicago was the proving-ground for its experiment with bravado. Their palaver went like this: 'Probably a lot of us will get shot. But for every one of us that goes down, there'll be five to take his place'; or: 'If you have anything short of a mortal wound, you are expected to fight on. We're going to off the pig.' And there it was – 'how far are you willing to go?' was a rhetorical question. All those years of pushing for a leftist solution down tunnels of *persona*, experiments with passion, passivity, jail, mind expansion, carnality led up the way now to the Final Therapy: nothing less than *dying* for *The* Revolution. All the guilt and shame of being a white American radical, a punk and a failure, gathered to the logic of the Big Dare. It was a casting off of family, character armour and dissatisfaction with a sweeping gesture of challenge to the self, one final sexual thrust for fame – in the very language of Weatherman – *Wargasm*.

The proof of it came with the Days of Rage. 'We now find the government guilty and sentence it to death in the streets', their leaflet promised. Politically, this threat was meant to enlist the alienated white youth culture that was supposedly turning on to violence and going wild in the streets. The cadres would lead the way – just like the Viet Cong – and *The* People would join them once the battle was on. They predicted a turnout of 10,000 in Chicago; 800 appeared, mostly Weathermen and, by the second day, only 300 were left raging. Still, this was no reason for despair and only meant they would have to fight that much harder. One leader summed it up (and, in doing so, probably summed up the history of the US Left): 'We're going to win by not thinking of losing.'

It was another 'first'. The first-ever white youth culture *aggression* against the State for political purposes. At a given signal they moved through the streets, trashing (random smashing) as they went, taking out windows, cars, an occasional citizen. They boasted sixty cop casualties at the end of the action. Astonishingly, the police were caught by surprise; they never expected that leftists would have the nerve. Neither did the leftists. The Wargasm was dazzling, the very idea that it could be done after all. They were now carried along on a wave of drummed-up moral logic: '. . . if they shot a bunch of us, even if the people hated us, they wouldn't stand for it because we're white.' After a few hours, they burned themselves out and scattered.

On another raging day, women cadres, some fifty in number, got *their* shit together. Armed with motorcycle helmets, clubs, long poles and Viet Cong flags, they worked themselves up to fever pitch in a Chicago park. Bernadine Dohrn, already chief Weatherspokeswoman, announced: 'For the first time in history women are getting themselves together. We're not picketing in front of bra factories now. We're not . . . engaged in self-indulgent bullshit . . . A few buckshot wounds mean we're doing the right thing . . . Bullets are not going to stop us . . .' Then they sped off like furies, chanting the piercing cry of Arab revolutionary women they'd picked up from *The Battle of Algiers* (a film which had a tremendous impact on their movement). But the pigs stopped them on the edge of the park, disarmed and subdued them in a matter of minutes. Ms Revolution – unlike the 'heroic' Arab ladies – broke into tears.

290 arrests were made in the few Days of Rage and these heroes were dubbed – naturally – the Chicago 290. This left fewer and fewer warriors as the days went on, and the actions diminished to a squeak. In the instant analysis and *mea culpa* syndrome that followed, one weathered man talked against violence for its own sake, the very kind they'd once been turned on to in the Marlon Brando film, *The Wild One*. It was a macho scene, man, after all. Another answered a jibe about the rage deflating so quickly: 'We're only learning.'

They were learning their parts in the upcoming Passion Play of the Urban Guerrilla.

The Days of Rage left Weatherman breathless in a cyclone of court cases. It was impossible to raise the staggering legal fees; also, jail sentences were surely in the offing and would wipe out the group's core. On top of this, they felt the Chicago action was not strategically sensible, whatever else it may have achieved by way of exposure and excitement. The very *plan* of it was suicidal; there was no repeat performance.

It was necessary to think again. At this point (late 1969) Weatherman became disappointed with white working-class youth (who failed to rally round the Days of Rage) and gave up altogether on the white movement. Without the support of large numbers, the brigade would have to hone down its revolutionary vision and get off the streets. It would now have to attack from an underground vantage and thereby aid the struggle of the blacks and the Vietnamese. This meant an entirely new orientation, and they chose the established model for it – the urban guerrilla. Third World revolutionaries like the Uruguayan Tupamaros or Al Fatah seemed to be striking blows *that really worked* against the empire. An important theoretical text, made available to them about that time, was 'The Minimanual of the Urban Guerilla' – by a Brazilian, Carlos Marighella – which describes the essence of the game: 'To conquer the art of dissembling. Never to fear danger. To behave the same by day as by night. Not to act impetuously. To have unlimited patience. To remain calm and cool in the worst conditions and situations. Never to leave a track or a trail. Not to get discouraged.' Judging by the Days of Rage and their aftermath, Weatherman struck out on nearly all these criteria. They had to learn now that one of the greatest 'sins' of the guerrilla was 'to boast about the actions he has completed and broadcast them to the four winds'. Instead, the process required being *nobody*, cutting your hair, changing your name, living out of town. It was not designed to *gain* converts; alas, the whole mystique of the urban guerrilla was based on the idea that he *already had* the love and the support of *The* People – and who could count on that in the US? The number of radicals now had to be broken down into 'affinity groups' of six to fifteen members. (It was the same pattern followed by the CP in 1920 and 1949, with the important exception that the Communists had Russian professionals to show them how it was done.) Underground was also a step up from the lingering mentality of going to jail to prove some moral premise. If you were a true revolutionary, it was now argued, you were *outside*, doing your thing.

All this brought a new and long-overdue vigilance. The breakdown into small striking-cadres was designed not only for efficiency, but for security as well. The informer had been back in vogue for some time already. Out of some forty prosecution witnesses in the Chicago Conspiracy Trial, thirty-four turned out to be undercover agents, and defendants were amazed to see old 'pals' and revolutionary 'leaders' paraded before them as spies. In 1968 Weatherman-to-be, Mark Rudd, was busted by his own personal bodyguard (Jerry Rubin was also nailed by this tactic). The FBI was on top: 'Nothing the SDS does surprises us. If they are going to have a rally, then we know what kind of tactics they are planning and we are ready for them . . .' Radicals tried to outmanoeuvre the Feds by leaving plans to the last minute, but this did not allow enough time for spreading word of a demonstration. After a *New York Times* reporter testified for the Committee about the 1968 SDS Convention, the 'straight' media was barred from further meetings; but newsmen managed to pose as hippies or buy off SDS members for info. In 1968 SDS was clever enough to establish a phoney 'sabotage and explosives' workshop at their convention to divert the undercover agents while the real business of the day transpired elsewhere; the measure of the success of this ploy is that J. Edgar Hoover believed it and cited the workshop time and again in the years following.

Paranoia about infiltration was another cause for Weatherman submerging. This decision was announced at their National War Council held in Michigan in December 1969, at which the birth of the new 'Weather Nation' was celebrated. A huge cardboard machine-gun hung from the ceiling over the gathering, a touch of unintentional self-parody. The group now entered a new phase, seeing themselves as 'vandals in the mother country' and 'tools of necessity' bent on clandestine marauding in the 'belly of the Amerikan beast'. When their first bomb struck, the next June, the FBI put a price of $2,000 a head for info leading to their arrest; the FBI also announced that it expected Weatherman to try to kidnap high officials and foreign diplomats. Many who had gone underground were fugitives from their Days of Rage indictments, making capture an even more delicious prospect. But the G-Men did not find it all that easy, and never managed to catch a significant Weatherman. For one thing, the group was learning primitive 'counter-intelligence' procedures, checking the backgrounds and keeping close watch on all brothers and sisters. One early method was the communal ingestion of LSD, a substance few cops could get into without revealing themselves; but this did not always work. Unmasked informers were sometimes beaten up, but never eradicated (as per instructions in the Minimanual). Still, the strictest security didn't always succeed. In 1970 an FBI agent posed as a disillusioned ex-Green Beret and managed to infiltrate a Weather collective in Seattle, the new 'bombing capital' of America. The group was obviously attracted to his military skills and, sure enough, he provided weapons training and target practice. He also supplied guns, potassium chlorate for bombs (as well as teaching the preparation of these) and dope. It wasn't until he appeared as star prosecution witness in the Seattle 7 conspiracy trial that anyone realized all the gear had been compliments of Edgar Hoover.

By the time Weatherman entered the explosives pageant, this was already an American way of life. The Permanent Subcommittee on Investigations cited 4,330 blasts in the period from January 1969 to April 1970. These had caused forty-three deaths (many of them novice saboteurs themselves) and $21·8 million in damage; there had also been 1,175 failed attempts and 35,129 threats. In this wonderful game there was a shining new pinnacle for the leftist hero to reach, higher even than the old high of going to jail – the new get-your-picture-in-the-post-office syndrome, climbing into the FBI's Most Wanted Top Ten. Bernadine Dohrn and another Weathergirl, Cathlyn Wilkerson, eventually got this honour on behalf of the Weather Nation. An earlier winner was Pun Plamondon, a big cheese in the White Panther Party who, along with John Sinclair, was cited for conspiracy to bomb a Michigan CIA building in early 1969; Plamondon immediately disappeared.

By January 1972 the Bank of America had been bombed thirty-nine times in various cities and burned to the ground in Santa Barbara, California, when a flaming trashcan was thrown through its window. The Capitol building in Washington suffered an explosion in response to Nixon's renewed bombing of Laos in early 1971. One radical got the notion to place bombs in safe-deposit boxes at banks across the country, causing chaos for the idea of their utter privacy. It was also discovered that many of the explosive materials got into leftist hands via dissidents in US military compounds!

One of the most spectacular displays of fireworks came at the University of Wisconsin in August 1970, when a group of 'weathery' fellows, called the New Year's Gang, took out the Army Mathematics Research Center (AMRC), causing $6 million damage and one death. It was not an isolated incident; the New Year's Gang had already fire-bombed an ROTC armoury, destroyed a monkey laboratory suspected of doing nerve-gas research and tried to bomb a near-by munitions plant with a stolen ROTC plane. Students claimed that the AMRC – funded by the Army – was into things like 'high-altitude infra-red surveillance equipment' used for – of course! – tracking down Che Guevara in the jungles of Bolivia! The Center had almost begged the bombing when, fed up with replacing broken windows, it installed new plexiglass shields which bounced back rocks. It was not yet at the expanded level of consciousness of the Berkeley Bank of America which simply changed its glass for brick, stem to stern, after three or four shattering years. (If only it could have changed its name!)

It was the Weather People, more than any other group, who were really getting their potassium chlorate together. After bombing the New York police building, they issued their first communiqué (urban guerrilla's method of informing *The* People about the political meaning of its actions). In it, Bernadine Dohrn announced: 'We're not hiding out but we're invisible.' The tough lesson was learned: outtasight. The dynamitards quickly followed up their June action by bombing a Manhattan Bank of America in July. On Columbus Day, 1970, the California National Guard were 'tipped off' that 'Weatherman will start attacking . . . every public building, aircraft, and military building throughout the state'. This was obviously someone's paranoia, but it attests to the cultural image Weatherman had conjured. In that particular weekend a courthouse, a National Guard armoury and an ROTC building were hit on the West Coast. For each of these actions, letters of explanation were circulated to the press. (These had been photostated to prevent them being traced to a particular typewriter – they were learning). One group wrote: 'As the beast falls, a new culture of life arises: our families and gardens, our music and acid and weed, their Bank of America burning to the ground.'

Despite its reputation for sheer terrorism, Weatherman was learning to attack and survive – the chief goal of the urban guerrilla. It had also learned that the game could no longer spin on improvisation, but demanded coordination and careful stratagem. Said one frustrated New York bomb-squad detective: 'In the old days when we caught a bomber such as George Metesky, the threat was over. Now, if you catch one, you haven't stopped the organization.'

The new efficiency led them to perform their greatest coup, the sparkling delivery of Dr Leary from minimum security lock-up. Despite the rumour that Weatherman got $25,000 for the job, the communiqué they issued indicated it was an act of real commitment. It said Leary had been 'captured for the work he did in helping all of us begin the task of creating a new culture on the barren wasteland . . . LSD and grass . . . will help us make a future world where it will be possible to live in peace.' The underground had mastered techniques of printing false documents, and provided Leary with a new identity. In the week the Doctor spent with Weatherman before his departure for Algeria, he shaved his head, grew a moustache and became a certain 'Mr McMillan'. But he seemed transformed in other ways, having walked full steam into the cowboy movie the Weather People were in the process of leaving behind. He packed a rod and swore he'd use it on anyone who interfered with his freedom. And, naturally – still and always the missionary – he projected his new image everywhere, expecting others to be where his head was. Referring to Joan Baez's pacifist husband, Leary declared: 'If David Harris has ten friends in the world, I say to you, get off your pious nonviolent asses and break him out.'

Weatherman's acknowledgement of Leary and the peaceful prospects of LSD – after the group had renounced the counterculture – showed that it was already (this was September 1970) in the process of another flip-flop. In March of that year three Weather People had been blown to smithereens while preparing bombs in a New York townhouse, all because they didn't know enough to install a safety switch and warning light. This had a stunning effect on their movement, and the Russian roulette and lack of experience suddenly acquired ominous overtones. In December 1970, Bernadine Dohrn issued a communiqué (by now these were on tape or accompanied by a thumbprint because of many bogus communiqués received) called 'New Morning', calling for an end to underground activity and a return to demonstrations and mass action: 'The deaths of three friends ended our military conception of what we're doing.' So – one year and three casualties after the guerrilla war was declared, it was more or less called off. But the communiqué did not really explain why it had taken from March to December to come to such an emotionally charged conclusion (with many bombings in between). More likely the humbled tone of the statement provides a better clue: 'Most of our actions have hit the enemy on about the same military scale as a bee sting.'

It was a failure of nerve. Weatherman continued to bomb sporadically in the next years, pulling off even a Ho Chi Minh birthday extravaganza (May 1972) in a ladies toilet at the Pentagon, flooding the Air Forces Data Services Center and damaging its computers. But the group's ability to sustain its crusade lay in ruins. Despite its occasional efficacy, bombing was just another *gesture* after all. Bernadine Dohrn had hoped 'to blast away the myths of the total superiority of The Man'. But it only knocked out the chief Weathermyth, the fiction of its own spunk. Even the fascination with death disappeared almost simultaneously with the mouthing of it. Nearly every bombing was accompanied by an advance warning or was directed solely at property. The ability to deliver hurt to others never got beyond the wish.

Weatherman seemed to many like the cathartic impulse of a lunatic minority; even in its heyday, there were never more than a few hundred hardcore cadres. But, in an important sense, the entire history of the American Left led up to this abortive climax. Weather People were not anarchists; they were, either directly or by social contagion, products of a heritage which insisted on voicing an alien and uncomfortable ideology, which admonished its adventurers and which watered down its rebellion with pacifism. All of this seethed in the folks who brought you Weatherman, and their failure to kill or even maintain their own fantasy of apocalypse can be laid to their coddling as middle-class white Americans – which they were still, despite all their therapy. As such, they were still striking back with a vengeance, grasping for power that was further from them than at any point in leftist history, calling their fight by wonderful dream-phrases when it was finally and utterly heat, mere vapour.

4

A political movement which could conceive of its own 'beginning', with little understanding of its antecedents, could just as logically arrange its own 'end'. Because the radical show seemed to go out in a blast, with leftists displaying few signs of regeneration, the latest in the series of instant analyses was that the whole thing was 'over'. Spoken or written obituaries sprang up like weeds

over a grave, asking, 'what went wrong?' or 'where are we now?';
some top radicals publicly denied the movement was finished,
but privately admitted things 'look pretty bad'. It was perfect
cultural whitewash for folks tired of being fooled, tired of defeat
and just plain tired.

Only the Old Left and hard-line Marxists seemed as 'alert' as
ever. PL had a firm grip on SDS (what was left of it) and continued to wait for the working-class uprising which was just
around the corner. One of the few anti-war groups still in business
by late 1971 was a Trotskyite stronghold called the National
Peace Action Coalition – Student Mobilization Committee. Even
the Communist Party had a kiss of life now in the gaining of its
first superstar member since the early fifties, sister Angela Davis;
because of her railroading by the Reagan administration, a
powerful campaign (the likes of which only the international CP
could muster) made her a radical household name. It was a kind
of victory to see all the adventurists and agitator-freaks get their
comeuppance ('we told you so, brats!'), while they, sober
Marxists, remained so riveted in place they never had to worry
about landing on their feet when the winds of change blew up a
twister.

Some New Leftists and gesture-makers still in spin were already looking ahead to the Big Comeback. The need to join
battered forces created new groups like the People's Coalition
which made strange bedfellows of Women's Strike for Peace,
Vietnam veterans, militant women, reformed Yippies and assorted
latest-phase artists – each still promoting their own issues. They
united only in reminding people that the war was still on and in
countering the image, in the eyes of the media and the liberal
establishment, that the Left was no longer anything but a nest of
mad bombers. 'Street people' were mostly off the streets now or
engaging in a further stage of the consciousness insurrection
called Merchandise Liberation. Jerry Rubin played bongo drums
for a short time in John Lennon's revolutionary pop group, and
also helped form the Rock Liberation Front, dedicated to keeping
the people's music free of capitalist impurity; this then fractured
into the Rock Liberation Front II which later became the Zippies
which also broke away from the Yippies. Much of Women's

Liberation had gone along private roads or descended into sheer psychic war against the opposite sex. Eldridge Cleaver, in exile, expelled Huey Newton and Bobby Seale from the Black Panther Party, who in turn expelled Cleaver from the same group. Academy Award actress, Jane Fonda, joined the movement as a Jane-come-lately and then married Academy Award protester Tom Hayden. Joan Baez separated from David Harris because of the strain of his being in jail so long for draft resistance. John Sinclair got out of prison in 1972 and his new Rainbow People's Party (formerly White Panthers) promised its first 'one-year plan'.

In the early part of the seventies, the fading movement staged a series of 'last stands'. The most significant of these happened in the spring of 1971 when folks came to Washington for the final showdown. The organizers were ex-Weathermen, ex-crazies, ex-SDS – under the leadership of stalwart Rennie Davis – known as the May Day Tribe. It was more than symbolic that they would hark back to May Day, for many who could – with a tear in the eye – remember the traditional meaning of May Day came along in force. These older folks were especially worried about 'alienating public opinion' and had to be assured that the event was not going to be another cowboy white trashing. It was planned as a wider foray into passive resistance, with three weeks of non-violent demos leading up to the finale scheduled for the first week of May. However, there was no guarantee that things would go sweetly. For one thing, 4 May was the first anniversary of the Kent State martyrdom and there was bound to be an emotion-packed response. Also, the goal of the final week was to close down the Government, and the Power was not likely to cooperate. This became evident when a permit to camp in a public park was revoked; it was discovered – surprise! – that nudity and dope-smoking had occurred. Now many who came for the pre-struggle rock concerts about-faced and went home, reducing the number of tribesmen. The original plan to create mass sit-ins at twenty-one major road junctions and bridges had to be severely limited.

If the movement hoped to play out another righteous romance here, the Administration was willing to oblige it with more than enough paranoia-fodder. 10,000 troops were put on the alert at seven military bases from Washington DC to North Carolina, in addition to National Guard and squads of local police. This included a battalion from an armoured cavalry regiment and a phalanx of US Marines. There were amphibious armoured cars at the ready (presumably to capture escaping protesters who were swimming out of town), and the use of troop 'insertions' by helicopter – as in Indo-China – was promised if things got hot (leftists threatened to retaliate on this one by flying kites and balloons to foil landings).

On the first big day, 4,000 rifle-proud troops knocked out any possible movement successes, and Marine helicopters landed without trouble at the Washington Monument to disperse crowds there. The demonstrators sat down *en masse* at crossroads and claimed the victory of holding six junctions for two hours. Where this failed, they put glass on the roads and let the air out of tyres or stood in front of moving cars. Several cars were overturned, and one was burned. Dr Spock was among a group that tried to take a bridge, but he was tear-gassed and hauled off under arrest yet again. One band of outlaws hurled bags of chicken-shit at the Pentagon. 7,000 were arrested on the first day and, by the end of the week, this had swelled to 12,000.

Across the Republic, some leftover California Weathertypes coordinated with the May Day demos by bombing a Pacific Gas and Electric plant, a Standard Oil refinery and – of course – two Banks of America. Meanwhile, back in DC, the siege came to a glorious end when someone managed to hang a Viet Cong flag from a balcony at the House of Representatives and a man stood naked on the steps of the Capitol building.

The most significant 'first' about the May Days was a hair-raising number called preventive detention. There were few broken heads and no 'apparent' brutality for the TV audience. Instead, the protesters were tear-gassed to a blindness, then corralled into a huge sports arena prepared in advance as a temporary jail. This served several purposes. It gave the police a peaceful, fair image. It kept many troublemakers off the streets (thereby weakening the whole point of the demo). Above all, it meant thousands of court cases, a fortune in bail money and legal fees for an already bank-rupt movement.

It was a stroke of reaction worthy of a Grand Master, and if there is any doubt who actually drew up the blueprint, there can be none at all about whose vision and style manipulated the event from start to finish. American repression at last became utterly professional under the watchful tutelage of one who had made a lifetime's business of it. Since he helped inaugurate the impotence of this protest generation, it was only fitting he should preside over its collapse and humiliation.

This wasn't his last trick by any means. Arrest was one thing, but there had been rents in the perfect fabric of judicial complicity such as the Chicago Conspiracy 7 going free on appeal. (Later there would be Angela Davis's acquittal and others.) Directly it had stopped the demo cold, the Justice Department announced it was planning a 'special grand jury' to investigate the May Day affair. This was made possible by the Organized Crime Control Act of 1970, which authorized the use of grand juries for investigating criminal activity. Upon receiving information and listening to testimony, a grand jury of well-picked, average citizens decides – in absolute secrecy – if a crime has been committed and whether an indictment should be made. A witness cannot have his lawyer with him in the jury room, he has no right to know the object of the investigation and he may not even be told if he himself will be a defendant should a criminal trial be necessary. On top of this, the use of the Fifth Amendment was effectively put out of action by a turn of the new law called 'use immunity'. In the past, a witness refusing to incriminate himself could be granted full immunity from prosecution – by a judge – and might then talk freely before the grand jury. 'Use immunity' provided that he could still be prosecuted later if evidence against him was obtained from testimony other than his own. This meant there was virtually no protecting a witness from a prosecutor asking him anything at all pertaining to the investigation; many just refused to talk anyway and were jailed for the term of the grand jury (up to eighteen months).

This sinister new twist of the legal apparatus was used in the Daniel Ellsberg-Pentagon Papers affair, against the radical Catholic priest, Daniel Berrigan and others. It was designed to

further cripple the Left and, specifically, to get Weatherman.*
Although the Government maintained that fugitive-hunting was
the domain only of the FBI, it had really got into the business
itself by granting special investigative powers to the grand juries,
who were easily manipulated by Administration-chosen Commie-
catching prosecutors. These hoped, for example, to threaten the
'underground support system' of Weatherman by gaining fraud
indictments against its surface contacts. Such people allegedly
purchased traveller's cheques, reported them stolen, cashed them
in and turned the proceeds over to the Weather underground.
Others may have helped by providing false identifications and
passports. But the most strategic reason for bringing these friends
of Weatherman before the grand jury was to collect as many
random facts as possible (by threatening non-talkative witnesses
with jail) and attempting, by computer, to piece together various
testimonies to solve the Weatherpuzzle. One Government prosecutor even admitted it was his driving ambition to get Bernadine
Dohrn (who by now was the ultimate fly in the male reactionary
ointment). In 1972 a standing indictment against thirteen key
Weather People was superseded by a new grand jury charge. But
they were still nowhere to be found.

The new team of hand-picked grand jury prosecutors took over
the political – if not legislative – function of the old HUAC, and
even stepped on the toes of the new Internal Security Committee.
But the grand jury prosecutors had far more power than the
witch-hunters and none of the publicity bravado. It was easy for

---

*The real test of Weatherman's myth-making power is that their bravado
was taken seriously by the President. At the very least, their impotent
gestures became the excuse for much of the work done by the White House
'plumbers' which goes under the false media-name 'Watergate'. It was
claimed that underground saboteurs had links even to the Democratic
Party, which led to the bugging of their headquarters. Clearly this was a
ready-made Red herring, an attempt to gain public sympathy for an illegal
government operation. But, at the same time, there can be no doubt that the
President's life-long obsession with radicals – the belief that they were out to
get *him* specifically – played a key role in the development of the 'dirty
tricks' department. He even asked the CIA – astonishingly – to determine
if such radical activity had a foreign influence. The President was unhappy
with the conclusion that it was completely 'home-grown' and decided to
launch his own investigation.

the public to be unaware of their existence or of the new jury powers – which was precisely the point. They could operate without drama and there was no way the Left might make spectacle of it. It was a brilliant delivery of undertakers for the self-proclaimed 'death' of the movement and a dance on its grave by Nixonculture.

Those who made a nice killing from the revolutionary sweepstakes generally hung around even after the so-called 'end' to mop up the spoils. And spoils there were indeed. Even the Nixon–McCarthy era couldn't boast so many casualties. These were not merely the drug cases and freak-outs and suicides of the 'cultural revolution', but also countless people whose political fervour had misfired or been abused. If the last great experiment with terrorism suggested some leftist death-wish, this was now to be compounded with post-*The* Revolution vulturism.

Parasites on the movement had long been in evidence and were integral to the nature of the new social/political changes. The gurus and shamans who sucked up much of the unharnessed cultural energy were often classical tricksters and dumbo-catching medicine-man frauds in some degree. But they could only have operated in a wide-open, accepting atmosphere (as it was *circa* 1965) and they made profit (emotional and otherwise) out of the confused dialogue between a political commitment that seemed futile and a mystical exile into (or out of) the self. They understood how to collect LSD casualties on the rebound and offer up more lasting rewards. So Krishna Consciousness and Meher Baba devotees and Maharishi Mahesh Yogi and a thousand others less enterprising were adjuncts to the scene, never gaining massive numbers, but patient and wealthy enough to sit out the political apocalypse, waiting to apply their spiritual first aid.

One movement regular who got 'healed' in this way was Rennie Davis; in 1973 he traded in his radicalism for a life at the toes of Guru Maharaj Ji, the fifteen-year-old boy reputed by his followers to be the incarnation of God on Earth. Davis had always been one of the most sober New Left leaders, working hard and patiently along practical tracks, avoiding the usual personality-crusades or ego-tripping. But his faith needs could no longer be satisfied by the movement and – like Louis Budenz some thirty years before – he arranged for himself a divine conversion out of the Left. Davis, naturally, maintained his public missionary spirit and – like past renegades – felt the need to eradicate his political efforts. He claimed his Chicago Conspiracy Trial was God's preparation for his current task of travelling the world, promoting the guru with stage discussions and public spectacles. Also: 'I'm going to do everything I ever wanted to do, now that I know that my revolutionary perspective of what causes suffering was wrong – that mind is Satan, mind is the anti-Christ.'

But none of these religious experts could mount a road-show like Jesus could, and it was only fitting that he would overtake all the swamis in the final stretch. The Jesus Movement did not only promise the usual pie-in-the-sky Big Finish, but also picked up on the symbols and materialistic accoutrements of the counter-culture (which the Eastern crowd could not readily do without blowing their cover). The new fundamentalists employed (and converted) rock musicians, started 'underground' papers modelled accurately on those already existing (one of these was called *Right On*), adopted the leftist clenched fist salute (but added a finger pointing up to Heaven). They also played the ecstasy game and kept up the general sense of pageant, making Hollywood their base and major fairgrounds.

Jesus Freakery came into vogue just at the collapse of the leftist surge and fed merrily on the general despair to nourish itself. One of its chief purposes was to kick away the crutches of the crippled movement. Jesus had long been a fighter of Commies, accepter and healer of renegades and Red-baiter extraordinaire. Now he disrupted rallies and SDS gatherings (where cries of 'The end is at hand' made a certain ironic sense). Those clergymen who opposed the war in Indo-China were castigated for leading their flocks astray; this was not a simple 'Jesus' peace is more lasting than a ceasefire' number, but calculated anti-Left propaganda. A cartoon from one typical Jesus paper showed a depraved, filthy hippie-SDS type, with 'Do It' stencilled on his shirt – Jerry Rubin as the Anti-Christ – molesting a clean and loving Christian and denying him the right to speak publicly.

Above all, Jesus was an antidote to liberation for those who still got high on guilt. Back came Puritanism with a vengeance, the total scorn of drugs (as if Jesus wasn't an opiate), suppression of pre-marital sex, anti-homosexuality and rabid, classical male chauvinism. For the disillusioned (many leftists among them) it gave the chase for therapy a new dimension, spilling over – without having very far to go – into 'salvation'.

Another breed of vampire got its kicks off the image of vibrant, liberated youth. Not only revolutionaries themselves – cashing in with published instant memoirs of a phenomenon they hadn't yet begun to fathom – but older sympathizers as well, opened up a Greenbacks of America revolution-market. This complex of articles, films, tomes, best-sellers, theses was usually guided by a desire to spread the message or give credence, comfort and support to young folks who had revived a 'defunct' Red Scare-killed movement. Many of the writers were teachers who had seen their students gassed and beaten and driven to despair; now they hoped to come to terms with conscience. But these works of outsiders-looking-in were filled with an optimism the 'youth culture' never possessed at its most starry-eyed. The makers of *The* Revolution were seen to be conjuring up an America that had supposedly eluded the elders, one which they imagined could hark back to Whitmanesque prophecies and founding principles.

Hollywood's attraction was neither so laudatory nor so intellectually perverse. In the heyday of the counter-culture it spewed a fountain of Technicolor wonders, like the *Strawberry Statement*, the film version of the Columbia strike and police riot, with every ounce of political dynamic edited away. The hero is a pretty innocent who 'joins' the student strike so he can make it with the leftist heroine; eventually, he exchanges his Robert Kennedy poster for one of Che and gets his head bashed at the Peace-In. Radical critics were furious at being so publicly plasticized. Yet if *The* Revolution had come to look like *Love Story* it was not entirely the fault of Hollywood capitalists, but also the indirect work of left-ish dreamweavers. It was only a matter of time before the former would purchase, overexpose and then dispose of the movement's already overblown premises.*

* The Left was incensed when Hollywood produced its version of *Che*, completely apolitical and romanticized. Firebombs and grenades were

The most hovering of all birds of prey, forever gnawing at the fringes of the Great Liberation, was the deadly 'Uncle Smack'. When all else failed, when the sweetest of experiments soured, when even the intoxication with literal death wore off, large numbers of once-committed people opted for a tried and true disappearing act. Some movement spokesmen, like John Sinclair, saw the rush into heroin addiction as part of a political conspiracy to debilitate *The* Revolution, beginning somewhere in the anti-LSD activities of police officials and winding up as a secret weapon in the crowded arsenal of Nixonculture. Sinclair saw the business begin when 'someone' started cutting pure LSD with deadly amphetamines, leading to an 'ADULTeration' of the youth culture. This was later backed by Nixon's 'Operation Intercept' which temporarily cut off marijuana supplies coming through Mexico; during this episode many kids fell to heroin which was plentiful at the time.

This version does not take into account the local counter-cultural 'rip-off' salesmen who would and did sell anything on the street, nor the complicity of the Mafia. But revelations of the late sixties, that eighty per cent of the world's illegal opium (used in making heroin) came from Southeast Asia (according to the UN Commission on Drugs and Narcotics); that the CIA was involved in the trade; that heroin was, for eight years, smuggled inside some returning corpses of US servicemen (many of whom had died from heroin overdoses, not just Viet Cong bullets) – all this goes one better than any conspiracy theory.

If it was not true that the Power employed heroin to silence the ghettos and the freaks, it was a wonderful myth that any repressive government would be proud to have thought up. It was the same level on which the US Government and the Left had always met – decadent fantasy – in their calculations of each other's motives.

---

tossed into cinemas showing the film and, in Detroit, SDS cadres captured the stage during a show and discussed 'economic imperialism' with the audience. However, in 1961, Errol Flynn (who'd fought with Castro and made his own film about it) carried a message to producer Darryl Zanuck, asking if he would be interested in making a film about the Cuban Revolution. 'Che' Guevara, the sender of this message, hoped the famous Hollywood producer would take up his offer.

For the Left, it was yet another thrill-packed version of *The* End. Whoever applied the Fix to movement stragglers and counter-cultural casualties, the Smack was only a symbolic departure. In all the probes, no self was got; at last, some just simply turned on so as to turn off. The struggle was at last – outtasight.

*

The weary Leary got no rest. Arriving in Algiers, he was first welcomed by Black Panther-in-exile, Eldridge Cleaver. Cleaver was the only major black militant to praise Weatherman (others dismissed it as 'Custeristic') and was naturally drawn to Leary's new 'ferocity'. After a short time, however, he discovered there was 'something wrong with Leary's brain', that he was still just a tripper and hadn't the clarity to be a revolutionary. The Doctor fled to Switzerland after a spell of 'imprisonment' by the Panthers.

It was only a matter of time before he would walk into a US Government trap, as he did in Afghanistan in 1972. The Feds had been gunning for him ever since his escape, and there were grand jury indictments by the score waiting for him. In addition his Brotherhood of Eternal Love had been busted for big dealing, and he was implicated. Said the Orange County District Attorney: 'I think the evidence shows that, under Timothy Leary's leadership, it has developed into a very sophisticated organization in terms of smuggling . . . If you have seen The French Connection *you are aware of these things.' For this apparent nonsense, Leary's bail was set at a cool 5 million.*

Once brought back to face all his trials, the good Doctor had to try and undo some of the 'damage' caused by his Weathertripping. He said he had spoken in the heat of the moment and vented a natural bitterness against the Power that bound him over: 'My so-called "militant" statements after escaping from the California prison were distorted, naturally, as by everyone with a political axe to grind.' But it was not so easily shrugged. For a brief moment of desperation he had become fixed by a political insight, published it abroad, urged it on others, allowed it to be absorbed. Now he was retreating from it and changing his mind. It was the story of The Revolution *in little. Changed his mind.*

Curtain Call

If all the home-grown remedies kept you anxious, failed to suppress unpleasant memory, you could still make that famous journey to the East. Most of the travelling swamis who brought their road-shows to town and played the local hot spots were suspect because of their Lincoln Continentals and the amount of time spent away from that original cave where they got their Nirvana together. Ex-Superguru Maharishi Mahesh Yogi set up headquarters in Los Angeles and pumped out lunch-hour meditation seminars for high-powered businessmen. He demonstrated how TM (Transcendental Meditation) could lower the capitalist temperature and even bring them more loot in the end (and he should know). The Pentagon also went for it as a cure for combat stress and might yet employ it for more fancy turns of terror. But Maharishi's comeback inside the establishment (he was once a king of the counter-culture) showed how he had lost ground among left-ish self-seekers. The spark of blessedness now seemed somehow extinguished in the US climate. No, if you wanted to get down to the nitty-gritty of enlightenment, you had to go out *there* and find it yourself.

While his old colleague and tripping-partner, Tim Leary, sparred with the law forces, Dr Richard Alpert was off in India discovering who he was. He had come out of the moneyed Jewish tradition, filled with the usual Portnoy anxieties, the drive to 'make it' and a homosexual 'problem' thrown into the bargain. He went through psychoanalysis and then got off the couch to become a post-Freudian therapist himself. After 'making it' as a Harvard faculty member, he met Leary and had a few of his internal tapes erased by a punch of the sacred mushroom. Together the two profs built an LSD movement and hoped to change the mind of America. But none of Alpert's experiences scraped right down to bone reality and this drove him through a complex of 'what next?' until he was flustered and strung out. In India a series of divine connections brought him to the Himalayas where he found, at long last, a guru who could *keep him high*. Whatever 'it' was – this old guy had it. Armed now with photos of his master to pray to and a new name (Baba Ram Dass), Alpert returned to the home front to make his impression.

Ram Dass did not have the capacity for original thinking that friend Leary had. But just as the latter seemed to step into quicksand with every move, Ram Dass had an inbred sense of being in the right place at the right time. When he re-surfaced in his new incarnation at the end of the sixties, spirits were in gloom. The psychedelic movement he helped to found was non-existent. His prediction of a Glad State was not borne out. Many leftists wanted out of the political fray without having to go through the blood in the hypodermic or the Blood of the Lamb; they craved simply peace with *honour*. They could relate well to Ram Dass. He was a familiar face on the scene and his odyssey was parallel in many respects to their own.

It wasn't his intention, however, to collect a flock or get into the surrogate-father racket; nor was he short on private capital. He was still in spin, with many plateaux up ahead, not yet ready to spread the word. In spite of this, he chose to bang out an autobiography/manifesto, *Be Here Now* (1971), which became a cult best-seller overnight; Jerry Rubin called it the most important book of the decade. In addition to the tale of Ram Dass's own enlightenment, the book was a self-improvement manual – out of the Yankee tradition leading down from Ben Franklin's 'wise-sayings' to the fab wisdoms of Dale Carnegie – tied to no real coherent world-view. Its eclectic philosophy oozed perfect balm for the wounds of weary revolutionaries. The message was nothing new – work on *yourself* – but a good deal of it related to specific political dilemmas: 'Political work is a noble way to spend your time here, so long as you do it without attachment, and with the understanding that it's not the whole game.' This tended to reduce commitment down to an exercise in 'karma', taking the 'struggle' out of the Struggle. It was OK to work for liberation movements as long as you didn't take it seriously. You could protest against and seek confrontation with an opponent – be he cop or politician – but you had to be able to *love* him, to humanize this enemy by recognizing we're all 'Us', there is no 'Them'. For folks who needed to wind down without feeling guilty, it was just what the guru ordered.

Here was also an answer to the terrible crisis and confusion that came with making *The* Revolution. The way to have power was to stop wanting it! You had to loosen your grip and let it flow. Revolution became a silent ballet; in true mystic fashion, the *way* you made it was more essential than the reason, and what you made of yourself in making the revolution *was*, in fact, the revolution. Ram Dass: 'What is important is that you get your house in order at each stage of the journey so that you can proceed.'

There was even greater comfort for those who craved a rest cure. The idea of 'be here now' was: don't get caught in the past and don't get hung up looking to the future – the work you have to do takes place *at this time*. So much for killing yourself to achieve leftist Utopias *someday* when Shangri-La was just a mantra away. If the future didn't count, then your *movement* was a collection of insights into yourself mounting minute by minute; these were not programmed to lead to anything, but society would eventually gain more fulfilled beings. Most of all, if you could be here now fully, there was no moral compulsion to hang on to nagging memory. The political failures of the recent past were all way-stations on your pilgrimage. Win or lose they got you to where you are and that is the only place you could be since 'every trip leads to the same place'.

Left-ish people were coming to similar conclusions, often without recourse to religion or authority-connections. The trail out of political activism led inevitably to becalmed vistas. The commune movement was swelling, 'just plain folks' were heading back to the good earth. Concern for the health of the environment – once part of the political charge – could now be put to the

286 The Radical Soap Opera

test. The usual outposts of involvement on the East and West
Coasts were abandoned for soothing ashrams and counter-
cultural villages springing up in New Mexico and Colorado.
People were experimenting with narrowing their Utopias, un-
hinging their 'attachments', moderating their desires, helping
themselves. It was a slice of mythic American pie that could be
perfectly accommodated in the do-it-yourself kitchen of Nixonculture (except for those damned welfare cheques that paid for all
this Nirvana!).

But the new new new 'working on yourself'-trip was only a
further stage in the unfolding autobiography, of which *The*
Revolution was only another – perhaps climactic – chapter. The
real difference now was that the craving for *high-speed* action
seemed to abate slightly. In the tried and true American pioneer
sense, Nature was acting as a purifier, exorcizing city demons
you'd picked up hanging out in corrupt vicinities. Even the
revolutionaries who were not literally out to pasture appeared
humbled in a novel way, almost recognizing they might have bit
off more than they could chew. It all could have passed for a
general stock-taking or a slow (though not necessarily strategic)
Spring Cleaning. Many people now in retreat would remain forever high or low. But, inevitably, others would miss the exposure
and adventure and come back to the streets. Just in case anyone
had a mind to start the show all over again, the broom of 'lessons
learned' would have its work cut out sweeping away the swill
cluttering the historical leftist brain. It was still far too early to
assess the impact of the past decade entirely, much less *plan* for
the future of the movement. But in the flux of a curious silence,
some prospects for work were beginning to suggest themselves.

The dream-spinners of the Left would have loved to march out
through their own devastation singing 'The Battle Hymn of the
Republic' behind Jeanette MacDonald. But there was no 'The
End' for it; history wouldn't even stop long enough for the
applause. Just as *The* Revolution could never really disown its
Red heritage, it failed to discard itself. With most of its supporting
fictions gone and masks cut away, the movement found itself with

little to build on – but perhaps more *real* than ever before. There was not much satisfaction in the wake of it but, by simple laws of dynamics, it was impossible to sustain the blown revolutionary posture without spluttering eventually to a whoosh. It was like a long-distance runner trying to break the sound barrier before mastering breath control. The rampaging ferocity of revolt was not a bad thing, and made for the sort of firepower that inflames dull patches of history. But it was far too intense. A good actor knows that proceeding on the basis of pure tension is to flirt with failure. He sometimes has to step out of his role for a brief second to achieve a modicum of relaxation – so as to make proper use of his energy. It was not something American revolutionary actors learned well because they had got drunk on confrontation. Their punch lacked rhythm, their timing went weird, they were overacting.

The misuse of its own physical dynamics demonstrated, in little, the movement's inability to understand the nature of change. When passionately non-violent people could talk the next year of killing for the cause and the year after sought forgetfulness in the self, it did not reflect political change of mind as much as Bedlam in the blood. Perhaps one of the virtues of the American Left had been its ability to shift between political and cultural effects, maintaining a freshness of attitude and knocking out the boredom of weighty ideology. But little use was ever made of yesterday's 'mistakes'; changes were not absorbed, but rather abandoned. This obscured the idea that where you have just been is crucial to an understanding of where you are now. Nor could instant analysis and memoir provide much clarity for political situations. There was nothing to see so soon, nothing at all but bolts of energy spurting off you as you wound down from seventy-eight to thirty-three and one third revolutions per minute.

The lush violins of nostalgia can never substitute for the hum of history. In place of an overview – which might just allow some small insight into future action – we lumber in the mucky wisdom of yesterday's cheap experiment and cripple all prospects with *longing*. And so *The* Revolution will sit upon memory and gain exquisite edges – how lovely it all was! Here comes a time – and we're quick at the brink – when we will sigh for the past glories (where are they now?) of last week.

Ram Dass's idea that you could smash the State without taking it seriously is a nifty bit of Eastern hocus-pocus. But it usefully undermines the myth of the Righteous Fight and provides a key to tactical thinking: it may not be necessary to be committed *all the time*. It may even be critical to apply the brakes purposely, to take the steam out of involvement before it blows out. This, of course, is a counter-revolutionary notion – it's not easy. There is no home-grown form of self-expression which helps take the edge off emergency. The inbred satire and ironic postures of European cultures can serve as shock absorbers, allowing for broad patches of relaxation and self-ridicule; a healthy measure of cynicism may even preclude the disillusionment that is inevitable when tackling the entrenched State. A failure to muster irony allowed the catastrophic Right hook that dropped the Left in the Red Scare. It was wide-eyed and wide-open. The same may be true as a cause for the more subtle and mechanical victory of Nixonculture, burying revolutionary passion under incessant ice-cubes. The Left is too raw, too feeble, too susceptible chiefly through its traditional sensitivity, but also because it has no distance from its extremely clenched fist. Without real 'character', without poise or cool for combat, the movement has been in ceaseless spin like a whistling top while the Power pushes the plunger and manipulates it at will.

With folks back to digging in the soil as well as the soul, it was just possible that the stuff of it, the very *material* world at their fingers, might provoke a necessary demystification. The Spring Cleaning would have to work in some highly decayed left-ish corners to get out the cobwebs that block a clear passage into the future. This would not be easy while shaman-worshippers and authority-junkies kept their heroes and holy rollers and supreme commanders in business. But if these could be swept away, so might the traditional romanticism and religious fervour. The hardest corner to break into would be the one that shelters pretence to significance, to ultimate victory over the forces of reaction, to the divinity of the movement. Sentiment covers this region and even grows a fungus here; it sprouts the idea that the re-dreaming of America is somehow worth a superhuman effort, worth all the casualties, worth the suffering that the rest of the world has known from the contagion of it. Once this last barrier to freedom and mobility is swept away, then nothing appears to be left and the Left appears to be nothing. Look again: it sheds its phantasms and works back from the bone.

A Note on Sources

This book makes no scholarly claims. Because of its style I have not made extensive use of quotations, nor have I – except where it is vital to the sense of an argument – acknowledged my sources in the body of the text. Still, the work has been heavily researched and can be documented. I have been through hundreds of secondary works to check my accuracy and gain a working knowledge of specific subjects. But I have not used secondary material to form the basis of my arguments; only in rare instances has it helped me to elaborate the information as I have written it down.

The bulk of the material has been taken from accounts written by participants in the political drama of each period. These are generally autobiographies and memoirs, but may also include texts parading as objective reportage. In some cases I have conducted interviews with people who were directly involved. Occasionally, in some of the later chapters, I have employed my own personal reminiscences of some Left activities from the mid-sixties. A vital source of information comes from thousands of pamphlets, leaflets, leftist newspapers and magazines, as well as US Government documents and publications. Again, nearly all of this material has been absorbed and baked in the general pie of my approach.

The difficulty of such a method is in coping with the abundance of delicious rumours, sensational exposés, political grudges, self-aggrandizing improvisations on the truth and downright lies. These have been of enormous value in helping me arrive at many of my conclusions about leftist expression. Despite the fact that I have retained much of this natural exaggeration for colour and effect, I have tried to recognize it for what it is and have indicated my scepticism in most cases where it occurs.

The following is only a partial list of works consulted, with a concentration on the central first-person accounts of each period. Only those secondary sources which I have relied on for significant backup information will be cited.

A Select Bibliography

I

CANNON, JAMES, *History of American Trotskyism*, Path Press Inc., New York, 1944.

CORNELL, JULIAN, *The Trial of Ezra Pound*, Faber & Faber, 1967.

DREISER, THEODORE, *An American Tragedy*, New American Library, New York, 1964.

DUNN, ROBERT W., ed. *The Palmer Raids*, Labor Research Association, New York, 1948. This short account provides the CP line on Palmer and the events of 1919, although it parades as an objective historical summary.

ENGELS, FRIEDRICH and MARX, KARL, *Letters to Americans: 1848–1895*, edited by Leonard E. Mins, International Publishers, New York, 1953.

Fighting Words, Selections from Twenty-Five Years of the Daily Worker, New Century Publishers, New York, 1949. The American *Daily Worker* itself, born in 1924, is always a source of useful anecdotes and political myths.

FOSTER, WILLIAM Z., *From Bryan to Stalin*, New York, 1937.

FREUD, SIGMUND, I have read extensively through Freud's books and papers, but for my purposes have concentrated on the following works: *Beyond the Pleasure Principle*, *Civilization and Its Discontents*, *Ego and Id*, *Interpretation of Dreams*, *Three Essays on the Theory of Sexuality* and *Two Short Accounts of Psychoanalysis* (including *Five Lectures on Psychoanalysis* and *The Question of Lay Analysis*) all published by Hogarth Press and the Institute of Psychoanalysis.

GOLDMAN, EMMA, *Anarchism and Other Essays*, Kennihat, New York, 1910; *Living My Life*, Plenum Publishing Corp., New York, 1931; *Red Emma Speaks*, edited by Alix Kates Shulman, Vintage Books, New York, 1972.

Investigation Activities of the Department of Justice, USA, Senate Documents, 66th Congress, 1st Session, Washington, 1919.

POUND, EZRA, *Impact*, Henry Regnery Co., Chicago, 1960; *Jefferson and/or Mussolini*, Liveright, New York, 1970; *Patria Mia*, Peter Owen, 1962.

SACCO, NICOLA and VANZETTI, BARTOLOMEO, *The Letters of Sacco and Vanzetti*, edited by Marion Denman Frankfurter and Gardner Jackson, Octagon, New York, 1928; *Commonwealth vs. Sacco and Vanzetti*, edited by Robert P. Weeks, Prentice-Hall Inc., 1958.

WHITMAN, WALT, *Democratic Vistas*, J. M. Dent & Sons, 1912.

Some useful secondary texts on this period are Theodore Draper's *The Roots of American Communism*, Viking Press, New York, 1957; and *American Communism and Soviet Russia*, Viking Press, New York, 1960. *The American Communist Party* by Irving Howe and Lewis Coser, Praeger, Boston, 1957, is valuable except where it suffers from a sneering anti-Stalinism. Gabriel A. Almond's *The Appeals of Communism*, Princeton University Press, New Jersey, 1954, provides a statistical study of membership in and defection from the CP. The best reference work on the entire subject of the American Left is the two-volume edition of *Socialism and American Life*, edited by Donald Drew Egbert and Stow Persons, Princeton University Press, New Jersey, 1952.

II

ANDERSON, MAXWELL, *Winterset*, Harcourt Brace Jovanovich, Inc., Washington, 1935.

BESSIE, ALVAH, *Inquisition in Eden*, Seven Seas Books, Berlin, 1967; *Men in Battle*, Veterans of the Abraham Lincoln Brigade, New York, 1939.

BRECHT, BERTOLT, *Brecht on Theatre*, Methuen, 1964.

BROWDER, EARL, *The People's Front*, New York, 1938.

The Civil War in Spain, edited by Robert Payne, Premier Books, Connecticut, 1964.

CLURMAN, HAROLD, *The Fervent Years*, Dobson, 1946.

DIES, MARTIN, *The Trojan Horse in America*, New York, 1940.

DREISER, THEODORE, *Dreiser Looks at Russia*, New York, 1928.

GATES, JOHN, *The Story of an American Communist*, Thomas Nelson, New York, 1958.

Hearings Regarding the Communist Infiltration of the Motion Picture Industry, US Congress, House, Committee on Un-American Activities, Washington, 1947. Further transcripts of investigations exist for 1951–3, concerning Communist activity specifically in Hollywood. These have also been excerpted in *Thirty Years of Treason*, edited by Eric Bentley, Thames & Hudson, 1971 and in a play by Eric Bentley,

Are You Now or Have You Ever Been, Harper & Row, New York, 1972.

HEMINGWAY, ERNEST, *The Fifth Column*, Penguin Books, 1966.

HOOVER, J. EDGAR, *Masters of Deceit*, J. M. Dent & Sons, 1958.

KRIVITSKY, W. G., *I Was Stalin's Agent*, Hamish Hamilton, 1939.

MATTHEWS, HERBERT L., *Two Wars and More to Come*, Carrick & Evans, New York, 1938.

MILLER, ARTHUR, *After the Fall*, Viking Press, New York, 1964.

MONTAGU, IVOR, *With Eisenstein in Hollywood*, Seven Seas Books, Berlin, 1968. Contains Eisenstein's complete scenario for *An American Tragedy*.

New Masses: An Anthology of the Rebel Thirties, edited by Joseph North, International Publishers, New York, 1969. I have also consulted specific issues of the magazine and its offspring, *Masses and Mainstream*.

ODETS, CLIFFORD, *Six Plays*, Modern Library, New York, 1963.

PISCATOR, MARIA LEY-, *The Piscator Experiment*, Southern Illinois University Press, Illinois, 1967.

ROLFE, EDWIN, *The Lincoln Battalion*, Veterans of the Abraham Lincoln Brigade, New York, 1939.

STANISLAVSKY, KONSTANTIN, *An Actor Prepares*, Theatre Arts Books, New York, 1936; *Building a Character*, Theatre Arts Books, New York, 1949; *Creating a Role*, Theatre Arts Books, New York, 1961; *My Life in Art*, Foreign Languages Publishing House, Moscow, n.d.

STRASBERG, LEE, *Strasberg at the Actors Studio*, edited by Robert Hethmon, Jonathan Cape, 1966.

TRUMBO, DALTON, *Additional Dialogue*, Bantam Books, New York, 1972.

VOROS, SANDOR, *American Commissar*, Chilton Co., Philadelphia and New York, 1961.

WEXLEY, JOHN, *They Shall Not Die*, New York, 1934.

The Writer in a Changing World, edited by Henry Hart, New York, 1937. This is the follow-up volume to *American Writers' Congress*, 1935.

Writers Take Sides, League of American Writers, New York, 1938.

For a general discussion of the HUAC there is Walter Goodman's *The Committee*, Penguin Books, Baltimore, 1969. The Hollywood Trials are all the rage now in the publishing world, but the best accounts to date by non-participants are Gordon Kahn's lefty-biased *Hollywood on Trial*, Boni & Gaer, New York, 1948 (dealing with 1947 only) and John Cogley's exhaustive two-volume *Report on Blacklisting*, The Fund for the Republic, 1956. An excellent bibliography for Spain can be found in Hugh Thomas's *The Spanish Civil War*, Penguin Books, 1965. Stanislavsky's US influence is well documented in a two-part edition of the *Tulane Drama Review*, T25 and T26, Fall and Winter, 1964.

III

BAEZ, JOAN, *Daybreak*, MacGibbon & Kee, 1970.

BENTLEY, ELIZABETH, *Out of Bondage*, Rupert Hart-Davis, 1952.

BUDENZ, LOUIS, *This is My Story*, New York, 1947.

CHAMBERS, WHITTAKER, *Witness*, André Deutsch, 1953.

CHESSMAN, CARYL, *The Kid Was a Killer*, Frederick Muller, 1960; *Trial by Ordeal*, Longmans, 1956.

DENNIS, EUGENE, *Ideas They Cannot Jail*, International Publishers, New York, 1950.

FAST, HOWARD, *Peekskill: USA*, Civil Rights Congress, 1951.

HISS, ALGER, *In the Court of Public Opinion*, Harper & Row, New York, 1972.

100 Things You Should Know About Communism, US Congress, House, Committee on Un-American Activities, Washington, 1949.

MCCARTHY, JOSEPH R., *McCarthyism: The Fight for America*, Devin-Adair Co., New York, 1952.

MATUSOW, HARVEY, *False Witness*, Cameron & Kahn, New York, 1955.

MARION, GEORGE, *The Communist Trial*, Fairplay Publishers, New York, 1950. This is a full-frontal CP version of the 1949 trial of the eleven Communist leaders; it attempts to make the Government's case sound absurd, an elaborate legal joke played out at the expense of innocent victims. The other side of the picture is presented by the trial judge, Harold R. Medina, who apparently felt it necessary to write a book defending his position, *The Anatomy of Freedom*, Henry Holt and Co., New York, 1959.

New Program of the Communist Party, USA (A Draft), Political Affairs Publishers, New York, 1966.

RAWSON, TABOR, *I Want to Live*, New American Library, New York, 1958.

ROSENBERG, ETHEL and JULIUS, *Death House Letters*, Jero Publishing Co., New York, 1953.

ROSSMAN, MICHAEL, *The Wedding Within the War*, Doubleday, New York, 1971. This is one of the most typical of the 'I was there' political autobiographies of the late sixties. A perpetual fund of sentimentality and Left righteousness.

SALINGER, J. D., *The Catcher in the Rye*, Penguin Books, 1958.

Spotlight on Spies, US Congress, House, Committee on Un-American Activities, Washington, 1949.

THOREAU, HENRY DAVID, *On the Duty of Civil Disobedience*, New American Library, New York, 1960.

Trial by Treason: The National Committee to Secure Justice for the Rosenbergs and Morton Sobell, US Congress, House, Committee on Un-American Activities, Washington, 1957.

One of the better general accounts of this period can be found in David A Shannon's *Decline of American Communism*, London, 1959. Of the numerous Rosenberg case accounts consulted, the more interesting ones tend to be fairly dogmatic on the crucial question of guilt or innocence. Those which presume guilt are *The Rosenberg Case* by S. Andhil Fineberg and Jonathan Root's *The Betrayers*, Secker & Warburg, London, 1964. The claims for innocence are naturally more numerous. The best of these is Walter and Miriam Schneir, *Invitation to An Inquest*, Penguin Books, Baltimore, 1973. Less convincing are: William A. Reuben, *The Atom Spy Hoax*, Action Books, New York, 1955 and John Wexley, *The Judgment of Julius and Ethel Rosenberg*, Cameron & Kahn, New York, 1955. Two fictional versions of the Rosenberg affair are Donald Freed's play, *Inquest*, Hill & Wang, New York, 1970 and E. L. Doctorow's first-rate novel, *The Book of Daniel*, New American Library, New York, 1971.

IV

The Digger Papers, published by the *Realist* magazine, New York, 1968.

GROGAN, EMMETT, *Ringolevio*, Heinemann, 1972.

JACOBS, PAUL and LANDAU, SAUL, *The New Radicals*, Penguin Books, 1967. Contains many New Left manifestoes, as well as a background analysis.

LEARY, TIMOTHY, *High Priest*, College Notes and Texts, Inc., New York, 1968; *Jail Notes*, Douglas, New York, 1970; *The Politics of Ecstasy*, Paladin, 1970.

LEARY, TIMOTHY, METZNER, RALPH and ALPERT, RICHARD, *The Psychedelic Experience*, University Books, New York, 1964.

LEARY, TIMOTHY, METZNER, RALPH, ed., *The Psychedelic Reader*, Selected from the *Psychedelic Review*, University Books, New York, 1965.

MAIROWITZ, DAVID Z. and STANSILL, PETER, *BAMN: Outlaw Manifestos and Ephemera, 1965–70*, Penguin Books, London and

New York, 1971. Contains essential manifestoes of Diggers, Mother-fuckers and other groups in the sixties.

Violations of State Department Regulations and Pro-Castro Propaganda Activities in the US, US Congress, House, Committee on Un-American Activities, Washington, 1963.

WINSTANLEY, GERARD, *The Works of Gerard Winstanley*, edited by George H. Sabine, Cornell University Press, Ithaca, 1941.

V

Hearings on Aid to the Enemy in time of Undeclared War, US Congress, House, Committee on Un-American Activities, Washington, 1966.

HOFFMANN, ABBIE, *Revolution for the Hell of It*, Dial Press, New York, 1968; *Woodstock Nation*, Vintage, New York, 1969.

MITFORD, JESSICA, *The Trial of Dr Spock*, Macdonald, 1969.

REICH, WILHELM. Unfortunately, most of Reich's works available in English have been 'revised' by Reich in his later orgone years. The surviving material is therefore often obscured and Reich's early work sometimes debased. Still, there is enough left intact to be of some value. In order to get an accurate picture of Reich's thinking, how-ever, it is important to read the majority of his writings. For the purposes of this book, the key texts, published by Farrar, Straus & Giroux, New York, are: *Character Analysis* (1949); *The Function of the Orgasm* (Noonday, 1942); *The Mass Psychology of Fascism* (1969); *The Murder of Christ* (1953); *Reich Speaks of Freud* (1967); *The Sexual Revolution* (1969); *Selected Writings* (1960). Also of interest are the *Annals of the Orgone Institute*, New York, 1947 and the *Orgone Energy Bulletin*, New York, 1949. Luckily Reich's early *Sex-Pol* writings have been published intact in an English edition, Vintage, New York, 1972, edited by Lee Baxandall. There are almost no significant secondary works on Reich in English. But for interest-ing biographical material see Ilse Ollendorff Reich's *Wilhelm Reich: A Personal Biography*, Avon Books, New York, 1969, and *Wilhelm Reich*, edited by Neill, Ritter, Waal, *et al.*, Ritter Press, 1958.

RUBIN, JERRY, *Do It!*, Simon & Schuster, New York, 1970; *We Are Everywhere*, Harper & Row, New York, 1971.

SPOCK, BENJAMIN, *Baby and Child Care*, Bodley Head, 1958; *Decent and Indecent*, Penguin Books, 1972; *A Young Person's Guide to Life and Love*, Bodley Head, 1970. Danger! Please keep out of reach of young persons!

We Accuse, Diablo Press, Berkeley, 1965. Speeches from Vietnam Day in Berkeley in 1965.

Literally dozens of anthologies of Women's Liberation writings have glutted the new women's market in publishing. One of the best remains Robin Morgan's *Sisterhood is Powerful*, Vintage, New York, 1970.

VI

BIRMINGHAM, JOHN, ed., *Our Time is Now*, Bantam, New York, 1970. Selections from High School underground papers.

BOYLE, KAY, *The Long Walk at San Francisco State*, Grove Press, New York, 1970.

Hearings (on SDS Activities), US Congress, House, Committee on Internal Security, Washington, 1969.

JACOBS, HAROLD, *Weatherman*, Ramparts Press, 1970. Contains important Weatherman documents as well as background material. For non-political insights into Weatherman see Thomas Powers's *Diana: The Making of a Terrorist*, Bantam Books, New York, 1971.

MARIGHELLA, CARLOS, *Minimanual of the Urban Guerrilla*, published anonymously.

SMACK! editors of *Ramparts* and Frank Browning, Harper & Row, New York, 1972. Excellent analysis of US traffic in heroin, and involvement of CIA.

Study of Campus Disorders, October 1967–May 1969, US Congress, Senate, Permanent Subcommittee on Investigations, Washington, 1969.

There are, of course, countless books published on the subject of the American Left in the sixties and its attendant 'counter-culture'. Many have got wealthy in this racket and have gained a splendid notoriety. Two of the most notorious are Charles Reich's *The Greening of America*, Penguin Books, 1971, and Jean-Francois Revel's *Without Marx or Jesus*, Doubleday, New York, 1971. Both of these were subject to ridicule by the Left when they were first published. But since, in two short years, their optimistic theses have been utterly disproved by events, there is no need to slander them further.

CURTAIN CALL

BABA RAM DASS, *Be Here Now*, Lama Foundation, New Mexico, 1971.